What is Europe?

21st Century Europe Series

General Editor: Helen Wallace

Drawing upon the latest research, this major series of concise thematically-organized texts provides state-of-the-art overviews of the key aspects of contemporary Europe from the Atlantic to the Urals for a broad student and serious general readership. Written by leading authorities in a lively and accessible style without assuming prior knowledge, each title is designed to synthesize and contribute to current knowledge and debate in its respective field.

Published

Andrew Cottey: *Security in 21st Century Europe (2nd Edn)*
Colin Hay and Daniel Wincott: *The Political Economy of European Welfare Capitalism*
Christopher Lord and Erika Harris: *Democracy in the New Europe*
Anna Triandafyllidou and Ruby Gropas: *What is Europe?*

Forthcoming

Tom Casier and Sophie Vanhoonacker: *Europe and the World*
Klaus Goetz: *Governing 21st Century Europe*
Ben Rosamond: *Globalization and the European Union*
Dermot McCann: *Political Economy of 21st Century Europe*

In Preparation

Citizenship and Identity in 21st Century Europe
Society and Social Change in 21st Century Europe

21st Century Europe
Series Standing Order ISBN 978–0–333–96042–4 hardback
Series Standing Order ISBN 978–0–333–96043–1 paperback
(*outside North America only*)

You can receive future titles in this series as they are published. To place a standing order please contact your bookseller or, in the case of difficulty, write to us at the address below with your name and address, the title of the series and the ISBN quoted above.

Customer Services Department, Macmillan Distribution Ltd
Houndmills, Basingstoke, Hampshire RG21 6XS, UK

What is Europe?

Anna Triandafyllidou
and
Ruby Gropas

 palgrave

First published 2015 by
PALGRAVE

Palgrave in the UK is an imprint of Macmillan Publishers Limited, registered in England, company number 785998, of 4 Crinan Street, London, N1 9XW.

Palgrave Macmillan in the US is a division of St Martin's Press LLC, 175 Fifth Avenue, New York, NY 10010.

Palgrave is a global imprint of the above companies and is represented throughout the world.

Palgrave® and Macmillan® are registered trademarks in the United States, the United Kingdom, Europe and other countries.

ISBN 978-1-4039-8682-5   ISBN 978-1-137-56065-0 (eBook)

DOI 10.1007/978-1-137-56065-0

A catalogue record for this book is available from the British Library.

A catalog record for this book is available from the Library of Congress.

From Anna to Bo Stråth, Stefano Bartolini and Tariq Modood,

*From Ruby to Loukas Tsoukalis, Theodore Couloumbis,
Thanos Veremis and Geoffrey Edwards,*

*As friends, colleagues and mentors they have inspired us to hold
our professional and academic ethics high, speak our mind and
keep cool no matter what.*

Contents

Preface

This book has a long story. It started in 2004 with an email from Steven Kennedy, who was Editor of the Palgrave Politics series. Together with Helen Wallace, they were launching a series on the New Europe. It started as an idea about a book critically discussing the question of what is Europe, and it also had a two-year delivery timeline.

We are now in February 2015. It obviously took longer than two years to complete this book that was for a long time a single-authored endeavour – Anna – and eventually became a joint project – Anna and Ruby.

Over the past decade, the idea of writing this book has always been incredibly fascinating and challenging, and sometimes even daunting. With Europe incessantly changing, and with euphoria giving place to a series of crises, trying to tackle the question of what Europe is has been increasingly complex, but also so much more politically meaningful.

While we have been writing this book, Europe has changed in many different ways. No surprise there really, as Europe has always been characterized with constant change. But the magnitude and range of dimensions on which changes have occurred during this decade have made the question of what is Europe all the more intriguing. The idea for this book was framed at a time when we were still riding the Euro-euphoria of the early 2000s. Very quickly this gave way to deep political crisis as EU citizens rejected the European Constitution in 2005, leading thinkers and intellectuals to some further soul-searching on what is Europe, on what Europe and the EU meant for Europeans, and on what this all meant for democracy in Europe. The celebratory mood of the continent's unification through EU enlargement to include Central and Eastern European countries, the island states of Cyprus and Malta as well as the formal start of accession negotiations with Turkey came to an abrupt end with the London and Madrid bombings of 2004 and 2005. The global financial crisis and the deep Eurozone crisis that followed severely impacted the lives of many EU citizens, challenging the very foundations of the

EU edifice. As we are finishing this book, Europe is in a rather sombre state facing the aftermath of the Arab spring, a war in Ukraine and regular tragedies at its borders, as young men and women die or drown as they try to reach Europe. It is also facing a disconcerting rise again of many '-isms': Euroscepticism, nationalism, populism and racism. Yet not all is bleak. We are also observing a rich democratic backlash from citizens and civil society against these divisive responses, calling for tolerance and respect for difference, for the need to respond to violent fundamentalism through inclusive policies, and for solidarity and social justice to continue to be values at the core of Europe.

Turning the idea into an actual manuscript has been fascinating as Europe kept being a moving object, but the task was not easy. There have been more requests to extend the submission deadline than any one of us can remember. There were always just too many other things going on. The joys and challenges of a mobile academic career do not leave much time for authored books. The book was always postponed as research project proposals, project deliverables, journal articles and job applications were each time taking precedence as more urgent and pressing deadlines. And, the joys and challenges of parenthood gave us even less time to dedicate to this book, as each one of us had two children during these years: Kimonas (2004), Alexandros (2010), Spiros Francis (2010) and Evangelia (2013).

A number of times, the reasonable decision seemed to be to cancel this book project and put it aside indefinitely. Bo Stråth, one of the persons to whom this book is dedicated, adamantly advised against it in 2005 by simply saying, 'talk with the Editor, plan out a reasonable timetable…and just write it!'. Loukas Tsoukalis gave similar advice seven years later.

Basically, we did not abandon the effort of writing this book despite the other trivial and less trivial tasks and demands of professional and family life precisely because Europe has been changing; it has remained both problematic and inspiring through these years, and it has kept us asking questions to each other about our present and future, as Greeks and as Europeans, and about the future of our children, these young Europeans with very mobile lives.

Through this long and uncertain path to this book's completion some people have been our stable reference points, our lighthouses, the people who give meaning to our lives, beyond jobs and books: Eugene and Loukas, our husbands, and of course our boys (Dionisio, Jason, Kimonas-Dimitris, Alexandros, Spiros Francis) and the little queen of the company, Evangelia! Our parents have been indispensable parts of this journey: Eva, Spyros, Dina, Dimitris, if it had not been for your support in the joys of parenthood, this book would never have reached this stage. We are grateful and we love you.

Just as importantly, throughout these years Steven Kennedy and Helen Wallace were incredibly supportive, patient and encouraged us to keep at it. And, when we submitted first drafts of the chapters, they provided the guidance of what sort of approach this book should take. We had been trying to write ready-made answers and thorough literature reviews; instead, Steven suggested we should provide the reader with the concepts, the history, the background and the tools to navigate through the questions rather than seek to make her or him experts on a subject in a single 30-page chapter!

We would like to take this opportunity to thank Vicky Valanos, with whom we have worked on many books, for being so responsive and meticulous and a copy-editor that is truly enjoyable to work with. Many thanks also to the anonymous reviewer of Palgrave who gave a lot of constructive criticisms, helping us improve the final draft.

Finally, although parts of this book have been written in different parts of the world, from Athens, to Naples, to Palo Alto, Komotini and Bruges, it is in San Domenico di Fiesole and the incredible environment of the EUI's Robert Schuman Centre that this book was able to take shape and meaning. Naturally, we remain responsible for all errors and omissions.

ANNA TRIANDAFYLLIDOU
RUBY GROPAS

Chapter 1

What is Europe?
An Introduction

It was nearly 30 years ago when Edgar Morin, a famous French philosopher and sociologist historian was writing:

> If Europe is law, it is also force; if it is democracy it is also oppression; if it is spirituality, it is also materiality; if it is moderation, it is also hubris and excess: if it is reason, it is also myth, even in the very idea of reason. (Morin, 1987, p. 23)

If one asked citizens the question, 'What is Europe?', they would probably disagree in their answers but many among them would assume that there is an absolute truth to be found – a definitive answer to be given. They would thus argue on the criteria or the historical evidence on which a definition of Europe could or should rest. Indeed, one might answer the question through reference to public opinion surveys, another may draw on historical works or quote the words of famous European thinkers, while many may privilege a politicized and ideological definition of Europe. More often than not, in such contemporary discussions, one would conflate the term 'Europe' with that of the 'European Union' (EU).

A basic answer to the question that we pose in this book is that Europe is a geographical *space*: it is a continent. However, Europe is also a *place*: it is a space that is culturally constructed. It is a reference to the European continent that includes cultural elements, a past that is both objectively (based on historical events) and subjectively constructed as European (the events are given a specific meaning and are put into a wider 'European' framework of meaning), and it also has a geopolitical power dimension (Europe is a contested and probably fragmented but still rather distinct global actor).

1

Why is defining Europe an important question today? The reasons are twofold: first, Europe has become a reality that cannot be ignored; second, Europe is relevant in the political, societal, cultural, economic and commercial fields, as well as in the domestic sphere and in the global arena. At the same time, Europe is in crisis – at all levels. A book that tries to answer the 'What is Europe?' question seeks to contribute to a debate on who 'we' the Europeans are, where 'we' come from and where 'we' are heading. This book aims to give the tools to readers to ask and answer the question themselves. It does not provide answers *tout court*.

Europe today is politically divided and without a sense of direction. Even though there is a wider acknowledgement that nation-states, while still important, are too small (economically or geopolitically) to face the challenges of the twenty-first century as single entities, Europe fails to inspire its residents as to the way forward. In some cases, the European integration project almost appears to be continuing simply out of momentum, or out of fear that scrapping it would be too costly. The reasons for which the European Community (today the EU) was created, notably to guarantee peace, are now largely irrelevant, as newer generations have faint memories, if at all, of war. The Younger generations appear to be more concerned with prosperity, and it is not clear whether prosperity and economic stability are easier to achieve at the European rather than the national or regional levels, with what benefits and, more importantly, at what costs.

The implosion of the communist regimes after 1989 and the end of the Cold War has left us without a clear ideological struggle between competing conceptions of 'good society'. At the end of the day, all questions of social justice and equality appear to be technical problems that require more efficient administrative implementation rather than new policies. Politics seem to not matter or to matter very little. In this absence of an ideological struggle, populist parties and extremist forces appear to be filling the void and gaining power. Worse still, terrorism, bred through social and economic marginalization, is occurring throughout Northern Europe.

In asking and answering the 'What is Europe?' question, this book seeks to shed light on the main differences and the tentative similarities that countries and people in Europe face, thereby pinpointing the main challenges that we share.

One may argue that Europe has become a central dimension of the wider societal transformation of modernity, since questioning what Europe is reflects also a questioning of what late modernity is, and how we orient ourselves towards the future (Bauman, 2004; Delanty, 2013). However, this book intends to take a somewhat different perspective: it aims to question the different facets of the Europe concept to reveal the internal diversity of the concept and not just its diachronic evolution. We wish to engage in a critical reading of the different perspectives on Europe: who decides what Europe is and what are the competing hegemonic discourses? We also seek to disassociate the concept of Europe from the current European integration project and consider how it can develop in new directions, deconstructing its past uses to inform our future plans. This does not mean ignoring the importance of the European Union project – actually this would be quite impossible. It does mean tracing its historical character and political limits with a view to opening up the horizon for considering anew the question of Europe.

Defining Europe

Defining 'Europe' seems to be an ongoing story that appears as an incessant effort to revisit the core existentialist questions of what makes up a definition of Europe. Throughout the course of the continent's history, politicians, political elites, academics and thinkers have been tackling and returning to this question in elaborate, critical, as well as in simplistic, populist ways. Here, we highlight the historical and ambivalent character of the term, and offer alternative views of Europe by putting current developments into perspective. We adopt a critical viewpoint with regard to social and political developments in Europe today, and more generally in the post-Second World War period. This book is distinctively European, in that it tries to emancipate the concept from the specific project of the EU and look both wider and deeper into the origins, evolution and future of Europe in a variety of levels and from an interdisciplinary point of view.

We argue that there can be no single definition of Europe. The dynamic nature of what Europe represents is not new, nor is it a trait particular to the more recent phase of European history, namely, the EU. Therefore, we take the position that Europe is a concept that becomes meaningful in relation to its specific historical context. Mikael Af Malmborg and Bo Stråth (2002, p. 3) have argued that Europe is the invention of nation-states. By this provocative statement they wanted to highlight not only that there are different national answers to the 'What is Europe?' question but also that Europe is essentially a constructed nation. Stråth, like Delanty (1995), among other-well known contemporary historians and sociologists, points to the diverse meanings that Europe has assumed in history. They pay, however, less attention to the fact that Europe may have multiple meanings also synchronically. At a given point in time, depending on the perspective we adopt and the situation in which we find ourselves, Europe may represent very different things. Thus, perhaps we should speak of 'many *Europes*' rather than of just one.

Not only has the definition of Europe varied through the past centuries and even decades – as historians and sociologists argue – but its content and meaning also varies in relation to the different realms of social life. Delanty and Rumford (2005) argue that Europe has become a dimension that cannot be ignored at both the societal and the political level. Rather, we would say that there are different Europes operating in various social realms: there is a Europe in culture and/or something called 'a European civilization' (even if its meaning is highly contested); there is a Europe in politics and a social Europe; there is also a Europe in history and there are boundaries to Europe that are constantly shifting and changing. From a conceptual viewpoint, there is no need – and it is not possible either – to define a single Europe, drawing together all these meanings and perspectives into a single container. From an ideological viewpoint, however, it is possible to provide not only a critical review but also a synthesis of what Europe is – and also of what it should be at present.

Brand Europe

The issue of the *European-ness* of its people and countries that are at the geographical or cultural margins of the current EU project raises the question of *power*: who has the power to decide what Europe is and who belongs to it? This is a question seldom dealt with in academic and media debates, perhaps because it is judged as self-evident or, by some, as less important.

For instance, decisions on who belongs to the EU are taken by the European Council, consisting of the member states, which consider themselves, and are largely recognized by other countries, as the legitimate owners of the 'brand' name 'Europe'.

Their ownership of the European-Union-slash-Europe as a geopolitical project is not argued on the basis of a crude power rhetoric. The political dimension of Europe's 'ownership' is largely framed into a wider claim of ownership over culture and symbols (Handler, 1988, p. 142). The Copenhagen criteria for new countries' accession to the EU, the political conditionality principles of EU international aid programmes, as well as the official EU negotiations' debate with associated countries, such as Turkey, or other Balkan states, supposedly reflect this value dimension rather than a crude difference in power. Nonetheless, this value debate presupposes a power dimension: the EU and the countries that currently belong to it have the power to judge whether other countries, nations, ethnic groups, territories, traditions, cultural forms or symbols are 'European'. And as Bourdieu (1991, p. 236) has argued, to name something is to bring it into existence. The political and symbolic power to assign the European label as a brand name that belongs to the EU has gone largely uncontested in recent years. However, this was not always the case and this is one aspect of the 'What is Europe?' question that needs to be critically explored with a view to uncovering how this power of naming has been used in the past and what its implications are today for defining Europe. Chapters 2, 4 and 5 on the Changing Shape of Europe, on Cultural Europe and on European Identity, respectively, tackle some of these issues.

Historical trajectories

In scholarly debate, some researchers have proposed theoretical or historical models from which a definition of Europe will emerge somehow 'naturally' and 'objectively' from *historical* inquiry. Europe has existed in history, albeit in different shapes and with different meanings or modes of organization. The EU is simply a landmark in the historical trajectory of the larger entity called 'Europe'. In effect, however, much of the political and public discourse assumes an a-historical perspective: it treats the EU as a development unique in history and once formed, destined to be there until the end of time. This implicit view that

ny media and politicians take for granted leads to the search
for absolute and timeless definitions of Europe often disguising
the power differentials and (geo)political dynamics behind them.

Adopting a critical perspective, Chapters 2 and 3 in this vol-
ume discuss the origins of the term 'Europe' and the different
meanings it has acquired over the centuries, as well as the different European unification projects that have developed in the last
100 years. More specifically, Chapter 2 looks at how the term
emerged, mainly as a geographical expression demarcating the
Christian world and how it changed in the mid-fifteenth century.
In particular, a milestone occurred after the fall of Constantinople
to the Ottoman Turks in 1453 and the colonial expansion
of European powers after 1492, giving way to the notion of
European identity as a system of 'civilizational values'. It is argued
that after the fall of Constantinople, when the Greek Christian
Eastern Empire disappeared and Europe was confined to the Latin
West, the idea of Europe began to replace Christendom and eventually became a new cultural frame of reference.

The meaning of Europe is examined during the period of
European explorations of other parts of the world, between the
fifteenth and eighteenth centuries, when the Christian universal
mission was replaced by the 'white man's burden'. 'Europe'
as a term is of course also linked to the Renaissance and the
Enlightenment. The Enlightenment philosophers identified with
the idea of Europe as the process of modernity and valued the
primacy of science and rationality. Europe provided the symbol
of the new universal civilization predicated by the Enlightenment.

The changes in the meaning of Europe during the era of
nationalism, notably in relation to both early nation formation
in the seventeenth and eighteenth centuries, and the more recent
nationalist movements in the nineteenth and twentieth centuries,
are herewith discussed along with how the term was used within
nationalist discourses to signify specific geographical areas,
values or populations.

A European value system?

Chapter 3 investigates the visions that Europe has stirred in recent
centuries among thinkers and statesmen. However, to understand the various visions that Europe has inspired in the minds of
European thinkers and leaders, it is necessary to understand the

political context within which these have been formulated and the drivers of these narratives. It is also necessary to trace the values and ideas that have been associated with these visions of Europe. Chapter 3 discusses what has inspired attempts at defining Europe and unifying it and the context within which these narratives co-existed, antagonized, impregnated and succeeded one another. The chapter offers a critical reading of the various projects of a united Europe promoted by different thinkers, intellectuals and politicians in the interwar period, during the rise of fascism and Nazism as well as in the post-war era and during the Cold War. We highlight the different variants of this imagined European unity and critically discuss its west-Eurocentrism, pointing to how such projects were perceived and conceived in Central Eastern Europe. The chapter concludes with a forward-looking reflection on the meaning and relevance of Europe in the near future.

European cultural dimensions

Complementing the political dimension of Europe, Chapter 4 discusses its cultural dimension. It actually highlights the ambivalence of any reference to a European culture or value system. We try to unravel European culture and what it represents, or rather what it has represented at different times, and in what ways these representations are relevant to the present. By navigating between the ideas of Europe as civilization, Europe as progress, Europe as modernity, Europe as unity and Europe as diversity, we explore the key themes that have been dominant in Europe's cultural battleground and their significance today. We also try to pinpoint some of the dissenters and exceptions to this theory.

We highlight some of the complexities and contradictions that make up the way culture is understood and explore the ways in which European culture has been defined, the heritages that constitute it and their relevance in contemporary understandings of European culture. We also present some efforts that have been made to attribute meaning and offer definitions of 'European' culture on the part of international and regional inter-state organizations, whose scope of competence covers issues of culture, education, democracy and cooperation. We also delve into Europe's relationship with the 'Other', in order to underscore the cleavages, contradictions and alternative visions that have been put forward as representations of European culture and European values.

Throughout this *parcours culturel*, we seek the dominant, the alternative and the dissenting definitions of what is included and represented within 'European culture'. Just as importantly, we explore what 'European culture' aspires to. This latter aspirational dimension is probably its most distinctive feature, as it has shaped its universalist and forward-looking dimensions. European culture acquires meaning when the commonalities, shared values and experiences of the past are constructed in a forward-looking manner. In other words, references to a European culture seem to mostly be made when its constituent parts claim their belonging to a shared cultural space in order to express a political vision of Europe and the ideals it represents – or ought to represent.

Political and public discourses also refer to the social dimensions of Europe, notably the welfare policies that aim at taking care of the most vulnerable populations in society, on the basis of a shared notion of social solidarity. However, such discourses hugely differ both among European countries and within each country. Any similarity among them must be understood in relative terms: national social models of European countries, and their ideological variants, differ significantly from one country to the other. However, they are more similar with one another than with the social protection models that exist in other countries outside Europe. Indeed, any discussion of the social dimension of Europe today must acknowledge both the different welfare models and value constellations that prevail in each society and the different historical experiences that, for instance, characterize Western/Southern European countries from their Central and Eastern European neighbours.

Loaded meanings

The different meanings and outlooks of Europe through history raise, unavoidably, the question of whether a European identity exists, or has ever existed, and in what form. Do the Europeans feel European? And if they do, how does a feeling of belonging to Europe relate to other important collective and political identities, such as national identity or indeed ethnic/minority identity?

This set of questions is unpacked in Chapter 5. First of all, we need to discuss what kind of identity is, or would be, a European identity. Should we expect it to be like a national identity? Should it have a similar type of cultural content, notably a language, a set of customs and traditions, a common civic culture, links with a historical homeland and a current political territory, a single economy and a wish to be politically autonomous if not for outright political independence? And if it is to be such a kind of primary political identity, have we seen this European identity take shape over the last two or three decades, when the communist regimes in Central Eastern Europe collapsed in 1989? Is it since then that Europe has been culturally and politically reconnected?

Or, should European identity be understood as an 'umbrella' type of secondary political identity that brings together a range of national identities that have some similarities in common, notably links to a common geographical territory (the European continent) and a certain link with a common European culture (see Chapter 4 on European culture and European values). This kind of secondary and mediated type of collective identity – mediated, that is, through national belonging – appears to have been a predominant feature of the European identity so far in the twenty-first century.

A second range of questions with regard to European identity considers the relationship between European identity, cultural diversity and democratic inclusive politics. Is European identity an 'open' identity that allows for the inclusion of migrants and minorities or is it a 'closed' one, as national identities often are? Can European identity help us, the 'Europeans', to understand ourselves better and clarify our relations with our 'significant others', whether these are minorities and immigrants within Europe or other nations, world regions, cultures or civilizations.

There are at least two implicit questions that are usually neglected in this debate. First, *who defines* what kind of diversity 'belongs' to Europe? In other words, who speaks on behalf of Europe? Is it the EU institutions? Is it the EU member states (or rather some of the EU member states in particular, such as Germany or France)? Or is it the people of Europe? The people, though hesitant as regards their attachment to the 'EU', do seem to be expressing a common European connection in the way they express commonly shared concerns or 'indignation' with EU and national policies and politics in the form of demonstrations, marches and mobilization in social movements.

Second, *what kind of cultural or religious diversity* is judged to be alien to the European continent and hence is not necessarily included in the 'Unity in Diversity' motto? Islam and Muslims are an obvious case in point here. For some politicians and a part of the public opinion in European countries, there is no such a thing as European Muslims or European Islam. Islamic traditions are alien to most of Europe. They have been the by-product of Arab expansion or Ottoman conquest in a more distant past and of recent migrations and colonial relations in recent times. But they are not considered as belonging to the European cultural and value area. However, Islam not only has a historical presence of centuries in Spain (800 years) and countries that were under Ottoman Empire rule (400 years), there is also a new European Islam that is the outcome of earlier labour migrations of the post-war period. However, as we discuss in Chapter 5, the question of whether Europe and Islam can belong together remains unsettled in public and political debates.

The geographical conundrum

Moving from geopolitics to geography, there are claims of *European-ness* by nations and people that are on the fringes of the continent and even beyond it, in Eurasia or in northern Africa. It is actually often unclear whether people wish to join an area of security and prosperity identified with the EU or whether they make reference to a cultural, historical or symbolic notion of Europe that brings with it certain value connotations. The question of the borders and boundaries of Europe is taken up in Chapter 6.

Europe's external borders, or boundaries that trace its periphery and limits, are not the only borders that matter; there are also borders within. These internal borders – whether functional, spatial, national, ethnic, religious, linguistic, ideological or socio-economic – are just as defining in terms of creating identities and attributing substance to the concept of 'Europe'. These internal borders, in many cases much more than the external ones, have structured both the course of Europe's history and also the perceptions the rest of the world holds about Europe. Finally, there are borders that are not even situated at the borders at all, at least in the geographico-politico-administrative sense of the term (Balibar, 2002, p. 84). In effect, informal, cultural or ideational borders may exclude or marginalize some socioeconomic groups from access to certain policies, privileges or rights.

Understanding Europe's internal and external borders is therefore fundamental to any attempt at defining what Europe is, what it represents, and what it aspires to. We try to tackle the issue of borders and boundaries in Chapter 6 in order to trace and identify some of the constitutive elements that define 'Europe', the changes that have occurred to these elements and how they have transformed and influenced what Europe represents. William Walters (2009) has argued that debates about the frontiers of Europe are necessary political interventions which interject elements of fixture into the fluid, diverse and ambiguous space that constitutes Europe. Thus, Chapter 6 highlights the politics of power behind different configurations of Europe's borders and boundaries and, through this, offers some insight on how others perceive Europe.

The political power map

The question of power poses two further interrelated questions: one concerns the political dimension in defining Europe and the other, the existence of a European culture and of a set of European values. Chapter 7 discusses the political dimension in defining Europe. This is particularly challenging not just because of the inherent complexity of politics but also because of the diversity that characterizes the political features in or of Europe. Unavoidably, we have been selective and highly subjective with regard to which political dimension we have singled out to discuss here.

Europe's political map is composed of a rich range of competing ideologies, from the liberal to the illiberal and from the democratic to the undemocratic, all with universalist aspirations and global resonance. It has been crafted through the coexistence of a long legacy of nation-building, of state-building, of improving democratic institutions and democratic governance and tumultuous experiences of different types of authoritarian rule. It has also been shaped by a history of tensions between the civil and the military centres of power and between the civil and religious centres of power.

The political map of Europe essentially emerged in the late Middle Ages. During the thirteenth and fourteenth centuries, the

Church's hegemony began to gradually be challenged by powerful rulers, and feudalism offered the frame within which Europe's nation-states emerged. The social structures of feudalism lay the groundwork for the political structures that established France, Portugal, Spain and England. Among the most important structures of this period were the assemblies that are the roots of Europe's parliamentarism, and the system of justice (that was separate from the feudal structure), which along with the reintroduction of Roman Law, enabled the systematic and organized record of judgements and administrative decisions. Thus, at the end of the Middle Ages, the emergence of these European nation-states along with the Roman-German Empire and the later establishment of the Austro-Hungarian Empire replaced the fluid political territorial organization, which had been regionalized and compartmentalized until then.

Southeastern Europe was perhaps the exception to this trend given the political fluidity that continued to characterize the Balkans, Hungary, Moldavia and Bulgaria, and the threatening rise of the Ottoman Empire in the east. Nonetheless, the interstate system that began to emerge in this historical period became characteristic of Europe and was then exported to the rest of the world, forming the basis of the organization of modern political life in all corners of the world and the building blocks of international relations. Capitalism also emerged in this period mainly in the urban centres of northern Italy and the Netherlands and undoubtedly defined the socioeconomic cleavages and ideological conflicts in all political systems over the next six centuries.

Ideological cleavages

Chapter 7 concentrates on the left wing/right wing division in European politics among 'Western European' countries. The chapter discusses the main tenets of the left wing/right wing cleavage in the 1980s, when the 'Iron Curtain' was still in place and the world was divided into capitalist and communist camps, and corporativist models of mass production were still largely functioning in Western European countries. It then examines how the left wing dimension was reconsidered in the post-1989 context to the extent that some thinkers announced the 'end of ideologies' or even 'the end of history', as Francis

Fukuyama famously put it. In the post-1989 context, the focus was on how the left wing/right wing cleavage was reshaped and/or intertwined with the notions of 'Western' or 'Eastern' Europe to that of a common 'united Europe'.

Peace, freedom, security and human rights are declared in political debates as core European political values. These general political principles, while important in defining the main common tenets of different political cultures in Europe, are not exclusively European. The way these are codified and conceptualized in contemporary politics and policies is undoubtedly defined by the European experience, history, philosophical heritage, legal and political systems. Nevertheless, peace, freedom, security and human rights are values that are part of all cultures and civilizations, even though they may be defined, prioritized or understood in different ways. The European or Western reading of these values as universal is often criticized by cultural relativists underlining that certain societies may prioritize social over political rights, or respect for tradition over certain individual rights or even nationalism over peace. In this respect, it is worth reconsidering the debate over the European character of these principles mainly to uncover the 'cultural property' and historical arguments that underlie it.

Europe and (in)equality

A social dimension is inherent to the discussion about what Europe is. The social dimension involves conceptions of equality and inequality, solidarity and community or indeed responsibility and autonomy. It includes ideas about rights and obligations of the citizens towards the state and of the state towards its citizens. The social dimension is fundamentally about what we consider a 'good' society and lies at the heart of the functioning of democracy and citizenship. Social protection provided by the state enables all citizens to function as such and creates the institutional links between the individual and her/his family, on one hand, and the state and society, on the other.

Thus, in Chapter 8, we concentrate on the political framework and cultural connotations of concepts such as community, solidarity and social cohesion. We argue that the current concept of social solidarity is strongly based on the concept of national citizenship that purports a high level of community cohesion and solidarity among fellow nationals. However, there are a number of related developments that need to be taken into account when discussing the social dimension of Europe. These include the withering-away of the Fordist system of production and its replacement by a post-Fordist world that is much more volatile. The increasing cultural diversity of European societies as the result of post-war migrations in Western Europe, of post-1989 migration in Southern Europe and of the revival of nationalism and ethnicity in the post-1989 period in Central and Eastern Europe. The declining demography of Europe also needs to be taken into account.

Last but not least, a discussion of social Europe needs to engage with the post-1989 context and the rise of neoliberalism as a dominant if not hegemonic paradigm for socioeconomic relations. This temporary disruption of the ideological struggle among different conceptions of social solidarity and justice has transformed social justice struggles to technocratic debates about whether one system of welfare payments or entitlements is more effective than another. This has had important implications for the normative and political foundations of the European welfare systems and the values and self-conceptions of European societies. Interestingly, in the present day, we are entering yet another phase, after the acute financial crisis that Europe experienced in the late 2000s and early 2010s. This is a phase where the hegemony of neoliberalism is challenged, and the importance of social protection and social solidarity is being considered anew, albeit in a completely different framework.

The geopolitical context

In defining what Europe is, the *geopolitical context* of the answer is important. In the former EU15 countries largely in the western, southern and Nordic parts of the continent, Europe was often synonymous with the EU. However, in some countries, such as the UK or Sweden, Europe or the EU is something 'out there', across the Channel or further south. To the new member states (those that joined the EU in 2004, 2007 and 2013) and the associated countries, Europe is both geographically and symbolically or historically wider than the EU. A large part of the elites but also lay people in these countries consider(ed) themselves European, regardless of their membership of the EU.

The same is true for Switzerland, Norway and Iceland, who may define themselves as part of the European continent but wish to maintain a certain autonomy from (even if in parallel also a close connection with) the EU. From a geopolitical perspective, Europe also entails the Council of Europe (CoE, founded in 1949), an international organization that today includes 47 countries and 820 million citizens from the westernmost to the easternmost corners of the European continent. One should also not neglect the role of the North Atlantic Treaty Organization (NATO); with 28 member countries today, it was created also in 1949 to safeguard the freedom and security of its members through political and military means and which ties most European countries to their allies across the Atlantic. More than just creating a security community, NATO has defined a significant part of Europe's presence in regional and global affairs on security issues. It has also influenced the ways in which much of Europe has responded to the numerous traditional and emerging security challenges that it faces.

Since the 1990s, both the CoE and NATO have seen their membership expand significantly to include the former Warsaw Pact countries, and during this time, their mission has also evolved. The CoE's mission in promoting the rule of law, democracy and human rights has been crucial, particularly in the early days of the political transition in Central and Eastern Europe, while NATO has had to reinvent its mission of cooperative security since its prime *raison d'être* (notably the Cold War context) ceased to exist and other geopolitical challenges emerged in Europe and beyond.

Europe's position in the global context is discussed in Chapter 9. We consider the Cold War era and the different *Europes* that existed during this timeframe. More specifically, on the one hand we examine the role that the Warsaw Pact and the Soviet Union's hegemony played in Central and Eastern Europe. And on the other hand, we discuss Western Europe as part of the Transatlantic Partnership and its development into the European Economic Community. We then examine the present geopolitical role of Europe in the world, given the tectonic shifts that have taken place in global politics since 1989. We question whether the idea of Europe can be distinguished from the EU or whether the EU has indeed monopolized the notion of Europe in its geopolitical dimension. We then analyse the position and role of the EU in the post-1989 and in the post-9/11 contexts and its responses to important critical junctures in international politics. We discuss the civilian and normative dimensions that the EU developed and the extent to which it attempted to assert itself as an alternative pole within the West, exercising soft power and multilateralism.

Ambitions to establish itself as a normative global actor; the importance it has attributed to the promotion of the triptych of democracy, human rights and rule of law in its external relations through its conditionality approach; its importance in the global economy; and its emphasis on regional cooperation and improved global governance constitute part of the story, suggesting an evolution towards Europe acting as a single entity in global politics. The other part of the story consists of a fragmented and divided Europe in global politics, a Europe unable to formulate a common foreign policy and a political power risking increasing irrelevance in global politics. In this context, Chapter 9 seeks to assess whether there are common elements bringing European countries together in international relations. Is there a distinctive European view on issues of war, peace, security, environment and general global politics or is there only an EU and separate national viewpoints?

Europe in and beyond the EU

During the first decade of the twenty-first century, the idea of European unity and of a distinctive European political project underwent, yet again, another set of crises. The early part of the decade, between 2002 and 2004, was pregnant with enthusiasm, at least among a large part of the national and European elites. They were excited with the emergence, through a process of public consultation and deliberation among representatives of the member states, of a Constitutional Treaty for Europe. Since the spring of 2005, ideas of a European unity and political project hit an all-time low, but this is not new, as European cynicism has occurred several times during the post-war period. The rejection of the Constitutional Treaty by the Dutch and French voters prompted all EU member states to enter a period of reflection on what the EU is or what it should become in the near future. Social and political discourses concentrated on whether the EU should pay more attention to the deepening dimension, addressing issues such as unemployment and social exclusion, or whether it should be more concerned with the widening perspective, notably furthering the enlargement process.

In the post-Constitution period, the 'reflection' exercise led to yet another socio-political arrangement with the Treaty of Lisbon. Overt conflict among the member states was avoided and so was radical change. At the same time, European institutions (such as the European Commission or the European Parliament) engaged in endless efforts to overcome the democratic deficit through web consultations and conferences aimed at non-governmental organizations (NGOs) and other stakeholders. Also, discussions about issues of public concern, such as gender equality, societal cohesion or the protection of the environment, were encouraged by European institutions in order to enhance citizens' awareness of their 'democratic ownership' over Europe. They emphasized the several types of goods and services that can best be addressed at the European level because of their transnational nature.

Times of crisis at the doorstep

This political and institutional crisis was then followed by an economic one. Triggered by the Greek soverign debt crisis in 2009, the foundations of the Eurozone were shaken to the extent that a real existentialist crisis challenged the EU. The end of the core European value of solidarity was proclaimed with public debate falling back into simplistic distinctions between northern and southern Europe, between centre and periphery, between creditors and debtors. Talk of a two (if not more)-speed Europe multiplied, based in principle on economic arguments of growth and fiscal stability, but essentially relapsing to cultural and religious stereotypes. In this discourse, there exists an implicit (and at times explicit) differentiation of 'Europeans'. Simply put, there is a core Europe composed of 'first class' Europeans who are virtuous savers, law-abiding, well-organized liberals and generally Protestant; and there is a second category of Europeans who consume more than they produce, and are debt-ridden, corrupt and disorganized.

In these discourses, Europe is lost or completely subjugated to the actual project of the EU. The term 'Europe' is used as a tautology: all EU countries are European countries and the reverse is true. Thus, the Europeanness of countries like Ukraine or Belarus that most people would geographically identify as Eastern European is denied because they do not meet the socioeconomic and political criteria necessary to become associated states or to open negotiations for EU membership. The same is true for some of the Balkan countries. Thus, Albania's or Serbia's *European-ness* is still under 'evaluation', while the European character of neighbouring Slovenia, Bulgaria and Croatia is 'confirmed' through their EU membership.

However, in those cases, the meaning of *European-ness* is not even debated – the power of current member states, or more precisely of certain member states, to decide who or what is properly European goes uncontested. The question of what Europe is or can be, within or beyond the EU, only comes to the fore when the Turkish membership question is debated. On these occasions, the cultural, geographical, religious and political contours of Europe and of traditions or values that are labelled 'European' emerge in the public and political debate. Such contested cases raise the question of how to define Europe and whether there is a geographical, cultural, social or political Europe that goes beyond the EU. It is through such debates that the concept of Europe is emancipated from the EU and its specific policies and power arrangements.

The question of Europe is also raised when it comes to questions of values or principles rather than political matters. The 2006 controversy over the depiction of the Prophet Mohammed in cartoons published originally in the Danish press and later re-published in several European dailies is a good case in point, as is the 2015 tragedy over the *Charlie Hebdo* satire and the killing of their editorial team by three Islamic extremists.

In 2006, the controversy started in Denmark, but soon acquired a transnational character to the extent that it attracted the attention of government elites in the Arab world asking for an apology from the Danish editor and/or government. Once the question of apology became a public concern (several months after the cartoons had been published originally in the Danish daily *Jyllands Post*), editors and journalists throughout Western Europe mobilized upholding or criticizing their publication. Concomitantly, the issue was given publicity in the Arab media (Soage, 2006) and citizens across Arab countries also mobilized, protesting against the cartoons. These protests led in some cities of the Middle East to violent outbursts and the burning of Danish embassies.

The 2015 *Charlie Hebdo* events were much more dramatic, as three extremists attacked and killed almost the entire editorial team of the newspaper in the latter's headquarters in Paris. The killing was presented as punishment for the cartoons that this small left-wing magazine had published through the years referring also to Islam and the Prophet. While the killings involved French citizens and a quintessentially French magazine, *Charlie Hebdo*, the crisis took an international turn. Five days later, on 11 January 2015, a huge rally in memory of the victims and against extremism was held in Paris and other French cities, gathering a total of 3.7 million people, among which were representatives from 40 countries, including African and Asian, predominantly Muslim, countries' leaders.

Both crises, in 2006 and in 2015, were not only international in nature but also specifically European in that they called into question important political principles such as freedom of expression and respect for other religions, as well as the limits of implementing these principles in practice.

In both the case of Turkish membership to the EU and the cartoons crises, the question of 'What is Europe?' becomes important through contrast to real or imagined threatening 'significant others', notably Muslim countries and Islam in general, even if several thinkers and some politicians recognize that there are European Muslims too. Paradoxically, both the European Muslims and the Muslims outside Europe become pivotal in answering the 'What is Europe?' question, freeing the debate from the EU straitjacket.

Europe writ large becomes relevant also in the realm of transatlantic relations. The partnership between the USA and Western Europe created a 'security community' (see Adler and Barnett 1998) that defined the course of the twentieth century in political, military, financial, economic, scientific and cultural terms. With the end of the Cold War, this community started to change and widen through the processes of EU and NATO enlargements. Over the past two decades, this community has been both enhanced and rendered more vulnerable, as Europe has changed. These changes have as much to do with the challenges posed by the continent's reunification and the EU's difficulties to widen and deepen; the challenges of post-communist transition for the countries of Central and Eastern Europe; and the challenges of post-conflict reconstruction for most of Southeast Europe, as with the global changes following 9/11, the consolidation of China's economic power and the global financial crisis.

Friend or foe?

Throughout all this, Europe becomes relevant through the direct or indirect efforts of the US political elites to contest the EU as a political player and to lure individual countries into privileged bilateral relations with the USA. On several occasions, the USA has sought directly or indirectly to foster instability and internal divisions within the EU. It happened in the case of the Iraq War with the G.W. Bush Administration's distinction between 'new' and 'old' Europe, and an argument that is frequently put forward is that US support for Turkey's EU membership essentially aims at putting an end to the project of political union. US diplomatic and military support for Kosovo's independence has also been seen in this light.

The transatlantic community renders Europe relevant in another dimension, as it points to tensions within what could be termed wider Western values of democracy, liberalism, freedom or secularism. Some issues, such as the death penalty or the possession of guns by individual citizens, have become exemplary of such tensions between a more European and a more North American current in the wider area of 'Western' values.

There is a majority of US citizens that tends to support the death penalty, as well as the right of citizens to possess and carry machine guns. Although there is strong internal contestation of these values, as there is contestation of the lack of a welfare safety net for the more disadvantaged sections of the US population, there is a distinct American tradition of individual freedom and individual responsibility that can be referred to as a support for both the death penalty and the policy about guns.

European countries, by contrast, have legally committed themselves to condemning the death penalty and severely restrict the possession of machine guns. They also support human rights in more fervent ways than the USA, although here again we see that practices are not always consistent. While intellectuals, the media and political parties condemned the Guantanamo base and generally the US policy on prisoners of war in Iraq and Afghanistan, European intelligence services cooperated with the CIA for the unlawful detention and interrogation of citizens or residents that were suspected to have played a part in terrorist plots, without upholding the necessary judicial scrutiny and procedure. Nonetheless, there seems to be a culture of human rights and respect for human life that expresses itself by condemning the death penalty and by defending civil liberties even at the risk of loosening public security measures that is stronger on this side of the Atlantic than in North America.

At the same time, compared with Europe, the USA is a society where religion and religiosity are more prevalent, where references to God are considered an integral part of pre-election campaigns. The high level of religiosity in North American society was also evident in the management of the cartoons crisis there. The North American media refused to re-publish the cartoons insulting Prophet Muhammad on the grounds that these constituted unnecessary offence to the religious sentiments of some people. This concern was stronger than the concern of upholding freedom of expression. In Europe, by contrast, there was much less concern about religious sensitivities and the entire debate focussed on the balance between freedom of expression and freedom of religion, leaving the question at the end unsettled.

Concluding remarks

The above reflections suggest that the idea of Europe as a cultural, political or geographical entity is currently largely subsumed under the notion of the 'European Union', which has become hegemonic in Europe and abroad. Nonetheless, there are important matters and dimensions that are not and cannot be covered by a single discourse on European integration and that become apparent mainly when Europe is contrasted with 'Others', other nations, cultures or continents, because they are too close or too distant symbolically and/or geographically from Europe. In exploring the 'What is Europe?' question, this book also explores how Europe is viewed from these 'Other' continents and nations, notably from the Near or more distant East but also from the West (North America in particular).

Overall this book is forward thinking: it looks into the past to better understand the present and to think about the future in innovative ways. It reviews past scholarly literature and research evidence on Europe with a view to clarifying the power dynamics behind naming Europe and to highlighting the diverse *Europes* that exist within and beyond the current European unification project. The book seeks to emancipate the concept of Europe from the hegemony of EU discourses and also to analyse some of these discourses critically. It also argues against an excessive Eurocentrism in the public debate and in the scholarly literature, obsessed with defining Europe. Rather, such a debate reveals the uncertainty and fuzziness of a European cultural or political entity and of a European identity. However, such an uncertainty is not, in our view, necessarily a bad thing. Such uncertainty could contribute to a self-critical and reflexive attitude within European countries.

Chapter 2

The Changing Shape of Europe

History is obviously not merely a simple record of a series of facts. It is an effort at understanding, interpreting and reinterpreting specific events, or, even more so, humanity at work. It sits on a fine line between objectivity and subjectivity, between an account of actions and our individual perspective of them. Our historical perspective is tainted by ideology, by time and distance. It is essentially a series of arguments that are debated, a selection of events presented by the historian in an effort to understand the why and how. We may actually distinguish between history as the product of critical inquiry into the past and history as 'our story', as a narrative that offers an awareness and understanding of the present, an explanation of the drivers of social change and, implicitly, a way to the future. This distinction between history as an academic endeavour and history as a meaning-making narrative may appear clear-cut in theory, but in practice, it can be fuzzy. Even a critical academic inquiry includes some degree of narrative. Ultimately, the historian does not stand in a historical (or ideological) void, s/he is also historically situated.

This book's attempt to examine the different shapes that Europe has taken through the centuries adopts a critical perspective while also recognizing the limits of the 'objectivity' of such an account. By reviewing some of the core debates that have defined Europe in history, we try to understand why and how the meaning of Europe has shifted. Undoubtedly, the book's reading of events is tainted by the authors' individual perspectives and possibly also by their expectations. Why? Because any account of history implicitly carries a promise of carrying the truth and the most plausible explanation about a series of events in order to inform, educate and most importantly, offer the possibility to learn from the past. The truth is, we hardly ever do. Nevertheless, we always hope to because it is hard to steer clear from the common

Western bias that refers to history in order to measure progress and that hopes to use history to improve the present, avoid repetition of mistakes, and overcome crises.

In this chapter we first outline the different geographical and cultural shapes that Europe has taken through the centuries, starting from the mythological origins of the word Europe, and tracing its evolution through antiquity, Roman times, the onset and expansion of Christianity, the age of Empire, the French Revolution, the wars of the nineteenth century, the overall process of industrialization and nation formation in the different parts of Europe, and concluding with the ways in which the two world wars have shaped our contemporary understanding of Europe, and shaped the origins, or rather the wish, for a united Europe. However, this is not a chapter on European history or on the history of Europe; it is a chapter on the changing locations and shapes that Europe has taken throughout history with a view to highlighting the relationship of the term Europe with other influential notions in each historical period such as classical Greece, the Roman Empire, Christianity, the *mission civilisatrice*, modernity, and so on.

The changing shape of Europe in history

In this section, we explore the different meanings of Europe over time and in different realms of life – that is from a cultural, religious, political or economic perspective. Providing a comprehensive history of the idea goes beyond the scope of this book; it is, however, important to note that the term Europe has had different meanings and uses in different historical periods and that these meanings and uses were determined by the cultural and geopolitical frameworks of each historical period and of the political and economic powers emerging within them. This brief summary of the evolution of the notion of Europe in the past 25 centuries aims less to give a complete account of the definitions and connotations of the term, as this would be impossible in a single chapter and has been eloquently done by others (Perrin, 1994; Delanty, 1995; Pagden, 2002; Perkins, 2004; Delanty and Rumford, 2005). The aim is rather to show how the concept of Europe is a product of history and has occasionally acquired its own reality and symbolic power. A discussion of the meaning and uses of the term Europe provides important information about what is not Europe and who were the other cultural, political or geographical entities that were distinguished from Europe.

Hellenic Europe

The name Europe is a transliteration of the Greek work *Ευρώπη (Evropi)*. The name finds its origins in Greek mythology: *Evropi* is the name of a young woman, daughter of the Phoenician king Agenor (king of the city of Tyre on the coast of Sidon, in present day Lebanon), who was abducted by Zeus, the supreme ruler of Mount Olympus and of the pantheon of gods who resided there. Zeus, known in Greek mythology for his weakness for beautiful young women, seduced and abducted Europe disguised as a white bull. He brought Europe to Crete to bear their offspring. There, she later married the king of Crete. The place where she arrived was to take her name, Europe, and their offspring would be called Europeans (*Ευρωπαίοι – Evropaioi*), or so the story goes.

This myth has been the subject of various interpretations from ancient times until the present day. The ancient Greek historian Herodotus argues that the myth reflects the economic and military rivalry between the Cretans and Phoenicians: Europe, a Phoenician princess, was abducted by Cretan merchants who took her to be a bride to their king Asterius (Pagden, 2002, p. 34). The story and the myth is actually repeated in the case of Troy and the abduction of beautiful Helen, wife of Menelaus, the king of Sparta, supposedly an act of revenge by the Asians towards the Europeans, specifically the Greeks. According to Herodotus, the fact that the Greeks started a war, the famous Trojan War, for the honour of a woman, was something specific to the Europeans because apparently Asians would not take the rape of one of their women as something worth waging a war over (Pagden, 2002, p. 34). Already in this ancient interpretation of the myth we find both a geographical demarcation of Europe and a cultural distinction between Europe and Asia.

Europe was referred to by Homer as the daughter of Phoenix in line with the narrative, while in ancient Greek mythology in general she was frequently mentioned as the sister of Asia and Libya (Africa). The three sisters symbolized the three land masses. It is the very same Herodotus who notes that he could not understand 'why three names, and women's names at that, should have been given to a tract which is in reality one' (Herodotus, Histories, VII, 104 cit. in Pagden, 2002, p. 36). His argument is occasionally taken up today by scholars, who note that Asia and Europe are in reality one land mass and that it is only our Eurocentric view of the world that makes us define contemporary Europe as a continent, separate from Asia and Africa (Pocock, 2002).

Regardless of which version of the myth is valid, it is clear from the writings of Greek historians like Herodotus or first-century cartographer Strabo that Europe was geographically located in the south-eastern part of the Mediterranean basin, quite far from where the geographical and political centre of Europe lies today. Naturally, that was the result of the ancient Greeks' own geographical location and of the limits of their knowledge of the world that surrounded them. Europe was centred on the Aegean Sea and was largely synonymous to Hellas, notably the Greek peninsula and its surrounding islands in the Aegean and Crete. Perhaps unsurprisingly given the maritime character of the Greek civilization, Europe was centred on the Aegean Sea and more widely on the Mediterranean Sea. It was less centred on land, nor was it a continent of any sort. It was rather the shores surrounding the well-known and well-travelled south-eastern part of the Mediterranean where the Greeks developed their colonies.

It is in these foundational myths and early conceptions of Europe that we can already identify some of the core features that characterize the idea of Europe today: notably the belief that Europe is the cradle of democracy and the prototype of man-made civilization based on the combination of nature with the rule of law.

First of all, the past and present distinctiveness of Europe lies to a large extent on the basic distinction of the ancient Greeks between the 'Hellenes' and the 'barbarians'. While during classical Greek times Persians came to epitomize 'the barbarians', the term was used in a rather expansive way to refer to all non-Greeks. This opposition was based on a complex set of factors which combined climate, natural environment and race (*ethnos*). To put it simply, those farther east and south in Asia and Libya were seen as intelligent and sensitive people but also lazy, lethargic and ultimately corrupt. The natural features of their environment supposedly created a predisposition for despotic rule and apathy. On the other hand, those living farther north from Europe (the Mediterranean basin that is) were thought of as brave and hard-working but also unthinking, uncultivated people, who were ultimately uncivilized (sic) (Pagden, 2002, p. 36).

Greece (and in relation to it Europe) was considered to lay in between the two extremes, thus symbolizing 'civilization'. It was the place where the temperate climate and the landscape combined to form a people and a culture that had the best of both worlds. They were intelligent and peace-loving; they cultivated the land; and brought together the force of nature with the power of the law. The Greeks/Europeans were the freest of all people because they obeyed the law rather than the will of their master. Anthony Pagden wonders how and why the ancient Greeks, who were chauvinist in their attitudes, came to include in their conception of civilized people other non-Greeks, notably the other 'Europeans' in the Mediterranean basin. He comes to the conclusion that this happened because the peoples of the south-eastern part of the Mediterranean were interdependent for their survival and flourished through trade and exchange (Pagden, 2002, p. 39). In summary, it was this unique combination of climatic and territorial features that were considered to define Europe, that is, the Mediterranean basin and the Greek peninsula and islands, as the centre of the known world and the cradle of civilization. The dividing line with both north and south was their intemperate climate and their 'barbarian' attitudes and way of life.

While it is clear that the Greeks were distinguished from the Asians, who were seen as barbarian, it is less clear whether the Greeks were also called Europeans or whether, as Aristotle writes, the Greeks were opposed to both the Asians and Europeans, who were both seen as uncivilized (The Politics, 1962, pp. 136 and 269 cit. in Delanty, 1995, p. 18). Delanty reviews several ancient Greek thinkers including Plato, Aeschylus, Herodotus and Isocrates to show that there is uncertainty about whether the term Europe had any geographical or cultural meaning for the ancient Greeks. He questions whether the Europeans were seen as part of the Greek culture and civilization or whether they were also considered as barbaric, even if to a lesser degree than the peoples of Asia. The conclusion is indeed dubious. Some classical thinkers identified Greece with Europe and Persia with Asia; others distinguished between Greeks and non-Greeks, including in the latter category both Europeans and Asians; others still completely ignored the term Europe.

Three points are worth considering here: First, Europe had its origins outside the borders of contemporary Europe and even outside the borders of ancient Greece – indeed the mythical origins of Europe and its cultural and political distinctiveness had more to do with Asia Minor than they had to do with Europe itself. Second, Europe was born out of its opposition with Asia, much like Hellas contrasted itself to Phoenicia and Persia. Europe was based on the notion of Hellenism that implied an opposition and a dualism between civilizations combined with a strong ethno-centrism. What is today called the oriental 'other' finds its roots in these proto-conceptions of Europe. Third, the concept of Europe as a cultural community, which is today inextricably linked with that of classical Greece, was largely unimportant at the time. It gradually emerged as classical Greek civilization came into contact with Christianity (Peckham, 2003).

The concept of Europe in antiquity starts emerging as a distinct geographical and political entity after Alexander the Great. As Alexander appropriated the Greek language and culture, united the Greek peninsula under Macedonia and brought, through his conquests, the Greek language and culture much farther east, a broader concept of Europe that referred to the south-eastern part of the Mediterranean including Asia Minor started to emerge. However, Alexander arrived much farther than any conception of Europe would reach – he even left Greek settlers in India – but his expansion of the Greek cultural influence eastwards brought about the use of the term Europe for the wider region and emancipated the term from classical Greek references to the barbaric Europeans. Interestingly, the core of Europe moved eastwards, and was centred on the Aegean Sea and Asia Minor, areas that in more recent times are considered only peripherally European (Perrin, 1994). These territories were perceived as culturally and politically 'European' for many centuries because they belonged to the Roman and later the Byzantine Empires.

The concept of Europe emerging at the time of Alexander the Great is largely built on the contrast to the Oriental 'other', which included the Persians and beyond Persia, and the other Asiatic civilizations. In other words, even these early conceptions of Europe were subordinated to a concept of the West, albeit that the western frontier was further to the east than it is today.

Reconsidering the meaning and uses of the term Europe in ancient times suggests that Europe was rather unimportant for the ancient Greeks, and for the Persians for that matter, and that if any sort of reference to Europe existed, it was centred much more to the east than it is today. Much of the connection between ancient Greece and Europe in modern times appears to be the work of modern 'European' intellectuals since the Enlightenment, when the link was reconstructed through references to ancient Greek civilization. As Tsoukalas also argues (2002) the Hellenism of modern Greece was largely imposed on it by Western Europeans while modern Greece had more to do with the Orient culturally and politically. The construction, however, of the link between ancient Greece and Europe has now served as a legitimizing myth for the Eurocentric interpretation of European civilization as unique and universal in the same way that ancient Greeks believed that their own culture and civilization was unique and superior to all others.

Roman Europe

With the fall of Macedonia and its defeat by Rome in 197 BC a new era started, not only for the Greek peninsula, but also for the wider Mediterranean basin. While Rome was the centre of the empire, the heart of the empire remained in the eastern Mediterranean. As Pocock notes, the Roman Empire was not continental, it was Mediterranean. It signified the 'hegemony of a central Italian people over all three of the coastlands – Asian, African and European – first defined in the ancient Mediterranean and has been carried deep into the hinterlands behind each' (Pocock, 2002, p. 59). Indeed the Roman Empire was characterized not only by its maritime routes but also by the roads that the Romans travelled and built into the European continent as far north and west as present-day England.

During the Roman times, the idea of Europe was of secondary importance. The governors or citizens of the Roman Empire did not think of themselves as European even if they might recognize that Rome was situated in Europe. In the early Christian era, Christianity was also associated with the Roman Empire; to be a Christian was to be a Roman, not a European as was later the case. At the same time, what are now known as Europeans were called 'Franks' (indeed these terms survive to this day in the languages of Syria and Iran, in Egypt but also in colloquial Greek).

The Roman world introduced a codified legal system and developed a network of cities and written cultures that allowed trade and connections between peoples and places as far afield as contemporary Britain and Iraq to develop. The Mediterranean basin was a central point of reference and indeed a sea that united people rather than divided them. The contemporary division between east and west was much less pronounced then. By contrast, the division between north and south, both in geographical and cultural terms, was felt more acutely: the Alps were much more of a natural frontier than the sea could be. The Roman Empire integrated important Hellenic and oriental influences rather than any occidental traits. 'Europe had not yet been "westernized"; nor for that matter, had the East been "orientalised"' (Delanty, 1995, p. 20).

While the empire depended for its survival on the vast areas of Asia, Africa and Europe over which it exercised authority, its legal and political character was shaped by Greek philosophy and by the belief in the rule of law. The belief in the importance and power of law was such that, according to Nicolet (1988, p. 28), the Romans thought that 'the political realm of Rome and the human genus had been made one'. In other words, the Roman Empire largely continued the Greek quasi-mythical belief in the uniqueness of the Mediterranean environment and culture and in the superiority of the Greco-Roman civilization.

Even after its division into two parts in 286 AD, the (western part of the) Roman Empire was pretty much 'Eastern'. It comprised territories in Africa (the western parts of North Africa) and the Iberian peninsula. Greece, the Aegean Sea and Asia Minor remained in the eastern part of the empire, with the Italian peninsula becoming a natural dividing line. When Constantine transferred the capital to Constantinople in 330 AD, the city was meant to be the new Rome and its inhabitants called themselves Romans. At the same time, the western and northern parts of the Roman empire were quickly lost to the 'barbarians' of the north. Thus, the political and cultural epicentre of the Roman world and the conception of the Occident shifted eastwards (Pocock, 2002).

The cultural and political definition of the West and the East and the geographical demarcation of these terms, then and today, differ significantly. When the capital of the Roman Empire was transferred further east, this did not signify that the empire became 'oriental' (as the Greco-Roman civilization continued to contrast itself to the barbaric 'Orient'). Rather, it meant that the relevant centre of power moved eastwards.

This evolution was gradually subverted by the collapse of the western part of the Roman Empire, the dominance of the Gothic tribes and the eventual combination of Gothic and Roman law into a new system under the influence of Latin Christianity (Pagden, 2002, p. 43). Constantinople acquired an identity of its own that was more Eastern, and Greek language prevailed over Latin even though the latter remained the dominant *lingua franca* in the western part of the Roman Empire. At the same time, the 'Western' world as we understand it today started emerging and with it the notion of the European Occident, which came to be contrasted to Byzantium. In other words, the Orient started to move westwards and Asia Minor ceased to be perceived as 'occidental'.

While the role of the Byzantine Empire declined geopolitically after its failure to recover its western half, its civilizational role has been crucial: through its eastern and western roots and its reference to Rome it provided the continuity necessary for Christianity to emerge as the wider civilizational framework in Europe. However, the claim of Byzantine emperors on the Roman tradition, and their self-conception of their rule and of their empire as the natural heirs of Rome and its political and legal culture, indirectly pushed the western part of the empire and the emerging notion of Europe towards Latin Christianity.

The division and gradual collapse of the Roman Empire actually left two different legacies, an eastern and a western. It is only in the sixth and seventh centuries that the notion of Europe emerges as a geographical entity and slowly as a cultural entity that designates the former Western Roman Empire and, to a large extent, what we understand today geographically as Europe. However, the concept of Europe was at the time inextricably connected to and used interchangeably with the term Christianity.

Christian Europe

The passage from the proto-concept of Roman Europe to the Christian conception of Europe is important both politically and culturally. Europe finds its first unifying trait in the Greco-Roman legal and political culture, in the Roman legal system,

and in the Greco-Roman tradition of cities as political and
economic centres. Pagden (2002, p. 40) notes that although the
majority of the population of Europe was rural, the cultural
outlook of Europe, derived from its Greco-Roman past, was
conceived as ultimately urban. Indeed, Mediterranean and
Roman civilization was characterized by sophisticated urban
societies developed in the Greek, Roman, Arab and Iranian
worlds (Pocock, 2002, p. 60). Many of today's words that
describe social and political life are etymologically derived from
the Greek term *polis* (politics, polity) or from the Latin term
civitas (civil, civility, civilization), both of which make reference
to the urban environment (Pagden, 2002, p. 40).

While early Christianity spread not only north of the
Mediterranean, but also in many directions towards North
Africa, Arabia and Ethiopia, reaching as far as India, it was
the organization of the Christian church under papal authority
that gave Christianity an institutional and political weight. The
organization of the Catholic Church contributed to the spread of
Latin as a common language in the west, while Greek remained
a lingua franca in the eastern part. Europe's cultural reference
remained tied to the West, to Latin and Catholicism. Its connection with Byzantium and the former eastern part of the Roman
Empire was much weaker, if existing at all. In fact in the modern
Greek national narrative, Byzantium is considered to be Greek
in its culture and Christian in its religion, hence it is quintessentially both Greek and European. Its oriental influences and links
are re-interpreted through the emphasis on its Greco-Roman
culture. However, in many parts of what we now call Europe
while the Europeanness of ancient Greece is not only accepted
but reinforced, the European character of Byzantium is put into
question.

The passage from a Roman to a Christian proto-conception
of Europe is mediated by the Jewish tradition. First and foremost the influence is cultural, as Judaism lays at the origin of the
Christian tradition. Judaism supersedes the polytheistic nature of
the Greco-Roman world, and proposes one almighty God that
is made in the image of man and can redeem humans from sin.
The Jewish belief in salvation through personal redemption
introduces one of the basic cultural elements of Christianity
and actually reinforces the importance of the individual as an
autonomous agent (originally found in ancient Greek political

thinking). Brunkhorst (2005) argues that Judaism also inspires the critical spirit of later Europeans through the Jewish rejection of Egyptian rule and the divine power of the Egyptian pharaoh, and their adherence to a higher law regulating their society. While Judaism and Christianity developed in separate directions as religions, their contribution along with that of the Greco-Roman tradition laid the seeds of what is now known as European civilization.

The idea of Europe however emerged more forcefully as a point of reference together with Christianity in the struggle against Islam. The religious revolution that took place in the seventh century in the fertile crescent of Asia brought about a major change in the geopolitical and cultural map of Europe and Asia. After the death of the Prophet Mohammed in 632 AD, his followers spread though Arabia and conquered the Persian Empire of the Sassanids (present-day Iraq, Syria and Palestine). The Arabs conquered most of North Africa during the seventh and eighth centuries, and in 711 AD defeated the Visigoths in the Iberian peninsula and conquered the lands south of the Pyrenees. Their empire also spread eastwards and reached India. Under these circumstances the limits of European and Christian civilization shrank to the Pyrenees and the Bosporus and attention shifted to the Islamic rather than the barbaric northern threat.

Indeed, the notion of Europe became deeply entrenched in this period with that of Christendom and acquired meaning by contrasting itself with the Arabs and the Islamic world. The Abbaside caliphate that replaced the Umayyads lasted between 750 AD and the mid-thirteenth century. As a result of its non-Arab expansion the caliphate transformed into an Islamic political system and its centre moved from Damascus to Baghdad, linking the Middle East with the other parts of Asia and North Africa. However, the Arab world absorbed much of the Greco-Roman civilization that had thrived in these territories and became to a large extent the natural continuation of this civilization in the sciences and philosophy during the centuries of Arab ascendancy. Arab cultural influences also reached Europe in the period until the sixteenth century when Arab civilization entered a period of decline. In the ninth century, with the annexation of Crete and Sicily, the Mediterranean basin became dominated by the Arabs and the European continent was put on the defensive.

It is in this period that we note clearly the migration of the concept of Europe from its water-based definition around the South-eastern Mediterranean to its continental definition, not only as the land that is separated from Asia by the Bosporus straits but also as a continental mass. The European continent then embraced Scandinavia, the British Isles, France, the Iberian peninsula, Italy, the Low countries, Germany, Austria, Poland, Hungary, Bohemia, Moravia, Slovakia and Croatia but not the territories where the concept was born, notably the southern part of the Balkan peninsula, the Greek archipelago or Asia Minor (Jordan, 2002, p. 75). Christianity became the glue that unified the different peoples and cultures of the former Western Roman Empire and its more northern territories in what is now known as the European continent. The Barbarian tribes that had conquered the former Western empire, among whom the Franks were the most important, converted to Christianity. Hence, they were no longer conceived of as a threat to Europe.

The emergence of the concept of Europe is intertwined with the rivalry between Latin/Catholic Christianity and Orthodox/Greek-speaking Christianity. The double legacy (one eastern and one western) of the Roman Empire was further perpetuated and reinforced during the ascendancy of Christianity. The emergence of the northern and western conception of Europe was increasingly detached from its proto-concept linked to Greco-Roman civilization. It denied any connection with the Middle East and contrasted itself to the Jews, and emphasized its Christian character in opposition to Islam. During the Dark Ages of Arab and Muslim ascendancy (fifth to ninth centuries), Christianity emerged as the special trait that qualified Europe and the Europeans, the idea of Rome as the centre of the western world was abandoned and the cultural and political centre of the 'Occident' moved west and north.

It is this defensive move to the west and north under pressure of attack from the south and the east that created Europe not only as a geographical but also as a cultural and, to a certain extent, a political entity. Although during these centuries (especially the tenth to thirteenth) the feudal system of production prevailed and there was no central political authority in the continent (Jordan, 2002), a sense of cultural unity was provided by Christianity, which was actually suitable to the agrarian world based on the ethics of obedience and hierarchy. Thus in the Dark

Ages, Europe emerged to describe a Christian Commonwealth that was opposed both culturally and politically to Islam.

This was when the east–west divide in the Mediterranean became more important than the north–south division. Moreover, the identification of Europe with Christianity and of the Orient with Islam led to the development of 'a moral-religious divide with the Occident signifying civilization and goodness and the Orient barbarity and evil' (Delanty, 1995, p. 26).

During the Middle Ages, the concept of Europe remained dependent on the wider notion of Christendom, notably the Christian world. Dawson has argued that it was because of Christendom that Europe first became conscious of itself as a society of peoples of common moral values and common spiritual aims (1952). The mobilization of the medieval kingdoms for the recovery of the holy lands in the Middle East provided both a legitimizing myth for their rulers and a common cultural reference that brought together people with different languages and ethnic traditions. The crusading ideology both prepared and prevented the emergence of a political concept of Europe. The reason was that while on the one hand it highlighted what the peoples inhabiting the continent had in common, on the other hand it gave them a non-territorial identity. Christianity was a universal identity and indeed a non-territorial one by definition. Moreover, the temporary occupation of Jerusalem by the crusaders (1099–1187) gave Christianity a meaning and a mission beyond the borders of the continent.

The pervasiveness of Christianity in Europe and the use and relevance of the term Europe until the fifteenth century should not however be overestimated. Until that time the Byzantine Empire provided also for a political expression of Christianity which, however, was increasingly identified as oriental and non-European. Besides, after the defeats in Manzikert by the Ottomans in 1071, the loss of Bari to the Normans in the same year and the looting of Constantinople by the crusaders of the fourth crusade, the empire lost much of its power and glory and entered a phase of decline until its dismantling by the ascending power of the Turks in the mid-fifteenth century.

Given the lack of territorial continuity of Christian lands and taking into account also the universal aspirations of the Christian religion, Christianity was not seen as synonymous to Europe but extending beyond it. It was rather in opposition to the Muslims on one hand and the Byzantines or Eastern Christians on the other that the notion of Christian Europe emerged.

The High Middle Ages were by and large marked by the opposition between Christian and Muslim powers in the African-Asian-European geographical complex. In the Latin West, the medieval kingdoms and their princes were put on the defensive in what they considered their lands. They eventually failed to capture in any enduring way the Holy lands but also saw their own territories shrinking as the Turks advanced into the Balkans and the Black Sea in the fourteenth century already. The fall of Constantinople to the Turks in 1453 is taken as an event of epochal significance that marked the start of a new era in Europe and Asia. The dismantling of the Byzantine Empire showed tangibly that Islam and the Ottoman Empire were now part of Europe. Not only had Asia Minor become 'oriental' politically and religiously but Turkey was also in what was thought of as Europe.

During this period, the only western victory over Islam took place in Spain when the king of León and Castile recaptured Toledo from the Arabs in 1085. However, it was not until 1492 when Ferdinand and Isabela conquered Granada that the Iberian peninsula was won over by the Christians, and it was only in the late seventeenth century that the western powers managed to regain control of Hungarian territories in the East from the Ottomans and reverse the trend of Islamic expansion.

References to Europe mostly appeared in public speeches of European princes and the Pope in the context of the Islamic advance and the Ottoman Empire. Yapp (1992, p. 141) notes that Pope Pius II said when he first heard of the fall of Constantinople 'now we have really been struck in Europe, that is, *at home*' [emphasis added], which shows both that Europe had a geographical meaning by then, as a continent, but also that the Pope considered himself and Christianity as intimately linked with Europe. This is by no means to say that Europe was a popular term or a strong collective identity felt by the people inhabiting the continent. Nevertheless, these scattered references to Europe and the Europeans in the discourses of the political and religious elites of the time mark the emergence of a political and cultural notion of Europe.

Overall, until the late fifteenth century Christianity was the most important cultural referent in the continent, while the term

Europe had more of a geographical and less of a political or cultural meaning (see Bartlett, 1993; Le Goff, 2005). However, the end of the Middle Ages, the continuing (and relatively unsuccessful) struggle against Islamic invasion from the East and the expansion of European powers to the west to discover new lands brought the concept of Europe to the fore.

Missionary Europe

Europe developed as a cultural notion in the fifteenth till the seventeenth century by reference to two fronts: the continuing opposition with Islam and the Ottoman Empire to the east, and the European expansion to other continents. These struggles forged Europe as a geographical and cultural idea, gradually emancipating it from Christianity. There were several social processes that took part in the emergence of this new concept.

The expansion of western powers overseas to explore and dominate new lands and yet undiscovered resources, and the accompanying missionary zeal of European explorers and their rulers played an important part in the development of a self-conscious understanding of the princes and kings of Europe as 'Europeans'. While the motor behind expansion was largely economic and political, their 'mission' was legitimated through culture and religion. The European powers embarked on a mission to 'civilise' the 'savages', notably the populations that inhabited southern and central America, the Indian continent and Sub-Saharan Africa. It was in this outward and expansive move that Europe started acquiring a meaning of its own, one that was entrenched with Christianity but also embraced a larger set of civilizational values that were later identified as specifically European (Delanty, 1995, p. 30).

During these times, the idea of Europe as a set of values, epitomized by the dominance of man-made civilization over nature, gradually developed. This idea of Europeans being the only peoples who have brought together crafts ($\tau\acute{\epsilon}\chi\nu\eta$ in ancient Greek) and nature ($\varphi\acute{\upsilon}\sigma\iota\varsigma$) had already been developed by the ancient Greeks. During the age of discovery this view was re-appropriated by the European powers and further reinforced with racial connotations. The different phenotypic features of the 'savages', their hitherto unknown mores and traditions, the need to find a unifying myth for Europe; these were all elements

that contributed to the formation of a racial ideology of supremacy of the Europeans (aka Whites) over other 'races'. This racial
ideology was developed in and through the ideology of the
'white man's burden' to conquer and civilize all other places and
peoples (Mudimbe, 1988), even if there were individual cases
in which people from other continents were absorbed into the
indigenous population of Europe.

This racial connotation of Europe developed also through
reference to the Turks and Muslims at large, who became 'orientalized'. Actually, it may be more properly referred to as a
racialized and ethnicized process. This is not to deny that the
Ottoman Empire allowed for people of different religious domin-
ations to self-organize and actually self-govern to some extent
(the millet system), but rather it is to emphasize how the notion
of Europe acquires a certain meaning through specific historical
processes. The flight of Greek intellectuals from the conquered
Byzantine cities to the West reinforced the notion of Europe
over the idea of Christianity. Given the internal division of
Christianity between Latin West and Orthodox East, Greek writers found the term Europe more appropriate when talking about
the continent (Hay, 1957/1968, pp. 87–8).

While many among the Greeks and the Turks continued to call
the 'Europeans' Franks, a discourse on Europe emerged within
the continent in relation to German identity and the continuation of the Holy Roman Empire tradition. As early as 962 AD,
Pope John XII crowned Otto Roman Emperor and protector
of the papacy. The German Empire came thus to fill the power
vacuum that had been created after the dismantling of the Holy
Roman Empire in the west. It sought to take advantage of the
Holy Roman Empire tradition to unite the counts and princes of
Central Europe under German suzerainty (Delanty, 1995, p. 40).
Although its territories did not quite cover the entire continent,
its spiritual unity with the Papacy in Italy and its opposition to
the Byzantine power and tradition gave it a certain degree of cultural power and unity. It was in this Germanic idea of unity that
a cultural notion of Europe was forged in the continent.

These developments suggest, on one hand, the ascending and
expanding character of the concept of Europe in the fifteenth
to seventeenth centuries and, on the other hand, the degree of
internal diversity that characterized it. Unlike Islam, which in
the Ottoman Empire and its Islamic law found a unitary cultural

and political expression, Europe and Christianity remained fundamentally polyphonic and diversified. First of all, as many thinkers have suggested, the socio-cultural characteristic of Europe was not its political uniformity through the mastery of the emerging states but rather local particularism, (Jordan, 2002, p. 77). By this we mean the separation of cities from the countryside, the emergence of an urban population, a bewildering variety of local cultures and, overall, the opposition of society to the state. These features marked an internally differentiated social and political landscape with multiple small centres of power. This is what some have called the revolutionary traditions of Europe (Tilly, 1993).

This political pluralism was matched by discord within the Church. Although Latin Papacy exercised a certain degree of hegemony in Western Europe, it failed to transform it into a single bloc. In the late Middle Ages the One Hundred Years War between England and France prevented the formation of a mega-state in Western Europe. Moreover, a tradition of anti-Roman Catholicism developed that culminated in the Protestant Reformation. Indeed in the very centuries (sixteenth and seventeenth) when the cultural and political concept of Europe started emerging, the continent was more internally diversified and divided than ever before.

Given the internal conflicts and discord that characterized the continent, it comes, to a certain extent, as a surprise that 'Europeans' needed additional internal enemies against whom to consolidate their ethnic and religious identity. Indeed, it remains difficult to explain why, as the Muslims were readily available as the number one threat for Europe, the Jews were also picked-up as scapegoats. Hostility against the Jews went hand-in-hand with witch-hunting and the chasing of heretics. The challenge posed to Protestantism's establishment in Northern and Western Europe challenged the power and unity of the Catholic Church, thus rendering minorities important for the forging of a positive in-group identity (Atkin and Tallet, 2003). Through the persecution and oppression of minorities, such as the Jews, the Roma and the presumed witches (often women), the Church and the 'good' and 'faithful' people could reinforce their identity and power.

Cohn (1993) notes that minority persecution started in Europe in the early twelfth century at the same time with the first victory of the King of León and Castile over the Moors in Spain.

The fight against the infidel enemy acquired an ethnic and racial connotation: the victory had to be complemented by the ruthless expulsion of the Moors and the Jews from Spain. The Spanish kingdom had to be 'purified' from foreign cultural and ethnic elements. Indeed the denial of the Moor civilization in Spain is apparent to this day (Zapata-Barrero, 2006). It appears that this racial/ethnic purity discourse gained currency in the continent and particularly turned against transnational minorities such as the Jews and the Roma. Witch and minority hunting was also a form of constructing unity within.

The early concept of cultural and political Europe was thus forged through the expansion of European powers in the West and the defence of Europe and Christianity in the East but also at the same time through internal processes of building cultural and religious unity in opposition to internal minorities.

Modern Europe

The origins of a modern concept of Europe are mainly to be found in the age of European exploration and colonial expansion to other continents. The shift of attention from the eastern frontier, where little success was achieved, to the western frontier that allowed for the military and economic expansion of the western powers was decisive in shaping the concept of modern Europe. Even though the roots of a European consciousness among the elites were located in the opposition to Islam, it was the West that created a western secular identity that is largely understood as distinctively European today.

The adventurous discoveries of Britain, France, the Netherlands, Spain and Portugal and the empires they built in the Far East and the Americas along with the spreading of science and technology innovations in the West (the compass, the printing press and gunpowder – all invented in China earlier but adopted in Europe from the thirteenth century onwards), created the appropriate socio-economic environment for a secular identity to emerge. The ancient legitimizing myth of the Greek civilization's mastery over nature was re-appropriated in modern Europe.

The trading colonial empires set-up by the western states gave an unprecedented impetus to Western Europe, which abandoned the declining agrarian-based economies for the mastery of the seas. Indeed, the European powers' dominance over the seas was also a way of limiting the power of the Islamic civilization because the Ottomans never managed to truly dominate in this domain.

The expansion of European powers to the west had important repercussions in the internal balance of the continent. The 'discovery' of the Americas and the opening up of new routes to India favoured maritime and mercantilist states in Western Europe. Central European empires such as the Habsburgs continued to focus their attention eastwards. They actually developed a feudal system of production in the twelfth century, when feudalism was dying out in Western Europe. This led to an uneven, albeit complementary, mode of socio-economic development within Europe. In Central Eastern Europe the mode of development was characterized by the persistence of empires, which were poly-ethnic and multicultural, remained largely anchored in the agrarian mode of life and production (providing for the wheat that was indispensable to feed Western European populations) even if, for instance, the Austro-Hungarian Empire developed cosmopolitan metropolises and trade centres in Vienna and Budapest. However, overall Central and Eastern European territories did not develop technologically and politically into sovereign states and their trade remained limited. Dominated by the fear of the Islamic threat, they only entered modernization much later than Western Europe. Cahnman (1952) actually sees the contrasts between the 'Oceanic' Europe of the Western states and the 'Continental' Europe of the Centre-East and the Empires.

It was however this westward expansion and flourishing of European powers that brought about an important ambivalence in the term: since the period of colonial expansion, Europe came to become synonymous with the West. The West signified also the New World, the new territories, the mastery of the seas, the development of science and trade. European identity emerged as a secular 'Western' identity rather than as an overall European one, not least because the Central Eastern European territories were following a different path of socio-economic and political development. It was in this close link of Europe to the West that we find until well into the twentieth century a difficulty in emancipating and distinguishing the cultural and political idea of Europe from that of the West, which included North America.

The cultural roots of the emergence of modern Europe are to be found in the fifteenth century Italian Renaissance and in its sixteenth-century Northern European counterpart. The ideas of humanism blossomed in the Renaissance, offering an integrating world view and advocating civic participation in government that would become the basis for a modern idea of Europe (Nauert, 2006). The change that started with the Renaissance was accelerated by the religious wars of the seventeenth century and the Reformation. Indeed it was a combination of commercial interests, geopolitical antagonisms, religious differences and power politics that caused the Thirty Years War (1618–1648) eventually dragging into it all states, princes and emperors in Europe. The war started when the Austrian Habsburgs tried to impose Roman Catholicism on their Protestant subjects in Bohemia, so it was initially a religious war. However, it eventually involved France and its rivalry against the Holy Roman Empire; Spain and its Eighty Years War with the Netherlands (1568–1648); Russia; the German princes; the Swedes; the Danes; and the Poles; as well as the Swiss. The series of Treaties signed in the region of Westphalia (in Munster and Osnabruck) during 1648 marked the end of these bloody conflicts in the continent (even if France and Spain remained at war for another 11 years) sowing the seeds of an international order where state sovereignty prevails over empire.

The shattered unity of Christendom provided the necessary space for the emergence of secularism. The socio-economic changes that took place in the seventeenth and eighteenth centuries, which culminated in the final crisis of the *Ancien Régime* in 1789 and the French Revolution, brought about a new social and political order in Europe. After the Napoleonic years and the brief restoration of the Old Order by Metternich in 1816–1848, nation-states started consolidating as the new form of government. Civic values and the notion of 'citizen' had been reinforced through the American Revolution in 1776. They became the dominant cultural framework of 'the West', a framework more appropriate for the European states that had transformed into world powers. This cultural framework sought to bring together a Christian humanist ideal with a universal value system based on rationality, science and progress. In fact this is the cultural framework of European modernity even if its reality was far less noble at times than its ideals.

These changes did not completely overthrow the cultural and symbolic power of Christianity. Rather, they led to a new synthesis that brought together the ideas of progress, civilization and Christian redemption (in the Protestant sense) along with a sense of unity through exclusion. Europe could not be unified through reference to any common ethnic or cultural traits. It could, however, be contrasted to common 'others'. Thus, a sense of European identity emerged through several forms of racism, such as anti-Semitism but also white racism regarding people of 'colour' (the 'negroes' and the 'indios' among others).

The socio-economic development of Europe, the French Revolution and the turn to secularism did not reinforce an idea of European unity but rather the existence of separate and sovereign nation-states. Indeed, while a common European cultural framework did emerge through the Renaissance and the Enlightenment, that cultural framework was to be carried forward by the political entity of the nation-state. The ideal of Europe was based on the political notion of the nation-state and the 'peoples' of Europe as 'nations'.

It may actually seem ironic but when the historical context favoured the emergence of a cultural concept of Europe, because the relevance of Christian unity had receded and the Enlightenment had constructed a notion of a common European heritage, the process was hindered by two alternative developments: the contemporary emergence of the concept of 'the West' and the development of the nation-state as the political unit that characterized European modernity.

On one hand, the break with the Orient, the colonial expansion of Western powers and the overall geopolitical division of the wider Euro-Asian region led to the emergence of the concept of 'the West' as a powerful alternative to Europe. The West resonated well with the modern European states because it reflected their links to the New World and the colonies. It also expressed the geopolitical and economic division that had emerged within the continent between the eastern, still primarily agrarian, territories organized into Empires (Austro-Hungarian, Ottoman and Russian) and the Western mercantilist and gradually industrializing economies. The West also reflected the division of Christianity between the Latin/Protestant West and the Orthodox East even if it downplayed the intra-European rift between Catholics and Protestants. In short, 'the West' better reflected the geopolitical, economic and cultural organization of the continent in modern times. The emerging, thus modern, idea of Europe was explicitly or implicitly defined as 'Western' Europe rather than Europe *tout court*.

On the other hand, the idea of Europe was also contested by the emergence of nation-states. The European unity, which in any case had always been a myth, could now only be conceived through the political prism of the nation-state. The nation-state was itself a product of modernity even if it was culturally rooted in pre-modern times (Smith, 1986). It provided the political framework for the capitalist mode of production; it created national markets large enough to sustain industrial growth and to promote trade (Hobsbawm, 1990, pp. 9–46). The creation of nation-states also promoted national visions of Europe (Delanty, 1995, p. 76; Stråth, 2000; Af Malmborg and Stråth, 2002). National political elites associated the idea of Europe with competing nation-states: Bismarck considered Europe to be centred on France and for this reason opposed the idea of European unity (Schieder, 1962). During the nineteenth century, Britain associated Europe with France and rather centred its political and economic interests on its colonies overseas, while Metternich interpreted Europe from an Austrian imperial perspective (Körner, 2000).

Europe emerged then as a regulative idea with the aim of reducing conflict and friction between the nation-states of Europe (Delanty, 1995, p. 77). The notion of a common cultural heritage was politically expedient. It provided for a normative framework that would frame international politics. Nonetheless, this was a framework regulating a zero-sum game between the world powers of the time (France, Britain, Austria-Hungary but also Russia, Germany, and Austria). It was a negative unity that was achieved rather than a positive one (Pocock, 2002). Let us, however, delve a little deeper into this question of a Europe of nations and the wars that tore it apart.

Europe of nations

Studying modern Europe cannot be separated from (or, actually, can hardly be distinguished by) a review of the rise of nationalism and the nation-state as the main political entity. While the international system of government based on sovereign states emerged with the Treaty of Westphalia in 1648, the true rise of nationalism as a political ideology in Europe starts in the late eighteenth century with the French Revolution of 1789 (influenced also by the American Revolution in 1776). The French Revolution was European in its consequences as it marked the end of the *Ancien Régime* and the beginning of a period of important societal transformation. This transformation was as much socio-political as it was economic. It was social and political in that the ideology of nationalism put forward the people as the source of political legitimacy, declared all members of the nation as equal in front of the state and promoted a strong notion of collective self-determination as the nation has to seek its autonomy where this has been denied.

The economic aspect of this transformation related to the rise and expansion of capitalism as the dominant mode of production. Indeed the period between 1850 and 1870 was characterized by an extraordinary economic transformation process. The industrial development and expansion of exports of countries such as Britain, Germany and Belgium was unprecedented. Indeed the potential of capitalist industrialization that had already started in the first half of the nineteenth century came to its full realization. Capitalism found expanding markets for its products and it is the first time that a single economic world was created, bringing together European countries and their colonies in different parts of the planet. While the main technical innovations of the first industrial period had not required advanced scientific knowledge, in this period of capitalist expansion industry was penetrated by science and the links between the educational system and industrial growth became evident. The 1873 crisis and the depression of the 1870s temporarily slowed down this capitalist expansion; however, there had been sufficient fundamental change to alter the shape of European countries and to support the rise of nations and their nation-states. The late nineteenth century was a period of great transformation in Europe that brought together capitalism, nationalism and a certain opening towards political liberalism and democracy (Hobsbawm, 1996, pp. 34, 71).

The late nineteenth and early twentieth centuries have been characterized by a paradoxical coupling of the particular with the universal as nationalism spread beyond the geographical core of continental Europe. Nationalism was gradually accepted as a universal norm for the organization of peoples into political communities. Interestingly, the big nation-states of Europe were also those with large empires and, perhaps paradoxically, imperialism and nationalism became political allies within the nation-state. Nationalism underpinned imperial colonialism. Indeed, the nation-state building process was inextricably intertwined with colonialism even if different states pursued different cultural models of imperialism, with France seeking assimilation while Britain opted eventually for indirect rule through enlisting the support and cooperation of local elites.

Europe was also referred to by the short-lived pan-European revolutionary 'Young Europe' movement inspired by Giuseppe Mazzini, a famous Italian liberal nationalist. This movement exemplified the fusion between the emerging and fervent nationalism movements of the nineteenth century and the parallel emergence and usage of the concept of Europe (Bayly and Biagini, 2008). The unification of Europe under humanist and republican principles was seen as the natural continuation of the Italian, Polish and German liberation and unification struggles. In this context, Europe took the form of both unity and difference as it offered a platform for different nationalist movements that were seeking to assert themselves against the forces of counter-revolutionary conservatism. A vision of a united, democratic Europe was projected against the Holy Alliance of the European countries' monarchs.

Thus, modern Europe as a universal cultural framework was paradoxically formed by two competing universalisms: the universalism of Enlightenment philosophers on one hand, and the universalism of the particular, that of national ideologies, on the other hand. These two universalisms were inextricably combined in the ideologies of most European nations. Their cultural roots were invented or re-discovered by reference to Christianity and Europe, and their historical trajectories were connected to a real or mythical European past. Each nation formed its own narrative but Europe was prominent in most (Af Malmborg and Stråth, 2002). Greek nationalism held tight connections to the Enlightenment philosophers, and the classical Greek heritage was re-interpreted in the light of modern Europe. Italian nationalism was built on the Renaissance and on ancient Rome, which also held European connotations. German romantic nationalism saw Germany as the cradle of Europe and the heir of Latin civilization. French nationalism and republicanism also had strong European connotations, as the French Revolution was interpreted as a particularly European event.

Europe was thus (re-)invented in national ideologies and came to existence through these national narratives. A sense of cultural unity of Europe, however, was intertwined with the particular and unique narrative of each nation. The intellectuals' reconstruction of the definitions and uses of Europe in the past had little currency for modern 'Europeans' if it were not for their re-appropriation by nationalism. The term Europe, even if it became increasingly common from the mid-nineteenth century, acquired its meaning through the formation of nations. This is indeed the predicament of Europe to this day: how to exist in fusion but also as an entity over and beyond the European nation-state(s).

Total war Europe

It is war between European nation-states that has marked the contemporary notion of Europe and particularly Europe's twentieth century, more than peace or cooperation. Indeed the nineteenth century was marked by several localized conflicts; not least wars of national independence, particularly in Southern and Central Eastern Europe as the Austro-Hungarian and Ottoman Empire were gradually being dismantled by the rise of nations. But there was no large European conflict in the 'long' nineteenth century (notably between 1815 and 1914). Thus, despite the tensions that followed the economic crisis of the 1870s, a European war involving all the main powers of the continent was considered unlikely and was relegated to a historical memory or indeed a thing of the past (Hobsbawm, 1989, pp. 302–4). By contrast, the 'short' twentieth century, notably between 1914 and 1991 is marked by the invention of total war and by intense antagonism between European countries.

While it goes beyond the scope of this chapter and of this book to explain the origins of either the First or the Second World War, it is worth exploring how the notion of Europe has been predominantly shaped by conflict and division rather than by peace and cooperation, and how European conflicts have become world wars in the twentieth century. It is the very process of the industrialization and nationalization of Europe that carried the seeds of war (Hobsbawm, 1989, 1996). Industrial and capitalist development provided the technological means for a new type of war that would be a 'total war', notably a war that would involve the whole of society and that would produce extraordinary numbers of casualties.

At the same time, European colonial expansion in other continents, combined with the development of the capitalist world, had also upset the internal power balance within Europe. Thus, while in the early and mid-nineteenth century Britain was the undisputed world power both economically and militarily (controlling the world's maritime routes through its mighty navy that went unrivalled), by the late nineteenth century, Germany, France and Russia had significantly increased their military capacity. While capitalism required peace to prosper, it was the reshuffling of power relations that economic and industrial development provoked that brought about military antagonism alongside competition in trade. What was probably unexpected though was that a military conflict that started in Europe would lead to a world war.

The economic and political achievements of late nineteenth-century Europe, notably the rise of not only nationalism but also of political liberalism and democracy as well as industrialization, and the emergence of a cultural model of European modernity would be shadowed by the scale of destruction that warfare brought to the continent and the world. Modern Europe became, thus, an archetype of division and conflict rather than cooperation and exchange. European countries were divided into two camps, the 'German' and the 'French', and all states were forced to take sides. This process took more than 20 years from the formation of the 'Triple Alliance' (1882) to the 'Triple Entente' of 1907. The division however was then exported and projected in other parts of the world, notably in Asia and Africa through the colonies and through military antagonism over control of material resources in Asia and Africa. Perhaps more than debating how the specific domestic politics of Germany or Britain or Austria led to the First World War, it is interesting to look at how what were essentially European antagonisms were exported to the colonies and how conflict at the geographical fringes of Europe (the Balkan wars of liberation against the Ottoman Empire, the Italian conquest of Libya in 1911, the crisis over Morocco in 1911) fired back into its geographical core. This is not to undermine here the role and importance of the USA or Japan in either the First or Second World War but rather to note how conflict within Europe interacted and chain-reacted across the world through a combined economic, political and military short-circuit.

The political instability that followed the First World War and the great depression of the late 1920s and 1930s were fertile ground from which the Second World War emerged. Essentially, the failure of the League of Nations to guarantee peaceful solutions to frictions and tensions between the world powers, the failure of the victorious powers to integrate the losers, particularly Germany, the impossibility of forging alliances with communist Russia (which was supposed to be isolated behind the *cordon sanitaire* of the Baltic states, Poland and Romania) all brought with them the seeds of a new war. Even though it may be clear that the aggressive stance of Germany and Italy within Europe (and of Japan in Asia) triggered the Second World War, the whole process that led to it is best understood through looking into the two competing models for the reconstruction of Europe after the First World War. The Second World War was part of an ongoing struggle between two competing models for the reconstruction of Europe: the Western liberal democratic model and the Marxist Leninist socialist project. While the ideas of the latter originated in Western Europe, they were implemented in Russia after the 1917 Revolution. It was the struggle between these two ideologies and competing socio-economic and political models that created the space for the emergence of fascism but which also created the power to defeat fascism.

Fascist Europe

The short twentieth century in Europe has been heavily marked by the rise (and fall) of fascism and Nazism. As noted earlier, the socio-economic and political developments in nineteenth-century Europe had brought about not only the expansion of industrialization and capitalism but also liberal democracy as the prevalent mode of government in the continent. The legacy of Enlightenment had crystallized into a distrust towards authoritarian and absolutist rule and a commitment to constitutional government and an accepted set of civil liberties for citizens. As the Russian and Ottoman Empires were dismantled in the early twentieth century, the nation-states emerging out of them adopted democratic regimes, and despite ideological conflicts (between the capitalist or bourgeois forces and the then dynamically emerging socialist forces) they all agreed to the importance of the values of reason, science, education and individual freedom for everyone. Within this context, the First World War was seen as a brief interlude of bloodshed and barbarism that had actually confirmed the turn of all European countries towards liberal democracy. However, the reality was quite different. It is in the national politics and internal tensions of European democracies where the seeds of fascism and Nazism lie. It was the decline of European democracies that led to fascism, Nazism and the Second World War rather than some accident of history. Mazower's book *Dark Continent* (2000) explains systematically how some common themes, such as health and welfare, minorities, Eugenics and racism, ran through the different countries and led to the political developments of the interwar period. Both communism and Nazism were closely inter-related with one another and overall with the decline of liberal democracy. The inter-war years may be interpreted as part of an ongoing struggle between 'progressive' and 'reactionary' values and ideas that characterized Europe in that period. Such struggle was both international, in that it involved all the European countries, and internal, in that it cut across different political and ideological currents within each country.

While such a struggle involved both left-wing and right-wing political and ideological currents, in the interwar period and in the Second World War, liberal democracy and constitutional government were threatened from the far right rather than from the far left (contrary to what happened during the Cold War years, see further below). The political right forces of inter-war Europe, particularly fascist Italy and Nazi Germany, put forward an authoritarian, totalitarian, irrational ideology that glorified instinct and given attributes such as race and genealogy, against the liberal democratic and modern values that the Enlightenment, the French Revolution and the whole socio-economic transformation of the nineteenth century had forged into a 'European cultural model', recognizable as such.

Fascism also had a strong populist element of mobilizing the masses from below and creating an organic state where rulers and the ruled were forged into a single organic political community (a *Volksgemeinschaft*). Italian fascism and German national socialism interpenetrated one another and fascism adopted anti-Semitism and racism, which was initially absent from the fascist ideology. Interestingly, while fascism and national-socialism may be understood as reactionary forces that would have, if possible, wiped out the developments of the nineteenth century restoring the traditional order, they did not turn to the Church or King, the old sources of political absolutist power. They rather supplanted those sources with secular ideologies embodied in self-made men and supported by popular acclaim that were converted to actual cults.

Having said the above, it remains of course still puzzling why and how the struggle between progressive and reactionary forces could lead to such destruction, race-hatred, mechanized mass murder and atrocity of the scale perpetrated by Nazism in the Second World War (Kershaw, 2000). Hobsbawm attempts to make sense of the unthinkable in a concise passage in his *Age of Extremes*:

> The optimal conditions for the triumph of the crazy ultra-Right were an old state and its ruling mechanisms which could no longer function, a mass of disenchanted, disoriented and discontented citizens who no longer knew where their loyalties lay; strong socialist movements threatening or appearing to threaten social revolution, but not actually in a position to achieve it; and a move of nationalist resentment against the peace treaties of 1918–20. These were the conditions in which helpless old ruling elites were tempted to have recourse to the ultra-radicals... These were the conditions that turned movements of the radical Right into powerful organized and sometimes uniformed and paramilitary forces (squadristi; strom-troopers) or, as in Germany during the Great Slump, into massive electoral armies. However, in neither of the two fascist states did fascism 'conquer power'... In both cases fascism came to power ... in a 'constitutional' fashion. The novelty of fascism was that, once in power, it refused to play the old political games, and took over completely what it could. (1994, p. 127)

The dark moment of Europe, the rise of fascism and particularly of Nazism, was a product of its time, an episode in the long struggle between progressive and reactionary forces but it remains a puzzle why this should happen in Europe and not elsewhere. There are three possible explanations for this in which two are historically rooted. The first is that it was in Europe where the cultural model of modernity emerged, and hence perhaps the underlying political and ideological struggle between the 'new' and the 'old' was most intense. A second explanation was that the tragedy of the First World War and the economic and political uncertainty of the inter-war years made fascism and its promise of a total state that controls the economy and society, guaranteeing stability and full employment appealing to both elites and masses in many countries, not only Germany. A third explanation has to do with the special role that Germany occupied in this chunk of European history. Germany suffered a stark economic and political crisis after the First World War, and at the same time it was a country that by its size, geographical position and economic and military potential could not but play a major political role in Europe.

Divided and united Europe

Even though the defeat of Nazi Germany swept the danger of totalitarianism away and seemed to reconfirm the Enlightenment ideals as 'our common European values', liberal democracy in the European continent was challenged again, this time from the Left. Indeed, Europe emerged divided from the Second World War, as not only Russia but also a large part of Central Eastern Europe (notably all the countries east of the river Elbe, to the Adriatic sea, the Balkans [except Greece and the small European chunk of Turkey]) fell under the communist bloc. Albania, the Baltic states, Bulgaria, Czechoslovakia, Hungary, Poland, Romania and Yugoslavia moved into the socialist zone of influence under the hegemony of the Soviet Union and adopted communist regimes that severely restricted civil liberties and citizens' rights. Spain and Portugal were also under dictatorial rule until the mid-1970s, while Greece started with an imperfect parliamentary democracy, only to experience dictatorship in 1967 and eventually fully democratize in 1974.

In the post-war period, Europe was neither united under fascism nor torn apart by it, but it was divided along a Left versus Right political, ideological, economic and heavily militarized border that ran through the geographical heart of the continent. Germany itself was divided into two parts, one that belonged to Western Europe and another that belonged to the Warsaw Pact countries. The term Western Europe had, then, a strong political connotation rather than a geographical one: it demarcated the countries that were liberal democracies and free market economies. Eastern Europe referred to the socialist democracies that belonged to the communist bloc. This West and East division implemented initially in the heart of Europe was projected to different parts of the world, dividing the whole globe into two zones of influence, as negotiated between the great powers (Britain, Russia, the USA and France) in 1944–1945. This division remained stable until 1989. During this period, the notion of Europe was tightly linked to the notion of the West, which also encompassed North America. Europe was somehow weakened and submerged to the West; Western Europe was seen as the only Europe that could exist as Central or Eastern Europe was seen to have lost its 'Europeanness' under Soviet influence.

Paradoxically, but not surprisingly, division brings with it the seeds of unity too. The two parts of Europe forged a strong internal unity. The eastern part of Europe, notably the Warsaw Pact countries, united under Soviet hegemony into a common political and economic system of really existing socialism. The Western countries took gradual steps to forge an economic and later socio-political unity. Soon after the end of the war, in 1949, Western European countries came together to form the Council of Europe, an international organization whose aim has been to promote the rule of law democracy and human rights, albeit not through the transfer of sovereignty but rather mainly through international law. While initially the Council of Europe comprised only Western European countries, after 1989 it has gradually enlarged and expanded and includes today 47 countries and more than 800 million people. In 1957, the Treaty of Rome was signed establishing the European Coal and Steel Communities. Indeed the project that started as the European Economic Community (EEC) later evolved into what is today known as the European Union.

It was not, however, only the Cold War divisions that marked the post-war notion of Europe. More importantly, the self-understanding of (Western) Europe as a cultural model to be imitated, as a force of progress, was challenged by the very experience of the Second World War and particularly by the Shoah: the persecution and extermination of the European Jews. The gradual recognition of what had happened in the Second World War led to a critical reflection on this very European experience by thinkers such as Hannah Arendt (and her *Eichmann in Jerusalem*, 1963) or Adorno and Horkheimer's *Dialectic of Enlightenment* (1944). Adorno and Horkheimer (1944) and Zygmunt Bauman (1989) in his *Modernity and the Holocaust* sought to find the seeds of the Shoah in the instrumental rationality of the European cultural model. They looked at how technological and industrial progress combined with an instrumental rationalism can lead to such massive extermination, which, as Arendt (1963) argued, is difficult to explain even from an administrative and bureaucratic point of view.

This self-reflection on European modernity and on the earlier presumed linear path towards progress led to a rethinking of nationalism. For the first time perhaps in modern European history, nationalism was brought into question and was seen no longer as a force of progress but rather as a force of destruction. It would be an over-statement to argue that nationalism lost its political force after the war – quite the contrary, it remained the glue that tied political communities together. The fear of its destructive forces led to the creation of an international normative order supported by specific international institutions: the United Nations founded in 1945, UNESCO also in 1945, and the Declaration of Human Rights in 1948 in the effort to establish a new type of criminal act: the crime against humanity. These initiatives signalled a new phase in the self-understanding of Europe where nationalism retreated to some extent and became less of a defining feature of the notion of Europe. Rather it was the desire to reign in nationalism that characterized this phase.

The first decades after the war were marked by two contradictory tendencies. On one hand, the spectre of conflict and particularly of war between France and Germany continued. At the same time, European powers were involved in wars outside Europe that were part of the de-colonization process (for example France in Indochina in 1950 and in Algeria in 1962). On the other hand, the first couple of decades were also marked by collective amnesia in Western European countries. There was little discussion about the role of the resistance in different countries and who participated in it (Judt, 2005). There was also only a gradual and hesitant *prise de conscience* of what had happened to the Jews and the Roma under Nazism. In this sensitive political context, the project of European unification offered the advantage of being a memory-less project (Delanty, 2013, p. 237) because it signalled a fresh start aiming at peace and prosperity and with a light historical luggage. It sought to put the war behind and it also lacked a heavy historical memory. This was initially an advantage even if one may consider today that it is a fundamental weakness.

Does Europe make history?

A critical understanding of the meaning of the term 'Europe' today needs to take into account the evolution of the concept in history. Current political debates tend to neglect and obscure this historical evolution, treating Europe generally as a geopolitical, geographical or a cultural concept that has remained immutable in different periods and in different regions. Media and political debates tend to take Europe as a given, as a concept with a clear and stable meaning. However, what even the most recent social and political developments of the past 20 years show is that Europe is more about fluidity and change than about stability and clarity. The nature of the concept is historical, as indeed are all concepts, and in order to answer the question 'What is Europe?' we need to highlight and discuss the historical and contextual nature of the concept and to investigate the power games involved in its formation.

School textbooks, as well as the media, tend to project the contemporary meaning(s) of Europe into the past without paying attention to how the very meaning of Europe is historically and politically constructed. They thus fail to highlight and understand the different connotations of the term in different historical periods and in different places; they also fail to suggest that today, too, the concept of Europe serves specific political and symbolic purposes.

One question that we need to address before embarking on this brief historical excursus is the following: is Europe constituted in history or does it shape history? Should we consider

Europe as a malleable signifier, a name, that can lend itself to different uses and different users that shape it in line with their own beliefs and interests? Or has the idea of Europe acquired its own reality that is something more than the constructions in our minds? Europe has both a material configuration of land and water (not just an imaginary or cartographic representation of those) and a symbolic and discursive existence through which not only is it shaped by history but it also *makes* history (see also Roberts, 1967; Pocock, 2002, pp. 55–6).

It is this book's contention that Europe is shaped in history: Europe has been shaped for different purposes at different places and times and it is because of historical contingency that the term has survived to this day and has actually been transformed into a powerful symbolic and political factor. The power of Europe as a concept is not intrinsic to the name or to what it signifies. The notion of Europe does not contain some kind of inherent, ahistorical or universal value that makes us unable to do without it. It is the product of social historical processes that this book shall outline and review critically.

At the same time, we argue that Europe makes history. That Europe, as a concept, makes history does not mean that Europe fights wars or elects governments. After all, Europe is not an actor; it is neither a person, nor a group – it does not exist as a political or symbolic 'thing', but in our minds. Europe can make history to the extent that its meaning acquires a symbolic power that can shape people's views and actions.

The notion of Europe has become a relevant and nearly indispensable feature of contemporary social, cultural and political life, in the European continent and in other regions of the world. Here we adopt a social constructivist perspective: we look at Europe as a social reality that is self-constituting. Europe contains a set of discursive frames, worldviews, cultural models and systems of interpretation. These frames, models and socio-cognitive systems are both European and constitutive of Europe. They influence the making and interpretation of societal transformation – they are part and parcel of the emergence of new social realities and they shape these realities while they are also their integral part. Paraphrasing Castoriadis (1993, p. 9), Europe 'is a construction, a constitution, a creation of the world, of its own world'. Thus Europe makes and is made by history.

Europe and power

Making history involves symbolic and political power. Thus, if we argue that Europe shapes and is shaped by historical forces, it is necessary to discuss the power dimensions of the concept of Europe.

In an effort to disentangle the different aspects often bunched under the single term Europe in common parlance (and in some of the scholarly literature) much thought has been put into distinguishing between the idea of Europe and a European identity. These are neither identical nor have they been synchronic. The idea of Europe existed long before European identity as a political concept and/or as a form of cultural or political consciousness came into being, and before people started thinking of themselves as Europeans. Europe is a cultural frame of reference for the formation of identities and geopolitical realities, not an identity in itself (Hay, 1957/1968; Delanty, 1995; Mikkeli, 1998).

Delanty has eloquently argued that the idea of Europe has become a regulative idea that serves identity-building processes (1995, pp. 4–5). It could be understood as a collective representation (Moscovici, 1981): as a reproduction of reality that has at the same time prescriptive and regulative functions. It says something about how reality should be understood and how things should be organized. Thus, the idea of Europe prescribes the formation of a European collective identity.

It is difficult, however, to see how this happens if we look at the variety and internal diversity of the discourses that framed the term Europe in past centuries or recently, and the weakness, if not to say impossibility, of a European identity project to emerge. Perhaps Delanty's emphasis here is on the fact that European identity, to the extent that it is emerging, is based more on opposition to 'others', and exclusion of the 'other', than on a positive assertion of a self-identity (Delanty, 1995, p. 5). To put it simply, it is difference with non-Europeans that makes the Europeans distinctive rather than some common features that they truly share.

This point can be misleading as identity is based simultaneously on the process of constructing similarity and difference. The in-group consciousness is based both on the feeling that the members of the group share something in common and on the view that they share more in common than they share with outsiders. This is valid for national identity but not exclusively.

It is valid for all forms of political identities, and to this extent for European identity (Triandafyllidou, 2001).

Delanty (1995) goes even a step further. He suggests that Europe has become an ideology. Adopting Berger and Luckmann's definition (1984, p. 141) of ideology as a particular definition of reality that comes attached to a concrete power interest, Delanty argues that Europe is an ideology and indeed a nearly hegemonic one. Developments in the post-Cold War period actually tend to confirm this view. Dominant Western definitions of Europe have prevailed during the past 20 years, while counter-hegemonic discourses about Europe originating in Central and Eastern Europe, for instance, or indeed within Western or Southern Europe, have been relatively weak. The symbolic currency of these hegemonic and counter-hegemonic definitions of Europe has largely reflected the actual socio-economic and political power of the actors that (re)produced them. In other words, the political elites of the more affluent, politically stable and technologically advanced countries of Western Europe have generally imposed their own definitions of where Europe starts and ends and who and what constitutes a European over the less affluent politically and economically, in transition and technologically less developed Central Eastern European elites and citizens.

The problem with an idea that becomes hegemonic is that it cannot be easily chosen or rejected because it itself structures the choices and the epistemological framework within which these choices are made. Delanty (1995, p. 7) rightly argues 'Thinking, reading and writing about Europe are the intellectual modalities of power through which Europe is constituted as a strategic reality and a subject of knowledge'. The hegemonic character of Europe becomes evident not only in the power of some political and cultural elites to impose their definitions as universally valid but also in the impossibility of avoiding talking about Europe and characterizing peoples, cultures or territories as European (Pocock, 2002). Rejecting one's Europeanness is also a way of confirming the symbolic power of the idea of Europe.

Concluding remarks

The Enlightenment philosophers identified with the idea of Europe the process of modernity and the primacy of science and rationality. Europe offered the necessary 'space' for accepting confessional diversity within Christianity. It also provided the symbol of the new universal civilization predicated by the Enlightenment. A European identity became self-conscious only in the late seventeenth century and acquired its social and cultural content through the Age of Discovery. The Christian universal mission was thus replaced by the 'white man's burden'. The opposition between West-Christendom-Europe on the one hand, and East-Islam on the other hand was replaced by the notion of a Western European cultural identity that was defined as an outward movement through conquest of the New World and in contrast to internal (minorities, the Jews in particular) and external (the myth of the 'savage') 'others'.

The development of the notion of a European identity or culture was marked also by two inspiring 'others': classical Greece and the Roman Empire. Ancient Greece, with its polytheic tradition and tension between gnosticism and agnosticism, was seen as the precursor of the Enlightenment project. Furthermore, the Roman Empire, with its complex and changing relations with Judaism and later Islam, was also part of the European past. To put it simply, the notion of a European heritage by definition bore within it the seed of plurality and contradiction:

> If there is a heritage that can be described as particular to Europe, it is rather the tension between polytheist/pluralist and monotheist/fundamentalist tendencies, between heterodoxy and orthodoxy, in a constant movement from critique to crisis. (Af Malmborg and Stråth, 2002)

In other words, the idea of Europe as a cultural and geographical space developed in opposition to specific inspiring or threatening 'others'. These others (which became salient in different historical periods) included both external 'others' and Europe's own internal diversity, thus leading to the exclusion of minorities and to a re-interpretation of Europe itself through the national lens.

What we learn from this brief review of the evolution of the concept of Europe in different periods and in different realms of life is that it is fluidity, historicity and the need to adopt a critical self-reflective mode that should guide us in thinking about Europe. We also learn that Europe was historically much less important than many would consider today. It was never a driving force in history and it was never united by a positive point of reference but rather through the effort either to defend itself from threatening 'others' or to tame internal conflicts. Stråth in particular emphasizes that the distinctive feature of Europe, or of what we understand as European culture and history, is a self-reflective spirit. This is nonetheless questionable if we consider contemporary discourses on Europe and European unity (see also Pocock, 2002). In Chapter 3 we discuss the visions of Europe of those who believed in (the construction of) European unity and in a sort of European culture as unitary.

Chapter 3

Visions of a United Europe

What visions has Europe stirred?

Throughout history, Europe has been an elusive concept. Jean Monnet wrote in 1950:

> Europe has never existed...We must genuinely create Europe, it must become manifest to itself...and it must have confidence in its own future (Monnet, 1950).

Perceptions of what Europe is have inextricably been entangled with aspirations, often contradictory ones, of what Europe ought to be. Grand power politics, religion, nationalism and ideology have framed perceptions of Europe and have inspired very different visions of what Europe is meant to represent. Europe has often served as a narrative, told and retold by different actors, in different contexts and at different times, for different purposes and to very different audiences.

To understand the visions that Europe has stirred in recent centuries among thinkers and statesmen it is useful to explore the historical processes through which specific values and cultural traditions, such as Roman law, Greek philosophy, Hebraic ethics, Christian theology, scientific rationality, pluralism and democracy, became affirmed, thereby defining what European culture and civilization has generally stood for both within the continent and beyond. It is also necessary to identify the multiple political and ideological constructions and reconstructions of Europe as a concept since the eighteenth century. Understanding the various visions that Europe has inspired in the minds of thinkers and statesmen requires understanding the political context within which these have been formulated and what the drivers of these narratives were. In this chapter we discuss what has inspired attempts at defining, and specifically at unifying, Europe and the context within which these narratives co-existed, antagonized, impregnated and succeeded one another. Drawing from British historian Peter Burke's suggestion that Europe, 'is not so much a place as an idea' (1980, p. 21), we argue here that Europe has in fact been an intricate mosaic of visions. This mosaic has been characterized by a continuously shifting centre of gravity, distinguishing and differentiating between those who represent the 'meaning' of Europe from the 'others' and the 'foes'.

The concept of Europe has been associated with the accomplishment of a supreme state of peace and security. It has also been associated with a series of strategic alliances and unification projects. And yet, throughout the continent's history, references to 'Europe' have been fraught with dissent, division and 'otherness'. As discussed in Chapter 2, 'Europe' has been synonymous both with a divided continent and with a reunited one. It has represented a virtuous link between security, reconstruction and economic prosperity just as much as it has stood for vicious circles of nationalistic resentments and the decline of the West. Europe has embodied a continent of hostile Nations just as it has stood for a continent characterized by a unique political Union of like-minded States. Europe has been the 'dark continent' of division, rivalry, warfare and extremism within which antagonistic ideologies have clashed in vile ways. Yet it has also been the 'old continent' wisely representing democracy, liberalism, pluralism, unity, as well as universalist aspirations for peace, cooperation, good governance and social justice. Europe has been used as a reference for modernity, the Enlightenment, reason and science as well as revolutions and cosmopolitanism. It has also, however, taken the form of reactionary conservatism, despotic traditionalism and defensive, introvert nationalism. It has been synonymous with Christianity and Christendom, and with secularism and *laïcité*. These multiple sides of Europe have always coincided and have fed into one another leading to ambiguous, complex and contradictory visions of what 'Europe' is or, even more challengingly, what it ought to be.

Throughout history, the notion of 'Europe' has been instrumentalized by statesmen, politicians and intellectuals in pursuit of their political objectives. References to 'Europe' have been invoked to create a sense of unity and to nurture perceptions among the wider population of belonging to a wider community. Thus, depending on the context, specific shared affinities have been emphasized in some cases, while cultural and historical differences have been stressed in others. In the sections that follow, we discuss some of the most influential references to Europe that have been formulated by European intellectuals, statesmen and politicians. We try to situate these references in their historical context in order to understand what motivated these visions. We also try to show how the centre of gravity of the 'meaning' of Europe has shifted, repeatedly.

Why unify Europe?

So what has inspired attempts at unifying Europe? A simple response to this question would be that the unification of Europe has essentially been driven by a two-fold belief. First, that a set of common shared (generally perceived as rather superior) values exist. And second, that pooling together available resources may be advantageous and beneficial. Naturally, assuming that a set of values commonly perceived as quintessentially 'European' exists – though this too has been contested many a time – the questions that unavoidably follow are: *How* have these European values been defined? By *whom* have these values been defined? And what *mode of governance* is considered as best suited to pool together these resources and manage, or rather govern, Europe? These three questions are, of course, inextricably linked.

From the eighth to the seventeenth centuries, European values were largely defined in the form of Christianity. The Christian religion served as the unifying element of 'Europe' and Europe was imagined as a Christian commonwealth that differentiated itself from the Orient (see Hay, 1957/1968; Davies, 1996; Persson and Stråth, 2007). This differentiation was relevant vis-à-vis the Muslims, who were seen as infidels, as it was vis-à-vis the more 'Eastern' Christians of Byzantium and Russia. References to Europe's Christian core remain very vivid in contemporary understandings of Europe, as does a reflex, even patronizing, differentiation from all that lies to the East.

Even though Christianity was claimed as a unifying factor, in practice it led to major divisions and rivalries between European empires, each attempting to expand and impose its own authority in the name of Christendom. The European empires that shared the European geographic space rivalled each other in the way they referred to the concept of Europe. The Habsburg Monarchy's Catholicism, for instance, was heavily contested by France, which attempted to equate European culture with French culture while opposing the dominance of the Holy Roman Empire. At the same time, the Habsburgs' reign over Europe was also contested by Russia, which proposed an Orthodox and Slavic definition of Europe and an alternative path to modernity during the Romanov period, from the seventeenth, but especially during the eighteenth, century (Neumann, 1999; Boon and Delanty, 2007).

From the perspective of the Scandinavian peninsula, for a long period of time Europe was actually the rest of the continent and it was practically represented as the 'other' and associated with a rather negative connotation. Europe here stood for conservatism and Roman Catholicism, whereas Scandinavia's Protestantism stood for progress and freedom (Af Malmborg and Stråth, 2002, p. 15). This continued to be reflected well into the twentieth century, and actually even today, we have observed it become particularly prevalent in the scepticism expressed across Scandinavian countries towards the European Union. This scepticism was framed by a strong attachment to 'Scandinavian exceptionalism' and a self-image of being distinctively progressive societies founded on social democracy and a universal application of welfare rights (Lawler, 1997). Or, as Ole Wæver has distinctly and simply put it: 'Nordic identity is about being *better* than Europe' (Wæver, 1992, p. 77, emphasis in the original).

Höfele and von Koppenfels have described Europe in the early modern period as a 'patchwork stirred by centrifugal and centripetal forces' (2005, p. 7). In effect, this period of European history was one of pluralization, where the old perceived homogeneity of *Christianitas* offered by the Catholic Church was challenged by the Reformation and Counter-Reformation. During this same time, Latin and the doctrinal system of Scholasticism were losing their hold as the Renaissance unfolded. Indeed, throughout the seventeenth and eighteenth centuries, the unifying role of Christianity was gradually replaced by the emerging Enlightenment, ambitious to pursue a universal civilization project. The Enlightenment discourse had Europe at its core and absolute point of reference. Europe was presented as embodying scientific reason, progress, freedom of judgement and questioning of authoritative statements (what was called in

French *libre examen*) while further elaborating a counter-image of an authoritarian, repressive, traditionalist and mystical East (Af Malmorg and Stråth, 2002, p. 2). During this period, the concept of Europe gained currency and was given a map-based frame of reference. The relationship between geography and perceptions of one's own values and of their difference with the values of the 'other' became even more tightly intertwined. Geography became further politicized along east–west axes. The schism between Latin Christianity and the Eastern Orthodox Church was magnified during the age of the Enlightenment where Western Europe essentially 'invented' Eastern Europe as its complementary 'other'. As Larry Wolff has described, the intellectual centres in Western Europe, 'cultivated and appropriated (...) the notion of "civilization," an eighteenth-century neologism, and civilization discovered its complement, within the same continent, in shadowed lands of backwardness, even barbarism' (Wolff, 1994). This mental map of Europe distinguishing the capitalist core that lay in the western parts of the continent from the eastern parts that were considered 'backward' in socio-economic development terms, persisted as a very vivid reality during the twentieth century's Cold War. In fact, it seems to have survived well into the early twenty-first century even after three decades of post-communist transition.

As the Enlightenment brought with it an outburst of political, financial, technological and industrial innovation, the centres of culture, finance and political power shifted from Rome, Venice and Florence to London, Paris and Amsterdam. Gradually, the East–West mental divide of Europe came to override the North–South one that had dominated during the Italian Renaissance. Where exactly Western Europe became Eastern Europe, and where Eastern Europe met Asia is rather ambiguous. Though Eastern Europe was considered an integral part of the continent, it was also constructed as rather distinct from the more western parts based on a two-fold functionality that still rings very true today. Eastern Europe served as a space which would buffer Russia's outreach, and as a space within which to mediate with the 'Orient' (Wolff, 1994, p. 7). In the words of Iver B. Neumann: 'There are many "Easts" in the world, and none of them is without signification' (1999, p. 15). In effect, visions of Europe have been constructed around persistent efforts to 'purify' the concept of Europe by setting the boundaries between itself and the 'other', and by adopting a civilizationally superior, Eurocentric attitude towards 'others' in spite of extensive 'borrowing' and cross-fertilization of knowledge, goods and ideas that characterize all interactions between civilizations. There has been a tendency for a cultural imaginary that sees the world in terms of 'otherness', most notably in the form of the 'Oriental Other'. This process of othering has also taken place with parts of Europe itself, with the 'Eastern European Other' or the 'Southern European Other' distinctly distinguished by the 'core' throughout the centuries and up until the present.

Christianity and the Enlightenment have been two of the core pillars that have framed visions of why and how to unify Europe. They have left very heavy imprints on how Europe and its unification are understood even today. Nationalism and Revolution have been just as influential in defining Europe as have visions of its unification.

Starting with the mother of all revolutions, the French Revolution has deeply impacted both the definition of European values and visions of Europe. It has done so in at least three ways. First, it inspired people to transfer their allegiance from absolute monarchs to the nation-state. By underlining that the power of the nation resides with the people of the nation, the French Revolution spread the ideas that all men are created equal, that citizens have inalienable rights to liberty, security, property and resistance to oppression, and that governments exist to protect these rights. These ideas have since been considered to be at the heart of what defines (or at least ought to define) Europe.

Second, it ignited the Age of Nationalism, changing Europe not only ideologically but also in geopolitical terms. The political geography of the continent deeply changed through the erection of national borders that sliced territories away from Empires by trying to gather within these borders peoples who belonged to the same 'nation'. This paved the way to the creation of a Europe of Nations, and it came at a cost, and a rather high one as all national projects have been fraught with deep, angry and often violent frustrations of incompleteness and insecurities with regards to threats from within and without.

Finally, the French Revolution linked the idea of civilization to a specific model of development. In essence, the Western Europeans perceived themselves as being the most enlightened, free and unprejudiced peoples, personifying 'civilization' and thereby inspiring the model of development that was to be achieved by other less developed peoples on the continent and beyond (Wolff, 1994). We explore these perceptions further in Chapter 4, but what we suggest here is that nationalism basically brought national tints to the idea of Europe. Thus, 'Europe' was 'France' for French intellectuals just as it meant 'Germany' for Germans. For Voltaire, Europe was regarded as the most humane and free place in the world, and France as the most European of all nation-states. For Hegel, Europe represented the dynamic of progress and the supreme achievement of the idea of the world-spirit; the German world, and specifically Prussia, constituted its embodiment. This line of thought has consistently defined the way in which Western Europe, and more recently the EU, has interacted not only with 'others' further afield, but also with the 'other' more Eastern parts of the continent.

Russia, the most 'Eastern' of Europeans – also infused with its own internal 'Oriental Others' such as the Turkic speaking populations near the Volga or the Siberian Far East – has objected to this Western appropriation of the concept of Europe as representing progress and has alternated between an inherent understanding of belonging to Europe and a rejection of it. The sense of belonging to Europe has been well summed up by Fyodor Dostoyevsky quite simply as follows: 'Europe, as Russia, is our mother, our second mother. We have taken much from her, we shall take again, and we shall not wish to be ungrateful to her' (reference to Dostoyevsky, 1973, p. 1048 in Browning and Lehti, 2010, p. 41). Yet at the same time, the discourse coming out of Western Europe was critically denounced as an essentially imperialistic Romano-Germanic chauvinism simply hidden under the cloak of cosmopolitanism (Perkins and Liebscher, 2006). Russian nationalism, later followed by pan-Slavism, in turn also treated 'Europe' as the 'other', rejecting its individualism and materialism and proposing alternative models of civilization. These oppositions materialized in the tugs of war between Slavophiles and later communist revolutionaries versus Westernizers across most of Central, Eastern and South-East Europe. With Russian nationalism essentialized as ethnic, collectivist, authoritarian and infused by anti-Westernism, it in turn laid the foundations of anti-Western political thought, challenging Eurocentric historical models and cultural canons.

Returning to the questions outlined at the start of this section on how what we commonly refer to as European values have been defined and who has defined them, no discussion can be complete without reference to Napoleon Bonaparte. Napoleon attempted to unite Europe politically, administratively, economically and culturally (1804–1815). He conquered most of the continent but failed to unify it through the use of arms. His vision for a unified Europe laid the foundations for much that is declared as being associated with European unity today, and specifically with the European Union. He envisaged a vast federative European system within which borders would be dismantled in order to establish a single wider area where the same laws would be applicable, and where travellers would feel 'at home' wherever they went (Tsoubarian, 1994). Napoleon wished for a confederal system ruled by an Emperor (himself of course) with a unified army, a unified monetary system and a common system of legislation that would unify all peoples. These peoples were mainly French, Italians and Germans, who geographically belonged to the same nation but who had been separated for political reasons. In this administration, the French language would provide the necessary cultural unity. Napoleon's efforts at creating a European Empire were met with passionate hostility by Europe's other monarchs (Prussia, Bavaria, Württemberg, Denmark, Sweden, Austria and the Russian Tsar) who wanted to 'save Europe from Napoleon' (Franceschi and Weider, 2007, p. 65) and keep their power as well. His aspirations also clashed with Britain's core foreign policy principle of ensuring a 'European balance', which essentially meant preventing the excessive domination of any single European power over the continent. It is fascinating how such concerns still resonate strongly in European politics.

The end of the Napoleonic wars saw the Restoration of conservatism and an effort to return to the *status quo ante*, or, in other words, the way it was before the French Revolution. During this period (1814–1848), usually described as the Age of Metternich because of the Austrian Chancellor's influence over the continent, Europe was ruled by the Concert of Powers. This period of peace and stability between the great powers defined another facet of Europe and the values it represented. 'Europe' became tantamount to reactionary conservatism in society and political repression. This was personified in the Holy Alliance between Prussia, the Austrian Empire and the Russian Tsar, the so-called 'Northern Courts'. Europe came to be defined as a balance of power held together at the seams through treaties while reactionary despotic monarchs used force to crush the new ideas that had sprung out of the French Revolution. Yet, while this is the dominant narrative of what Europe represented during the Age of the Concert of Powers, it is not of course the whole story. Britain became increasingly estranged from the 'Northern Courts', their reactionary conservatism and absolutism. Together with France, Britain stood out as the liberal powers during this era of conservatism (though King William IV was disturbed with Lord Palmerston's policy of alliance with 'revolutionary' France).

In addition, during this very same time, revolutionary zeal, nationalism and the ideas of the Enlightenment were in full momentum in the south-eastern part of the continent. During the war for Greek independence that led to the modern Greek State in 1829, references to Europe were framed in terms of liberalism and nationalist aspirations, yet also of Christianity (as they were opposing the Muslim Ottoman Empire).

The Spring of Nations in France, Germany, Austria and Italy that followed soon thereafter marked yet another important phase in the evolution of the visions that Europe has stimulated. While each revolution was clearly national in its aims and rather particularistic in its causes, there were certain common 'European' traits. The revolutionary banner of '*liberté, égalité, fraternité*' echoed well outside the borders of France. Across the continent, the 1848 'semi-Revolutions' as described by Karl Marx, sought to democratize the political order and address the 'Social Question' posed by the existence of intense forms of structural poverty as a result of the Industrial Revolution (Dowe et al., 2001). Democratization, parliamentarization, the expansion of franchise, the multiplication of women's association, as well as an unprecedented degree of access to printed news changed political, civic and social life in European societies, particularly in urban centres, while feudal domination came to an end in rural areas. The demands for free and independent nation-states created wars of liberation, separation and unification but no nation-state arose as a winner from these wars, as the social forces were too weak and disorganized to overcome foreign and domestic resistance (Dowe et al., 2001, p. 19).

The second half of the nineteenth century saw the continued coexistence of two parallel processes on the continent: disintegration and unification. The eastern and south-eastern geographic periphery was on a path of fragmentation particularly after the Crimean War (1853–1856) and the increasingly frail Ottoman Empire vis-à-vis its millet's nationalist aspirations. Meanwhile, Germany's unification in 1871, its growing economic prosperity and Kaiser Wilhelm II's international ambitions fundamentally altered the European geopolitical landscape and defined the meaning of Europe, and all the connotations attached with the concept in both benign and malign ways, in the century that followed.

Thus, the close of the nineteenth century saw the end of an era aimed at maintaining stability and power and averting change. In 1888, Karl Marx and Friederich Engels wrote in *The Communist Manifesto* that: 'A spectre is haunting Europe – the spectre of Communism. All the powers of old Europe have entered into a holy alliance to exorcise this spectre: Pope and Czar, Metternich and Guizot, French Radicals and German police-spies' (Marx and Engels, 1998). This quote is a fine description of what Europe represented at the end of the nineteenth century. Europe embodied a balance of powers between supreme monarchs. It symbolized a union of traditionalists and conservatives, an alliance between the Church and dynasts, a coalition between those representing the political and economic establishment that benefited from the exploitation of a working class living in dire poverty and alienation. As the nineteenth century passed the relay baton to the twentieth century, Europe was the battleground between competing visions of aggressive nationalisms, ideologies and political projects on how to achieve freedom, justice, security, power and peace. We explore these further in Chapter 7 on Europe's political dimensions.

Twentieth century Europe: war and peace

In the twentieth century, visions for a Europe of peace through alliances between the great powers were replaced with visions for a Europe of peace through democracy. The magnitude of Europe's destruction and division after the First World War, the demise of the Great Empires and the triumph of the Bolsheviks in the 1917

Russian Revolution led to a profound re-examination of the causes of the causes of war and gave a dynamic impetus to the idea of a united, democratic Europe as the only way to guarantee peace.

In this context, Count Richard Coudenhove-Kalergi founded the Pan-Europe movement in the early 1920s that aimed at Europe's political unification. He considered unification in the form of a democratic federation of states as the way to guarantee a viable and lasting world peace. Essentially, unification was meant to protect European civilization from the 'non-Occidental culture of Bolshevism', while from an economic perspective it was the way to prevent American domination of world trade (Orluc, 2007, p. 96). French politician and diplomat Aristide Briand took up Count Coudenhove-Kalergi's ideas and suggested the creation of a regional union, a 'European Federation' with competencies in the field of economics. He proposed to set up a set of representative bodies within the League of Nations, which would aim to create a common market to raise the level of well-being of the peoples of the European community. Coudenhove-Kalergi's dream of a pacifist Europe, combined with the French proposal in the 1920s at the League of Nations for a united Europe that would ensure peace and economic prosperity, tend to be considered as the origins of what a couple of decades later inspired European integration. These aspirations, however, were short-lived as they were approached with cynicism and scepticism on the part of Germany, Italy and Britain, who viewed them as cloaked attempts at French domination. At the same time, they were confronted with the rise of nationalism, fascism, national-socialism, authoritarian forms of government and the re-militarization of the entire continent.

In the decade that followed, the unification project was hijacked by national-socialism and fascism. No longer a pacifist project, a united Europe represented the quest for *Lebensraum* (i.e. the vital living space for the Germanic people) and an affirmation of power through armed means as compensation for Germany's insulted ego. The ways in which winners and losers were treated in the Versailles Peace Treaty (1918) had far reaching consequences for Europe both as a concept and as a geographical region. Needless to say, it also had far-reaching consequences for the world far beyond the European peninsula of the Eurasian continent.

The unification of Europe by the Third Reich was pursued in the 1930s and 1940s as a vision of a racially re-ordered Europe, an Aryan-racist-imperialist proposition that aimed at strengthening ethnic Germandom. Nazism and fascism's ideas of *Mitteleuropa* were driven by economic considerations, certainly, but also by a deep racist ideology that wished for a Europe unified under an authoritarian nationalism built on traditional Christian values while rejecting, persecuting and ultimately attempting to exterminate all forms of pluralism and diversity (Lipgens, 1982). This required the ethnic cleansing of Eastern Europe and western Russia and eventually the final solution for the Jewish, Roma and Sinti populations of the continent (Morgan, 2003). The outbreak of fascist ideology and the consolidation of fascist regimes were the result of the backlash of ultra-nationalism and a counter-culture to the cultural and societal changes that had occurred at the end of the nineteenth century. Fascism also drew from the experience of colonialism. As Hannah Arendt has argued, the violence and racism that characterized imperialist expansion cannot be separated from the home societies, and it was easily transferable within European countries and was nurtured by 'scientific' justifications provided by 'social Darwinism' that had permeated mainstream European culture (Morgan, 2003; Woodley, 2010).

The Allied powers opposed Adolf Hitler's effort to establish this version of Europe in the course of the Second World War. However, within the Allied camp there were two different visions of the sort of Europe they envisaged in opposition to a fascist or Nazi Europe. And in each case, the unifying elements that would bind Europe together drew from a very different pool of ideas. One envisaged freedom and independence through a Europe of democracy, economic liberalism, pluralism and human rights. The other envisaged freedom and independence through class struggle, equality, social justice and the unifying banner of communism. The Allied victory catalysed the resurgence of the ideal of a pacifist Europe. The federal model that had been proposed before the war continued to inspire hopes for unification. Jean Monnet's practical functionalism and Altiero Spinelli's federalism indeed set the foundations for what was to eventually develop into the European Economic Community and later the European Union.

The Europe evoked and represented by the European Union in the latter decades of the twentieth century was the result of mergers between a number of geopolitical definitions of 'Europe' that have represented very different and largely opposing world views in the latter half of the twentieth century.

For one, there is Western Europe, which together with the United States, presented itself as the 'free' world, the 'First' world: in short, the 'West'. The transatlantic community that the countries of North-Western Europe (mainly Britain, France, the Benelux countries, the Federal Republic of Germany) forged with the USA came to stand for political and economic liberalism, democracy and first-generation human rights as well as a collective security community. Western Europe also represented the containment of a future renascent threat of a Germanic Europe, as in principle it cemented Franco-German reconciliation and inter-dependence between the economies of Western Europe. For this Europe, the 'other' was identified either as the communist threat and the Red Army from the East, or as a nascent Arab nationalism from the South, or eventually a few decades later, a fast-rising economic rivalry from Asia.

Then, there is Nordic Europe, representing what could almost be described as the most sophisticated version of modern Europe. Transparency, accountability, participatory democracy, civic citizenship and a strong attachment to individual political freedoms, independence and neutrality were coupled with a much-envied effective, inclusive and protective welfare state and a combative environmentalism. Among the Nordic countries, Finland stands apart with its 'special relationship' with Russia and then the Soviet Union, and its rather late industrialization, which led to a more liberal, noninterventionist economic mode of governance. Finland's particular concern to protect its territorial security while seeming unthreatening to the Soviet Union made it emphasize its neutrality consistently, presenting itself as a Nordic country with a statist, politically impartial, Western culture.

Moving to the southern part of the continent, and moving from west to east, it seems almost paradoxical that in the post-war period of liberal democracy in Western Europe, the two Iberian dictatorships of Franco and Salazar were able to survive and for so many decades. Yet they did, and Spain and Portugal were able to tie themselves with the European and Atlantic organizations that were gradually institutionalized after the Second World War. The repressive regimes of Franco and Salazar were tolerated by Western European countries and the

USA as a result of Cold War imperatives, as was Greece's rather dysfunctional liberal democracy that was established after the end of the country's civil war (1945–1949), its NATO accession and its subsequent consolidation in the Western bloc. Southern Europe was stereotyped as being more strongly attached to tradition, constrained by a more intrusive role of the Church (given the role of Opus Dei, particularly during the Franco regime, the strong presence of the Orthodox Church in Greece, and the influence of the Vatican in Italian politics), economically underdeveloped with an all-pervading, bureaucratically cumbersome and rather corrupt and clientelistic state. After the fall of Greece's colonels' *junta* and of the Iberian dictatorships, the focus shifted to the democratization and the 'Europeanization' of the Southern periphery. Their 'Europeanization' was essentially a modernization project and more specifically one aimed at adaptation to West European norms and practices (Gunther et al., 1995; Featherstone and Kazamias, 2001). Further east, in the far south-eastern peninsula of Europe, the Balkans personified the most pre-modern part of Europe, a tumultuous, explosive and divisive historical legacy of a region rich with linguistic, ethnic and religious diversity (Triandafyllidou, Gropas and Kouki, 2013; Sotiropoulos and Veremis, 2002). For the latter half of the twentieth century, South-East Europe was probably one of the most geopolitically sensitive areas of the continent, as it was simultaneously split between the two superpower blocs and engaged in three different political projects: part of it (Greece) participated in the regional integration project of the ECSC/EEC, another part participated in the federation project of the Slavs of the South (Yugoslavia), and yet another (Bulgaria and Romania) participated in the socialist Soviet project. As for Turkey, the Truman Doctrine announced in March 1947 paved the way for US financial support, which was much needed for the country's economic development (Martin and Keridis, 2004). This essentially cemented Turkey into the Cold War's Western bloc and was quickly followed with the country's accession to the Council of Europe in 1949 and to NATO in 1952, together with Greece.

Finally, Eastern Europe. Tightly paired together with the Soviet Union for the second half of the twentieth century and referred to as the 'Eastern bloc', the eastern periphery represented a different vision of Europe. Representing, in principle, equality and social justice, the right to employment and free access for all to public health and education, class struggle and a preference towards collective rather than individual rights, what lay on the eastern side of the Cold War divide also represented authoritarian rule. Nonetheless, for this Europe, the imperialistic, colonial and later neo-colonial Transatlantic, Western capitalist community driven by profit-seeking multinational corporations and human exploitation constituted the 'other'.

Just as the western side of the Iron Curtain pursued various forms of economic and military cooperation in order to advance its vision of a Europe of peace, security and prosperity, so too, on the Eastern side, integration was pursued through the Council for Mutual Economic Assistance (COMECON) and the Communist Information Bureau (Cominform). COMECON, formed in 1949 at the height of East–West confrontation and Cold War division of the continent, was complemented by the Inter-Party Communist Information Bureau and the Warsaw Pact and provided the basis for Europe's unique non-capitalist attempt at integration in all its history (Bideleux and Taylor, 1996, p. 174). COMECON's objective of intensifying the economic integration of its members through an International Socialist Division of Labour was in principle aimed at the harmonious and comprehensive development of all socialist countries. It also had as its declared objective the reinforcement of their unity. In practice, it did more to strengthen the radial trade links with Moscow and to realize Moscow's own security and power objectives than offer an alternative vision for European unity (Jones, 1980). Inspired by central planning and socialist principles, these institutions and their regional dimensions were more relevant to the USSR than the European model, hence the admission of Mongolia, Cuba and Vietnam. Moreover, the decision-making process across all sectors and on all subjects – from the arts, to science, to the economy – was centralized and located in Moscow, and even more specifically in the Politburo, rather than shared between Warsaw, Prague, Bucharest and Budapest. Finally, unity around a common ideology (Marxism/Leninism) and suspicion about the 'capitalist West' overrode any substantial reference or vision of a unified Europe. It was only in the late 1980s with the development of a vision of a 'common European home' orchestrated by Mikhail Gorbachev that things changed.

Europe: institutions and integration

Throughout the second half of the twentieth century, Western Europe positioned itself as the core of Europe: as the hegemonic definition of Europe. The institutions set-up by Western European countries largely dominated the meaning of 'Europe' and projected it beyond the geographic confines of the continent. These include the Council of Europe that was founded in 1949, the European Convention on Human Rights and the European Court of Human Rights, established in 1959. On the economic front, the European Coal and Steel Community (1951) set the ground for the European Economic Community in 1957 (and a few decades later the European Union). While the countries that could not envisage joining the EEC for political reasons set up the European Free Trade Association in 1960. The drive to promote economic, social and cultural cooperation and collective self-defence as East–West tension mounted, while taking precautions against the potential resurgence of any threat from Germany, also triggered institutions and cooperation in the security realm, notably through the 1948 Treaty of Brussels. It is interesting that just a few years later, in 1954, it was the Brussels Treaty, renamed the Western European Union (WEU) that provided the way through which the Federal Republic of Germany was integrated into the Western security system. Although a European defence identity hardly had any substance before the 1980s and1990s, Western Europe's unprecedented and unique experience at regional integration came to represent a novel approach to international relations, as it established institutions charged with finding supranational solutions to international problems.

One of the core architects of this approach was of course the influential French businessman and civil servant Jean Monnet, who sought to establish common interests in areas that had the potential to re-spark conflict through technocratic solutions. He argued that peace could only be ensured and entrenched through building institutions that would formulate common solutions to shared problems. The EEC, followed by the EU, became a unique experiment of regional integration, based on cooperation between member states, interdependence, institutional innovation and, above all, voluntarily pooled sovereignty. Monnet's technocratic and functionalist approach to European integration was shaped by the following assumptions: the obsolescence of the state, the danger of nationalism, the imperative to change the context of problems, the need for new institutions with which to anchor common interests through technocratic, incremental processes, and the fundamental notion of 'crisis', which would be the force that would drive Europe's political elites to embrace change and seek common solutions (Burgess, 2000, p. 49).

One of the other founding fathers of the EU, the Italian Altiero Spinelli, for his part envisaged a federal Europe, which would enable social reform. His version was tainted with a greater sense of urgency and, while he agreed that strong independent institutions were necessary for European solutions to prevail over national solutions to common problems, he considered it did not suffice to rely on economic considerations to push unification forward (Burgess, 2000, p. 36). Spinelli considered European unity on a federal basis as the most important political aim for the continent's future. He drew his inspiration from the ideas of the Italian liberal Luigi Einaudi, who had proposed a federal solution for Europe's problem of nationalism. Einaudi had criticized the League of Nations for failing to limit the sovereignty of its member states and had argued that only when the sovereignty of each European state was surrendered to a supranational organism would lasting peace be ensured (Burgess, 1995; Hewitson and D'Auria, 2012).

In the post-Second World War institution-building period, NATO became the organization that secured Western Europe's defence and cemented the security dimensions of the Transatlantic alliance. And it was the challenge of rearming West Germany via NATO in the early 1950s (accepted by Paris only after London and Washington committed that they would continue deploying troops on the European continent) that created the wider environment within which federalists (including Paul Henri Spaak, Fernand Dehousse, Alcide de Gaspari and Andreé Philip) and those who believed in the value of the community method for Western Europe were able to move European integration forward. European Political Cooperation (EPC) was launched and lay the foundations for the EU's security and foreign policy cooperation, which we examine in Chapter 9. The need for a peace and security project for Europe was perceived as more pressing than ever in order to keep the Germans 'down', the Russians 'out' and the Americans 'in', as NATO's first Secretary General, Lord Ismay, famously declared. French philosopher

Simone de Beauvoir framed it slightly differently in *La force des choses* (1963), claiming that 'Europe' was a myth used by the USA in order to restore German power as a counterweight to that of the USSR (Hewitson and D'Auria, 2012, p. 11). What is certain is that the destruction of the Second World War offered a 'ground zero' from which ideas of Europe could prosper.

Although the aims of Jean Monnet and Robert Schuman's European integration focused on reconciliation, economic reconstruction and peace building through the creation of new institutions, policy-making instruments, international treaties and law (Drake, 2000); in the words of Burgess, Europe, in the form of a European Economic Community/European Union, has remained a 'conceptual enigma' (2000, p. 254). Although the EEC/EU has clearly rendered the idea of Europe more tangible, ironically, the process of European integration has probably led to greater contestation over the meaning of Europe (Delanty, 2006b). This has been particularly the case when debates and discourses have rolled into discussions on identity as we discuss in Chapter 5.

Nonetheless, since the 1970s Western European countries have declared a 'European' community of values on the basis of liberal democracy, human rights, and rule of law, which was expressed in a very constrained manner through the launch of European Political Cooperation. The EEC positioned itself as the stronghold of European political values and culture with rather little contestation from the non-EEC European states. At the Copenhagen summit in December 1973, the nine EC Heads of State and Government officially declared the existence of a 'European identity' (Passerini, 1998, pp. 4–5), although talk of a European identity continues to raise more questions than answers and remains a contentious, if not irrelevant, topic in many member states almost half a century later. Nevertheless, by the late 1970s, the idea of Europe had taken the shape of much more than its initial function of post-war reconciliation, and much more than an economic alliance. In his 1978 Jean Monnet Lecture at the European University Institute, the President of the European Parliament, Emilio Colombo, spoke on the importance of enlarging the EEC to include Greece, Spain and Portugal. He underlined that:

> There is no doubt that the permanent absence of Spain, Greece and Portugal would in the long term damage the very

identity of the Community ideal. The contribution to European civilisation which these countries have made throughout their long history a no less valid contribution than that made by the existing members of the Community is such that if they did not join the ranks of those contributing to the ideals and culture of the Community, it would automatically be lowering its sights and be destined to become a mere regional trading area. Without the contribution of the Mediterranean area, Europe – and thus the Community – would be incomplete. (Colombo, 1978, p. 19)

The following year, the Jean Monnet Lecture at the European University Institute was given by Lord Ralf Dahrendorf. He argued that having moved from the 'first Europe', which essentially consisted of an extended interpretation of a customs union between the member states, to the 'second Europe' of the 1970s, which consisted of political success but also of institutional failures, it was time to move towards a 'third Europe'. Critical of the European institutions' cumbersome bureaucratic nature and the lack of democracy, he defined his vision of a 'third Europe' in the following terms:

> The meaning of the Third Europe … is neither primarily one of the end of civil war, nor even that of the nitty-gritty of prosperity by creating a wider common market. It is emphatically not the desire of some of the founding fathers to create another superpower either; to have as much decentralization as possible and only as much centralization as necessary, is a prescription for a humane society to which many, including myself, would subscribe today. (…) The meaning of the Third Europe, as it corresponds to the experience of a new generation of Europeans, is rather in two things: one is the irrelevance of borders for solving problems, and the other is the need for common decisions where there are genuine common interests. (Dahrendorf, 1979, pp. 7–9)

In the decade that followed, and under Jacques Delors' Presidency of the European Commission, Europe began to take tangible shape, largely through the 'relaunch' of Europe through the Single European Act (SEA, 1987). Following the 'Eurosclerosis' and 'Europessimism' that had characterized the 1970s, the mid-1980s witnessed a period of optimism and institutional momentum that led to the Single Market and the expression of member states' determination to transform their relations with a view to creating a European Union. As Andrew Moravcsik (1991) described, the SEA linked a comprehensive liberalization of trade and services in the European market with procedural reforms aimed at streamlining decision-making in the EC governing body. Although the pursuit of monetary union and a common defence were preferred objectives for Jacques Delors, he recognized that only the Single Market was politically feasible, so, adhering to the Monnet step-by-step functionalist approach, he focused on precisely that. Delors and the Internal Market Commissioner, Lord Arthur Cockfield, were able to bridge together business interest groups and national interests to push forward institutional reform. Jacques Delors' federalist vision for Europe also included plans for a Social Charter that would create pan-European workers' rights to match the liberalization of the markets. This social dimension, along with Delors' push for a European Union with a single currency and an emerging 'common foreign and security policy' in the late 1980s, was at opposite ends with Margaret Thatcher's political visions. For her, the EEC made sense so long as it consisted of economic cooperation among independent sovereign states. Her preference was for a 'wider', 'looser' European community that would include the 'great European cities' of Warsaw, Prague and Budapest (see reference to Thatcher's 1988 Bruges speech in Evans, 2004). When the Berlin Wall fell in 1989, the collapse of the communist bloc was recognized by Thatcher as an opportunity to reshape 'Europe' (meaning the EEC) by enlarging it into a politically looser free-market based community in which the Franco-German influence would be reduced and the organic link with the USA would be preserved (Evans, 2004, p. 109).

In spite of the resistance of Britain, the majority of the political elites in the other EEC member states saw a geostrategic interest and benefit in giving more substance and political weight to the concept of Europe at the end of the 1980s. The end of the Cold War and German reunification made the EEC the most suitable forum within which 'Europe' could be reunified. The dominant narrative that developed post-1989 was that the countries of Central and Eastern Europe were 'returning to Europe'. And this narrative did not only come from Brussels. It came from

Paris, Bonn and later Berlin, it came from Rome and Madrid, it came from Budapest, Prague and Warsaw, and it actually even came from Moscow. It thus came along with the resurfacing of the geopolitical concept of Central Europe: the continent's heartland had been dismantled as a concept after the Second World War, splintered by the Wall into two competing blocs until 1989. In his essay, the 'Tragedy of Central Europe', Milan Kundera (1984) passionately argued that predominantly Roman Catholic Poland, Hungary, what was Czechoslovakia at the time, Slovenia and Croatia had long been part of the 'West' and were arguably more 'European' than their Eastern Orthodox neighbours. The emergence of a debate on a Central European identity came to be considered as an important political process, offering a way out of the Soviet-type homogenization that had taken place during the Cold War. This avenue emphasized the 'European qualities' of the local cultures, in particular pluralism and democracy, hence 're-Europeanizing' the region while offering individuals an additional level of identity that would avoid 'the threat of reductionism encapsulated in political nationalism' (Schopflin and Wood, 1989; Neumann, 1999, p. 164). At the same time, Mikhail Gorbachev spoke of a *'common European home'* that idealistically seemed to revive the goal of creating a united Europe (1988). The democratic euphoria that dominated international relations in the beginning of the 1990s provided the context within which to explore Russia's coming together with the Euro-Atlantic community. This re-launched countless ambitious debates about whether 'a Europe from the Atlantic to the Urals' was indeed possible. Whereas in 1962 this famous statement by Charles de Gaulle had enraged Nikita Khrushchev (who saw it as yet another imperialist attempt to break up the Soviet Union), in the 1990s it became the slogan for Euro-enthusiasts on both western and eastern parts of the continent, and even more so across the Channel.

Enlarging the club – how far?

Yet, was such a wide vision of Europe indeed feasible in the 1990s? Or was it even desired? Officially and publically, the rhetoric was certainly there. But were the national governments of the EEC Member States as supportive of such an enlarged

EEC? Would the benefits associated with 'too much' widening outweigh the costs, or even the risks?

Ralf Dahrendorf was among those who were not convinced. In his book *Reflections on the Revolution in Europe* he argued that a 'common European home' indisputably ended where the Soviet Union, or whatever succeeded it, began for three reasons:

> One is that there is something deeply suspicious about yesterday's hegemonic power wishing to set-up house with those whom it occupied and held under its tutelage for so long; it is probably better to keep the grizzly bear outside. The second reason is that the Soviet Union, with all its European history, is a vast developing country which has a much longer way to go than others in its European orbit before it becomes a full part of the modern world. The third and most important point is that Europe is not just a geographical or even cultural concept, but one of acute political significance. This arises at least in part from the fact that small and medium sized countries try to determine their destiny together. (2005, p. 120)

While there was significant concern and deliberation about the sort of symbiotic relationship that was feasible or desirable between 'Europe' and what had been its most fearful existential threat in its eastern periphery, there was even more concern and deliberation about the sort of relationship that 'Europe' was to have with Germany, still perceived by many as 'Europe's' most important existential threat within. Treaty revisions, major redistribution policies through the EU's social cohesion and regional development funds, and impressive public diplomacy efforts on behalf of Bonn/Berlin were undertaken in order to calm fears among the smaller and more medium-sized EEC/EU member states about the forever recurring risk and threat of a 'German Europe' while ensuring the consolidation of a 'European Germany'. German Chancellor Helmut Kohl heavily invested in the Franco-German alliance as the core anchor of any vision of Europe, clarifying that German reunification was to be done within a politically united Europe, through the implementation of the Economic and Monetary Union (EMU) and the Social Charter. The reunification of Germany thus provided the catalyst for the most sophisticated attempt thus far for the continent's regional integration. Through the European Union, the founding member states largely defined what Europe was meant to represent in the twenty-first century. They defined both the form and the means through which it would be achieved. Through the EU institutions and processes, the countries of Western Europe articulated the political, legal, administrative, judiciary, societal and economic conditions that represented the ideal that had to be attained, as well as the path that had to be pursued to achieve it by the newly independent states of Central, Eastern and South-East Europe. Western European governments set the pace, the conditions and the processes that had to be followed and abided by (participation in the Euro-Atlantic security community first, association, and, eventually, adherence to the Copenhagen and the Maastricht criteria), and provided the means, the resources, the technical assistance and the narrative for the newly independent states to transition from communism, single-party rule and state-planned economies and be 'Europeanized' again.

The process of accession to EU membership for the countries of Central and South-East Europe involved deep institutional and political reforms in accordance with the agenda that was laid out through Brussels. The reunification of 'Europe' was pursued through the establishment of multi-party electoral systems, judicial reforms, support for freedom of the media and civil society building. Market liberalization, privatization and deregulation seemed to be the way through which to become European in a globalized world. Although NATO accession was a political priority for all, EU accession took a wider meaning beyond the security dimension and was essentially framed as a modernization project and a 'return to Europe' narrative. This narrative has been perceived by many as a form of paternalistic Eurocentrism that finds its origins in the eighteenth-century idea of Western imperialism as a *'mission civilisatrice'* (Lawson et al., 2010, p. 28). This same 'return to Europe' narrative had been used with the southern EEC enlargements a few years prior. On the occasion of Spain's EU accession ceremony in 1986, Madrid's Mayor, Tierno Galvan, had declared that 'we are more European today than we have ever been' (Eder and Spohn, 2005). King Juan Carlos I and Prime Minister Felipe Gonzalez had made similar declarations depicting Spain's EU accession as its 'triumphant passage to modernity and democracy'. The Nation had thus become 'European' and thereby 'modern' (Eder and Spohn, 2005, p. 118).

At the turn of the twenty-first century, the vision for Europe that was put forward through the EEC/EU was one of unity that celebrated diversity. The 'unity in diversity' motto from 2000 reflects the national, ethnic, linguistic and religious differences that define Europe. More specifically, it represents the paradigm shift that the European Union has attempted to achieve through its approach to integration. Diversity is thus not conceived in terms of a negative 'other' or a marker of separation, but as something positive that can function as a bridge of peace and prosperity. Respect for diversity does not only apply at the societal level; in fact, the EU has also, in principle, rendered this relevant for inter-state relations. The representation of small states and the principle of parity between all member states regardless of size and power – though often more challenging and challenged than is politically acceptable to acknowledge – has been crafted into all the EU institutions. Decision-making processes have been structured to require 'package deals' and coalitions to be built between smaller and larger countries for important decisions to be taken. The President of Estonia, Lennart Meri, spoke of the importance of this dimension of Europe's diversity as inherent to its nature and basically what distinguishes the concept of Europe that the EU represents from the reality that Europe, particularly the central and eastern parts, experienced in the twentieth century, when the larger powers annexed or dominated the smaller ones:

> Small states are the lubricating oil of Europe and the mortar of Europe. The survival and development of small nations is the key issue of the future of Europe. Europe needs small nations as much as we need Europe. Because the strength of the European Union does not lie in its size – the strength of Europe comes from its diversity. (Lennart Meri, President of Estonia, 'The Role of Small Nation in the European Union' speech at the University of Turku, Finland, 25 May 2000, quoted in Lehti and Smith, 2005, p. 1)

In spite of such ambitious and grand scale aspirations and declarations about Europe and the forms it should take in the twenty-first century, the question of what Europe actually is and what it meant in the minds of those who were already members of the Union and of the aspiring members remained full of contradictions and at the root of much discord and disappointment.

Much of this disappointment rightly stems from the Union's failure to avert a return to ethnic violence and aggressive nationalism at the heart of the continent. There was a tragic failure to respond in an effective, united and timely manner to the violent dissolution of Yugoslavia. The EU failed to enact and secure the ideal that it had argued it represented throughout the second half of the twentieth century: a European democratic peace. It was unable to protect human rights and peace within its south-eastern core, thereby affecting once again the notion and definition of Europe in its people's minds. 'Europe' was seen as still vulnerable to extremism and war, and the EU became associated with political weakness, disarray and a lack of unity. References to Europe as a 'political dwarf' dependent on America's military might deeply dented its aspirations to global power status. In addition, it led to two opposite realities and meanings of Europe that existed synchronously. On the one hand was the idea that had been nurtured through the EU that war was impossible between its member states, while on the other, war *was* being waged in Europe. The extreme contrast between the two realities that were juxtaposed next to each other in the same space and at the same time led people to associate Europe with peaceful prosperity, yet at the same time feel very unsafe and at risk. Paraphrasing Raymond Aron's famous description about the Cold War dialectic relationship between the Eastern and Western blocs as 'impossible peace, improbable war', Zaki Laïdi wrote about Europe in the post-Cold War period as a relationship between 'imperfect peace and unobtainable security' (1998, p. 98).

From 'how to unify Europe?' to 'what kind of Europe?' and 'how much Europe do we want?'

Eurocentrism has been unavoidably embedded in the historical trajectory outlined in this chapter. It is hard to think of a definition of the idea of Europe, or of a project aimed at European unification that is not imbued with Eurocentrism. Eurocentrism has been criticized for attributing to Europe the unique source of meaning, the world's centre of gravity and, to the 'West', a 'providential sense of historical destiny' (Shohat and Stam, 2014, p. 2). It is a pervasive mind-frame that divides all aspects of culture, history, science, politics, power and society in 'us/ours' and 'them/theirs' in a binary manner, bifurcating the world into the 'West and the Rest' and providing the ideological backing to colonialist practices and imperialist discourse. Essentially, it underpins implicitly or explicitly all readings of world or European history.

As Shohat and Stam have insightfully noted, Eurocentric discourse projects a linear historical trajectory of a sequence of empires from classical Greece to Pax Romana, Pax Britannica and so on, attributing to the 'West' an inherent progress towards democracy while representing its oppressive practices (colonialism, slave-trading, and so on) and dark periods in a 'sanitized form' of exceptional aberrations (2014, pp. 2–3). Thus, Eurocentrism has been criticized as presenting itself in racist or paternalistic discourse towards other societies, cultures or nations. Certainly, the ideas of Europe and the ways in which Europe has been envisaged have a strong Eurocentric foundation. They equally have a strong self-critical and self-depreciating basis. This coexistence is tightly knit and has enriched attempts to define what defines Europe and why.

As we have traced in this chapter, 'Europe' has essentially always been a political project. As such, there exist competitive visions of what Europe means and to what it ought to aspire (Jacobs and Maier, 1998). During the latter half of the twentieth century, the European Community/European Union gradually positioned itself as representing the realization of centuries-long aspirations (both declared and underlying) for European unity.

The EU came to represent Europe, thereby leading the bulk of the debate towards the question of 'What sort of Europe' do we wish for? How is Europe framed at present? As the project of European integration has evolved and consolidated itself through institutions, policies, treaty revisions and consecutive enlargements, how does it stand in our minds today?

The EC/EU has been considered the product of economically derived national self-interests and a way through which to renew the legitimacy of the European nation-states (Milward, 1992). It has also been positioned as the most appropriate means through which to assert Europe's relevance in international relations and to be able to promote its strategic interests through political and military means and exercise influence beyond its borders. Europe has also been framed as a normative power in global affairs and as embodying a distinctive Social Model founded on human rights, democracy, solidarity and the fight against inequality, intolerance, repression and discrimination both in Europe and internationally. In all these visions, there exists a degree of influence of the legacy of Europe's empires, a belief in the universal nature of European values and, implicitly, in a modernized and politically correct version of its older *mission civilisatrice*.

The dissenting view has sought to protect and re-strengthen the nation-state by restricting the role and powers of 'Europe', aka 'Brussels', these days. Expressed through different forms of Euroscepticism on behalf of populist parties from the far left and right or no-votes in European referenda, this perspective is important because of the questions it raises regarding legitimacy at the EU level and the challenging impacts that market integration and globalization have on national democracies (Leconte, 2010, p. 13).

Naturally, these perceptions of Europe are not the only two ideal types. European statesmen, politicians, academics and intellectuals do not neatly fall into one or the other of the two positions outlined above. Views of Europe are not binary and span across a wide spectrum of approaches. As a system of governance, for some, the EU is the most suited to the greater challenges posed by modernization, interdependence and globalization. Jan Zielonka (2006) described the EU as a neo-medieval empire, a 'meta-governor', mediating between a complex web of interlocking levels of governance, territorial units and democratic polities, which allowed for the 'two Europes' to come together following the end of the Cold War. Then there are those who are concerned that the EU may have 'overstretched' itself. They essentially admit that much of Europe's diversity cannot be integrated within a single governance project and raise the issue that perhaps there are limits to how much diversity can be feasibly managed. Finally, there are others who may be more concerned with the legitimacy deficit that the Union faces than the membership challenge; or, that a European reform agenda is long overdue (Emmanouilidis and Tsoukalis, 2011).

During the first decade of the twenty-first century, 'Europe' entered national political debates as a dimension of national identity and power. And as it gained momentum, it appears that the concept of Europe raised more questions than ever before. Attempts to understand and reassess what Europe actually meant in a globalized world led to debates in each member state (actual and prospective) on how national identities relate to understandings and visions of Europe, as well as the existence of one or many European identities. Increasingly, however, as the political, institutional and economic crises magnified after the mid-2000s, the questioning shifted from understanding the obstacles and impacts of Europeanization to whether the limits of how much diversity 'Europe' – meaning the EU – can digest had been reached. More importantly, as the economic crisis settled in after 2008, substantially constraining the EU's ability to procure and promise prosperity, 'Europe' became an ideological battleground. Perceived as a neoliberal project threatening the heart of social justice, welfare and employment rights across the continent, for Europe's left political forces the EU – simply referred to as Europe in all casual talk – has come to symbolize the dominance of global financial centres of power over democracy. At the very same time, for those wanting to open markets and to liberalize even further 'Europe' (the EU) epitomizes the continent's tradition of protectionist bureaucracies where vested interests stifle competition, innovation and entrepreneurship.

The coexistence of conflicting visions and perceptions of Europe is thus nothing new; it simply marks another phase of the history of the idea of Europe that has inspired aspirations of grandeur just as much as it has inspired contempt.

Concluding remarks

Having traced through some of the most meaningful and influential visions that have been formed about Europe, as Bo Stråth has argued, the question of what Europe *is* has no unequivocal answer (2000, p. 420).

Europe has been in a continuous discourse on unification. The idea of unity, either through hegemony or through consensus and cooperation, which is at the core of Europe suggests that essentially it is a political project. Europe has taken various meanings synchronically and diachronically, yet it seems that the idea of Europe has essentially taken three core approaches.

The first is fundamentally one of regeneration of Europe. These visions have looked to the past, often recreating or reinterpreting it, emphasizing the common roots of Europe's culture and identity, or its distinctive characteristics whose integrity had to be maintained. The second is one of preservation in the face of contemporary challenges from within and from the global arena. Finally, the third involves the generation of a new, different future (Hewitson and D'Auria, 2012). Europe frames a condition to aspire to, a political goal to be accomplished in order to break from the past or from conditions of degeneration, decline and weakness.

In all the forms that the idea of Europe has taken, Europe has been the 'self' and the 'other' bound into one. Although each of its constituent parts (countries and peoples) considers itself European and rightfully claims shared ownership of Europe's history, its values and civilization, this identity is simultaneously an elusive one because the centre of power is often seen, with a certain anxiety, as being 'elsewhere'. In short, Europe has often been 'so near and yet so far', a constantly shifting mosaic of ideas. The idea of Europe has been politically inspiring even though it provokes eternal dissatisfaction, perpetual frustration, and an unsettling concern pregnant with ambitious plans and grand desires of what it could be or what it ought to be.

Chapter 4

Cultural Europe

'It's culture, not war that cements European identity', wrote Umberto Eco in 2012. But what do we mean when we connect the words 'Europe' and 'culture'? In this chapter we try to unravel the connections between the two in order to explore what these have represented at different times in history and in which ways they are relevant at present. In recent decades, historians, sociologists, anthropologists, political scientists and philosophers have taken a strong interest in exploring the cultural dimensions of Europe and the signifiers of European culture, European heritage, the cultural identity of Europe and the extent to which it is different from or similar to 'Western' culture.

In this chapter we highlight some of the complexities and contradictions that make up the way culture is understood. We explore the ways in which European culture has been defined, the heritages that constitute it and their relevance in contemporary understandings of European culture. We also present some efforts that have been made to attribute meaning and offer definitions of 'European' culture on the part of international and regional inter-state organizations whose scope of competence covers issues of culture, education, democracy and cooperation, and how it has been distinguished from Western culture. We then delve into Europe's relationship with the 'other', the 'other' from without and the 'other' from within, in order to underscore the cleavages, contradictions and alternative visions that have been put forward as representations of European culture and European values.

Throughout this *parcours culturel*, we seek the dominant, the alternative and the dissenting definitions of what is included and represented within 'European culture'. Just as importantly, we explore what 'European culture' aspires to. This latter aspirational dimension is probably its most distinctive feature as it has morphed the universalist and forward-looking dimensions that are characteristic of 'European culture', and of the

90

cultures of Europe. European culture acquires meaning when the commonalities, shared values and experiences of the past are constructed in a forward-looking manner. In other words, references to a common European culture seem to be mostly made when its constituent parts claim their belonging to a shared cultural space in order to express a political vision of Europe and the ideals it represents – or ought to represent.

Against this background we explore the more recent transformations of the idea of Europe where the plurality of its cultural underpinnings have been recognized to a far wider extent than ever before. In effect, it seems that in the post Cold War context, the reunification of the continent was accompanied with the emergence of a post-Western understanding of Europe, along with an increased recognition of its pluri-civilizational background and its newer forms of cultural plurality.

Defining culture, yet again...

We must start with definitions. Defining culture is a Sisyphean task. Culture is a term that tends to be used loosely, so it has always been a challenge to define according to standards of science. The most commonly quoted definitions of culture offer simple common-sense definitions with references to the arts and other manifestations of human intellectual achievement. More complex definitions refer to values and ideals and aim at explaining individual and societal behaviours, or at changing them, or both. Anthropologists, in particular, have long insisted on the importance of understanding and scientifically defining culture because of its tremendous influence on humans and their behaviours. Studying the relationships between culture and society, between culture and humanness and the distinctions between culture and cultural systems has enriched our understandings of the concept of culture (see Blumenthal, 1940; Weiss, 1973).

Understanding the core dimensions of the concept of culture is necessary in order to attempt to tackle the bigger challenge of unravelling the multiple dimensions of Europe. So, while not intending to overlook the complexities that are associated with the rich definitions of culture, there are three dimensions that are most relevant in our exploration of the connections between culture and Europe. The first is a temporal dimension, then there is an economic dimension and finally there is a power dimension. Culture is defined as the heritage of the past, and as an inspiration for the future. Culture is perceived by some as the soul of society and by others a product to be packaged, branded and traded and a contributor to economic growth. And, culture is certainly about politics and power. As Ayn Rand simply put it in her last collection of essays, *Philosophy, Who Needs it?*, (1982) culture is a complex battleground of dominant ideas and influences – accepted in whole or in part – that allows for the existence of dissenters and exceptions. Culture may be regarded as an elitist affair, or it may take the form of popular culture, which either involves mainstreaming cultural products for the masses, or is a means through which to contest dominant groups, the dominant class or a dominant global (super) power. Culture has been approached as a foreign policy instrument through which to promote dialogue and understanding, and consolidate strategic alliances. At the same time, culture has been used to expand national influence globally and has therefore been reproached as a facet of imperialism. Yet, just as framings of 'culture' have created patterns of superordination, subordination and control, explicitly expressing the superiority of one culture over others, so too have 'sub-cultures' developed as ways to contest authority or the dominant cultural mainstream.

Culture has been understood as a process of making sense of life and the world, and, unavoidably, such a framing has ideological underpinnings. From a policy perspective, positive or negative socio-economic outcomes are often attributed to culture (as opposed to 'nature'), or at least to specific cultures, in order to explain human behaviours. This leads to some social groups and cultures being 'valorized' over others, often justifying the formulation of policies aimed at the 'adjustment' or the 'development' of these others. On the European continent the focus has been on historical minorities, immigrant populations and the Roma and Sinti people. Globally, the focus has been on what are referred to as Third World countries in international relations.

In 1952, in their classic *Culture: A Critical Review of Concepts and Definitions*, Alfred Kroeber and Clyde Kluckhohn classified definitions of culture under six headings: descriptive definitions that attempt to enumerate the content of culture;

historical definitions that emphasize an aggregate collection of joint social heritage or tradition; normative definitions that concentrate on rules and ways of behaving; genetic ones that characterize culture in terms of products, ideas or symbols; structural ones that define culture; and psychological definitions that explore cognition, meaning and its impact on the human psyche.

Clyde Kluckhohn (1949) further elaborated the concept of culture, offering a multifaceted and diffuse approach to the concept by referring to it as a way of life, the social legacy that the individual acquires from the group, as well as a way of thinking, feeling and behaving. In this sense, culture is not only a learned behaviour, it also becomes a mechanism for the normative regulation of behaviour and at the same time it is also an abstraction from behaviour. It is a set of techniques for adjusting both to the external environment and to others and it is a theory for anthropologists about the way people behave. Clifford Geertz (1973), on the contrary, approached culture in a more precise manner focusing on semiotics. He contended that culture is a context within which social events, behaviours, processes and institutions can be intelligibly, or as he argues, thickly, described. Drawing from Max Weber's vivid depiction that 'man is an animal suspended in webs of significance he himself has spun', Geertz has added that culture is precisely these webs (1973, p. 5). The analysis of culture thereby becomes an interpretative science in search of meaning.

Culture is of course also connected with the art of intellectual refinement or the pursuit of perfection, and is thereby linked to notions of progress, development, modernity and the essence of humanity (see also Baldwin et al., 2006). Thus, it often becomes linked with the term 'civilization', another over-stretched term that has provoked much criticism for its Eurocentrism but which has also opened the scope for fascinating work on civilizational pluralism (see Hann, 2011; Bettiza, 2014).

Whether culture is defined in structural or functional terms, whether it is about artefacts and objects or processes, it fosters a sense of belonging, thereby constructing or maintaining a group's identity. It integrates people just as much as it segregates them. It is about identity, representation, signification. It is also about power and ideology, thereby linking culture to projects of influence or even hegemony and to projects of political contestation and struggle.

These dimensions of culture are particularly insightful in the effort we have embarked on in this book. We try to unpack and disintangle some of the layers, interpretations and expectations that 'Europe' as a culture has evoked, inspired and defined. Geertz's approach outlined above becomes insightful and illuminating when discussing European culture because Europe is indeed suspended in webs of culture that it itself has spun, and through the exploration of Europe's culture(s) and our search for its meaning(s) we hope to come closer to answering this book's guiding question of how to understand Europe.

The interminable quest for definitions and the ever elusive concept of European culture

Definitions of culture become sensitive minefields when they relate to Europe. Does a European culture exist, and is it shared or common? Under what conditions does it express itself, and how it is represented? What values are associated with it? Who defines it and what does it mean to them? And, what sort of power relations does it imply? These questions are relevant not just for Europe, but for the rest of the world too, given how influential Europe and its (national) cultures have been across history and across continents. At least, until recently.

Geert Hofstede (2001) suggested that values refer to the desired or to the desirable, whereas culture is a collective programming of the mind that manifests itself as values. Europe has always presented itself as being all about culture and all about values. As we have discussed in the previous chapters, Europe and culture raise associations connected with the Enlightenment, belief in progress, freedom of thought and of expression, and tolerance. References to Europe and culture have become interlinked with the concept of democracy, human rights, the notion of rationality and free will. Europe and culture are also associated with education, as any reference to culture immediately ties our understanding of Europe with universities, science academies, libraries, museums and a rich humanistic cultural heritage in landscape, religion, the arts, music, literature and film.

The Council of Europe has tried to codify these dimensions into definitions, understandings and norms for all countries across the continent, in order to establish common behaviours and further enhance common values. Its initiatives and actions have aimed at recognizing the major role performed by culture in the progress of social knowledge, understanding others and respecting cultural diversity, while furthering common values. Together with democracy and human rights, the Council of Europe has positioned culture as a precondition for a satisfying life, and a source of fulfilment. On 19 December 1954, the Council of Europe adopted the Cultural Convention (Council of Europe, 1954) as the foundation for European cooperation in the fields of culture, education, youth and sport. Its aim was to encourage cultural cooperation in all its manifold forms, to foster understanding and knowledge between European countries, and to preserve their cultural heritage and treat it as an integral part of a broader 'European' heritage.

The Council of Europe, in effect, has tried to emphasize this 'broader European heritage' in order to unpack culture from its national affiliations and to strengthen an understanding of a shared regional cultural identity. UNESCO has also worked in this direction. By focusing on the continent's sub-regions, such as South-East Europe (opening a UNESCO office in Venice for instance) or the Iberian penninsula or Eastern Europe, it has strived to encourage wider understandings of a common cultural heritage that transcends or cuts across national geographic borders bridging peoples, practices, traditions and values at a regional or sub-regional level. Initiatives such as the proclamation of the route of Santiago de Compostela as the first European Cultural Itinerary by the Council of Europe in 1987, and inscribed on UNESCO's World Heritage list, are aimed at approaching culture as a commonly shared European good rather than an exclusively national possession:

> This route from the French-Spanish border was – and still is – taken by pilgrims to Santiago de Compostela. Some 1,800 buildings along the route, both religious and secular, are of great historic interest. The route played a fundamental role in encouraging cultural exchanges between the Iberian peninsula and the rest of Europe during the Middle Ages. It remains a testimony to the power of the Christian faith among people of all social classes and from all over Europe. (UNESCO World Cultural Heritage website)

But what does the 'European' descriptor refer to? Is there a transversal, shared dimension that cuts across national cultures? In short, are there enough similarities between national cultures to suggest that a European culture, distinct from the more general Western one, exists? Or is it an elitist construct always in the making and never quite autonomously defined?

European cultural history weaves together the Greek, Latin and Germanic heritages of European civilization. Pagan and Christian traditions are layered together with the history of the Sephardic and Ashkenazi Jews and the Jewish Diaspora, and with the Muslim heritage that ranges from the Moors in Spain to the Muslim minorities that are part of the Ottoman Empire's legacy across South-Eastern Europe. Narratives of European cultural history tend to commence with the Classical Greco-Roman period, and then trace the imprint of the Romanesque and Gothic architectures across Western Europe. The Renaissance and its humanisms, the Reformation, the English Revolution, the Age of Reason or the Enlightenment, and eventually the French Revolution all constitute the classical points of reference. More recent studies weaved into the narrative the ways in which the idea of Europe and its traditions have been influenced by 'the near others' and how these have contributed to European civilization's distinctive nature. Byzantium, the Ottomans, the Moors and the Levant, have been the most defining 'others'.

Studies in Europe's cultural history also explore the big ideas that transformed Europe, and the rest of the world by extension. Alongside narratives that linger on the trajectory of culture in the arts and religion – and particularly a Christian theocentric view of the world, we also encounter narratives of intellectual history and of the achievements of science and rationality. This historiography traces the rise of Enlightenment thinking and secularity to the big '-isms', from the birth of German Romanticism and Idealism, to Liberalism and Marxism. The rise of modern culture, expressed in the surrealist and dada movements and in the Bauhaus school; the totalitarianisms of fascism and national socialism and the phenomenon of mass, popular culture; the bridge between impressionism and Soviet-inspired socialist realism all the way to pop art and culture, which have made the twentieth century the fastest paced, most controversial, most multifaceted and most radical period of European culture thus far.

Yet, these narratives essentially zoom in and out of the national levels. They present a fascinating mosaic of cultures, trajectories and stories that took place concomitantly or in sequence across the European continent. They focus on particular nations, and move from one local setting to another in order to show the same-time interconnections, the dialectical relations or the differences. We could almost say that – if there is such a thing – what comes naturally to most historians, sociologists and political scientists is to deal with the continent's history, culture, societies, institutions and interactions at the national level and all the way down to the city level. What is more challenging is to explore and narrate these from a 'European' perspective. In which case, what would this 'European' perspective be? Would it be from a higher, eagle-eye perspective, or would it be from a point of view of synthesis? Or, would it be motivated by the calculated objective to derive support for a particular political project? European integration as defined through the EEC/EU's unification has certainly been the most galvanizing political project across the continent in this direction. It has triggered interest in rethinking, framing and debating European history as more than the sum of national histories, and European culture as more than the sum of national cultures. Against this context, we try to unpack what 'European culture' involves and to which values European culture refers.

'First among equals', Europe and the 'others'

The crudest reply to the question of 'What is Europe?' would probably be: 'Well, quite simply, Europe is not the "other"'. It would of course also be illustrative of the Eurocentrism that has characterized the idea of Europe.

All the way back to antiquity and Ancient Greece, representations of the 'other', collectively defined as Barbarians, have been used to distinguish between the 'in' and 'out' groups; that is, the us and them. These representations have defined the differences that distinguish the civilizations of the European continent from all the others. Herodotus' account of the Persian Wars between the Greeks and the Persians is the quintessential personnification of the clash of Europe's values with the 'Other'. The narrative presents this war as Europe's defensive fight for freedom, law, virtue, courage and piety against Asia's aggressive despotism, lasciviousness and arrogance (Burgess, 1997). It is also the battle that largely frames Europe's self-understanding and the roots of its conflicts with its surrounding worlds. References to the 'others' or the Barbarians are thus associated with two distinct emotions throughout the continent's history and cultural development: fear and superiority.

Fear of change that may be provoked through interaction with the 'other', whether foreign or from within, seems to be a rather common knee-jerk reaction for any culture. It certainly seems to have a constant, well-defined and ever-recurring place throughout European culture. These 'others' neither speak our language nor share our cultural and political values; rather the contrary, common parlance argues, they are undermining our culture and challenging our core values. In most cases they are perceived as 'lacking' culture, 'understanding' and 'reason' and thereby being either 'underdeveloped' or 'backward'. In this context, fear may take two forms. It may arise out of concern for the potential impact that the 'other' may have on our society's values, way of life and cultural identity. This fear is the underbelly of negative stereotyping and prejudicial attitudes that lead to discrimination and the expression of phobias in the public sphere such as anti-Semitism or Islamophobia. Alternatively, this fear may be associated with survival-related anxieties, such as economic concerns (for instance competition for access to scarce resources, or to jobs), or even actual physical safety or survival of the 'in-group' (Brown, 2010).

The twentieth-century poet Constantine Cavafy captures the effects of these fears while indicating that they are intricately linked with an absolute existential need for the 'other'. In his 1904 poem 'Waiting for the Barbarians', he describes a country where all of public life is at a standstill in anticipation of the arrival of the Barbarians. In Cavafy's poem, citizens wait in the assembly anticipating the arrival of the Barbarians; the emperor and his consuls are dressed to impress, laws are suspended and parliamentary debates cancelled awaiting the arrival of the Barbarian danger. And then, nothing. The feared 'others' never actually arrive, leaving a gaping hole at the heart of the country's life, suggesting quite simply that without the 'other' there is no reason for 'us', nothing tying us together, or motivating us, or defining who we are:

> Because night has fallen and the barbarians haven't come.
> And some of our men just in from the border say
> there are no barbarians any longer.
> Now what's going to happen to us without barbarians?
> Those people were a kind of solution. (Cavafy, 1904/1975)

Superiority, though certainly not an exclusively European trait, has been the other constant in Europe's cultural framing of the world. It has probably been most famously explained and criticized by Edward Said's *Orientalism*. He describes the way in which Europe defined its contacts with different societies and cultures as colonization, which expanded the continent's influence and its interaction with all corners of the world. Said has argued that the study of the exotic – either in order to understand the 'other', or to define the self in relation to the 'other' – essentially led to the construction of an artificial boundary between the west and the east, or the occident and the orient, or the civilized and the uncivilized. Thus, 'Europe' became tightly packed together with the 'West', '*l'Occident*' and 'Civilization', leading to facile conclusions as regards the superiority of cultures and race. These conclusions served the European empires' political projects of colonization well. A cultural hierarchy frame thereby progressively exoticized, disdained and demonized non-Europeans as a means to legitimize the expansion of their imperial authority in what was being discovered as an increasingly diverse and very unflat world. The construction of stereotypes based on notions of cultural hierarchy – quickly transformed into colour and racial hierarchies – infiltrated science, literature, popular perceptions and public speech. Regardless of whether it took the form of a duty-driven *mission civilizatrice* or a romanticized fascination with the exotic, it defined 'others' as lesser, backward and in dire need of being 'civilized' or 'Europeanized'.

So, does this neatly summarize the gist of Europe's relation with the 'others' and essentially respond to the question of how to define the existence of a European civilization? Obviously not. This would assume a reductionist approach towards European culture risking caricaturing it as a proud, narcissistic imperial culture confident of its sophistication and ecumenical value, and fearful of degeneration due to foreign influence. Although 'Europe' has expressed itself as the embodiment of civilization through its cultural accomplishments, particularly in the arts and sciences, nonetheless, Europe's relation with the 'other' has undoubtedly also included a very rich experience of exchanges and a strong admiration often expressed for other 'older' civilizations, and often tainted by various degrees of Orientalism. Between the seventeeth and nineteenth centuries, a wide scholarly interest and a spiritual enchantment developed towards China and Confucianism, towards Japan, and towards India and the sacred Sanskrit writings of the *Vedas* in particular (Reitbergen, 2014). It is also during this time that Europe's fascination with Egyptology developed along with an impressive growth in the translation and publication of Arabic and Persian classic texts.

Lumping together all the cultures of the Old Continent under a blanket reference to 'European civilization' poses a further risk. It would involve ignoring and dismissing the cultural and value hierarchies that have, whether implicitly or explicitly, defined relations and perceptions of one another between European peoples throughout history. Cultural racism, or any form of racism, is never directed only towards the very 'foreign' other; rather the contrary, it is often most passionate towards the 'other' that is in its closest vicinity. Thus, it is not just non-Europeans who have been approached from a standpoint of cultural supremacy. Members of minority populations within European societies, and in particular heterodox Christians, Jews, nomadic communities and Muslims, have been exoticized and demonized just as much, just as frequently, and have been stereotyped as 'backward' just as intensely. Minority communities across all European societies have been subject to centuries-long painful processes of stigmatization, forced modernization, assimilation and exclusion.

The need to intervene and redress 'backwardness' may be considered a defining feature of European civilization. Bancroft has described it as a moral imperative, a 'white-man's burden' to rid the world of backwardness (2005, p. 25). And, much of this is related to the understanding of progress and evolution that is associated with modernity that has its roots in Europe. The Enlightenment, along with the French and also the American Revolutions, promoted values of universal humanism and emancipation through which all men, regardless of class, religion, colour or nationality shared the same essential fundamental rights. The belief was in human progress where all, including the more 'primitive' peoples, would eventually receive the benefits of civilization (and Christianity). By the mid-nineteenth century, however, a modern form of racism began to spread, with 'race science' becoming the dominant epistemology that explained human history as well as the contemporary social and political order (Macmaster, 2001). Modernity's objective to revolutionize societies and their relation with space and time in a never-ending quest for progress, imposed a notion of backwardness in two directions. It has been directed towards non-European societies that were contemporary with European modernity (expressed essentially in anti-black colonial racism), and it has been directed towards the alien groups within that are perceived as defying the nation's moral order and generally all that was associated with the dominant understanding of European civilization.

Jonathan Sack's description of how these tensions played out against Europe's Jews in the context of the Enlightenment is illustrative in this respect:

> The Enlightenment presented European Jews with a messianic promise and a demonic reality. The promise was a secular and rational order in which anti-Jewish prejudice would be overcome and Jewish civil disabilities would be abolished. The reality was that the more Jews became like everyone else, the more irrational and absolute became the prejudice against them: they were capitalists, they were communists, they were too provincial and parochial, they were too rootless and cosmopolitan, they kept to themselves, they got everywhere, they were disloyal, they were suspiciously overloyal. The more assimilated they became, the more anti-Semitism grew. (Berger, 1999, p. 54)

Similarly, nomadic minorities across Europe, such as the Roma, Gypsies, 'Tinkers' and 'Travellers', have been racialized and extremely marginalized all across Europe. In the case of Ireland, as MacLaughlin (1999) has described, the defamation of 'Travellers' was coupled with the development of a rural fundamentalist nationalism that fused with Social Darwinism. This led 'travellers' to be treated as social anachronisms, located outside the moral and political structures of the Irish state and placed at the 'hostile' end of a continuum running from tradition to modernity. In Central and Eastern Europe, Roma have been reviled as 'social un-adaptables' as this 'backward' segment of society here too conflicted with the universalizing principles of modernity (Bancroft, 2005). Sociologists and political theorists such as Hannah Arendt or Zygmunt Bauman have explicitly linked modern racism with modernity. The institutionalization of nationalism in the modern European nation-state and the need for the populations of these territorial units to be defined vis-à-vis external 'others' and minorities who live in their midst, rendered race-thinking politically relevant and, indeed, expedient.

Culture has thus been tightly intermingled with race and the desire for hierarchy, order, modernity and the perceived comfort of generalized categorizations within Europe. As North-West Europe grew in military strength, in economic terms and in political capital, and long before the white–black hierarchy consolidated itself during the period of slavery, the juxtaposition of geographic and religious cleavages paired with imperial boundaries led to cultural hierarchies and explosive confrontations across Europe. According to Levine (1990), 'whiteness' or 'pallor' rather than the 'olive' Mediterranean skin portrayed purity and the aesthetic ideal, just as the highbrow more common among the Northern and Western European was associated with 'high intellect' or 'aesthetic refinement'.

Cultural cleavages and oppositions

The horrors of the two world wars and the Holocaust, led to the intellectual victory of cultural relativism and the deepest discredit of racism and the belief in the cultural superiority of one European nation over the others. UNESCO took a leading role in replacing 'race' as a theory of human difference with 'culture', seen as a non-hierarchical, and thus more suitable, means of conceptualizing diversity. UNESCO's work in the 1950s, expressed largely through the writings of French anthropologist Claude Levi-Strauss, framed the basis of the anti-racist policy adopted by the post-war international institutions and most Western European governments.

And yet, in spite of decades of intense anti-racism policies, since the 1990s we have noted a resurgent political right in Europe, steadily engaged in a rhetoric of exclusion of non-EU immigrants from Asia or Africa and the Middle East. Migrants have been increasingly construed as posing a threat to the national unity and security of the host nation due to their cultural difference (Stolcke, 1995). This rhetoric of exclusion is based on a 'radical opposition between nationals and immigrants as foreigners informed by a reified notion of bounded and distinct, localized national-cultural identity and heritage that is employed to rationalize the call for restrictive immigration policies' (Stolcke, 1995, p. 1). This racism draws from the unresolved tension in modern nation-states between the organic/ determinist (where group belonging is determined at birth) and the voluntarist (where attachment to the nation is the result of free association and is based on a social contract) ideas of belonging and underlines the incapacity of different cultures to communicate with each other. While the turn of the twenty-first century was accompanied with an intensification of the processes of globalization, it was also characterized by a shift in the rhetoric of exclusion and a discourse emphasizing the challenges encountered by liberal democratic approaches to governing migration-related cultural diversity. For many, the return to identity politics and cultural fears that followed the historiographic marker of 9/11, 'ought not' be happening in Europe precisely because of the Second World War.

The fact that the return to cultural, religious or ethnic racism was considered both within Europe and beyond as unthinkable is telling in itself. It is undoubtedly a normative conclusion based on the subconscious or implicit belief or expectation that European civilization is defined by progress and a historical dialectic evolution towards betterment, improvement, Enlightenment *tout court*. At the same time, the 'return' of fear of the 'other' has been taking place across the continent in parallel to the construction of a unique experiment in human political history, European unification. So, while European integration has been working towards inspiring and nurturing a sense of European belonging grounded on civic principles, rights and duties, and pooled sovereignty, the importance of boundaries, seen and unseen, has regained momentum against all efforts to the contrary.

Although the process of European integration in the various regional fora and institutions that have been set up has aimed at rendering borders into platforms of cooperation and exchange, the traditional function of exclusion has not been obliterated. While focusing on the dismantlement of internal borders as regards the movement of goods, capital, services and citizens, rendering them ever more permeable and irrelevant, external boundaries have been hardened. At the same time, new ones have been erected within, once again trigerring new debates about who really can and should belong to 'us' and who essentially will always be the 'other' and never quite

'European', regardless of whether he or she is born and raised within European societies. The infamous reference to the term 'Fortress Europe' – which has its origins in the military context of the Second World War – then resurfaced in the late 1980s by states outside the single market in relation to economic and trade concerns, only to be consolidated in the EU migration and security field since the 1990s. This has rendered extracommunitarian immigrants, in particular, the targets of rising popular fears and xenophobic rhetoric. This rhetoric initially came from the extreme right, but it has been increasingly mainstreamed into the more populist centre, expressing a growing concern over threats that cultural (and religious) diversity may pose to the cultural integrity of the nation (Stolcke, 1995; the Institute of Race Relations, 2008, p. 2). The revival of anti-Semitism, the growth of Islamophobia and anti-immigration discourses over the past couple of decades indicate the persisting challenges associated with managing diversity in increasingly diverse European societies.

Cleavages and divisions that run across cultures are not all structured along ethnic, religious or racial markers. Ideology is just as relevant and in fact fulfills two separate functions: it is an analytical tool to describe a particular society or state of affairs, and it offers a visionary dimension of the sort of society it ultimately wishes to construct. Ideologies have defined the socio-political and economic challenges that each society faces while also enriching our understandings and definitions of what we conceive European culture to be. They have claimed absolute possession of political truths in doctrinary ways and have aimed at (re)ordering social and cultural life in the image of proclaimed ideals. We are really spoiled for choice, considering the plethora of examples that exist to demonstrate the cleavages that separate Europe into a number of ideological cultures that transcend and cut across class, socio-economic situation, ethnic, linguistic or religious affiliation, gender difference, or age difference. As we discuss further in Chapter 7 when examining the main cleavages that have defined modern European politics, each ideological framework essentially offers a clear proposition of what 'Europe' is and what it is not, of what needs to be fought for, limited and obstructed, as well as what is to be achieved.

Thus, we have 'enlightened' and 'counter-enlightenment' cultures cutting within and across European societies. The former are inspired by the Enlightenment and promote rationalization in society and politics along the lines of liberalism, secularism and anticlericalism, democracy and free-market economics. They contest authority and tradition in pursuit of social utility and progress, and privilege the exercise of power through modern political parties. Note that here too we speak of 'enlightened' cultures in the plural, as the Enlightenment was not a unique, consistent and continuous pan-European movement, but rather a series of interconnected multiple, national Enlightenments.

These 'enlightened' cultures are contrasted to the reactionary political cultures, identified by Sir Isaiah Berlin as 'Counter-Enlightenment' (McMahon, 2001; Mali and Wokler, 2003), which are relativist, historicist, vitalist and irrational as exemplified in the writings of German philosophers J.G.A. Hamman, Friederich Jacobi and J.G. Herder or Italian Giovanni Battista Vico. The Counter-Enlightenment has united critics from the right and the left. From the conservative right, the Enlightenment has been depicted as the '*ur*-source of modern totalitarianism, the godless font of the Terror, the Gulag, and other atrocities committed in the name of reason' (MacMahon, 2001, p. 12). From the left, Enlightenment is responsible for hegemonic reason, totalizing discourse, racism, misogyny and, ultimately, the Holocaust and modernity's shortcomings. Overall, these political cultures are pre-democratic, nationalist, defensive, and rather ambivalent towards capitalism and its market forces, favouring clientelistic networks of power. While in Western Europe they were spearheaded by the Catholic Church, in the south-east periphery of the continent they have been described as the 'underdog culture', bearing a strong imprint of the Orthodox Church (Diamandouros, 1993).

Alongside these cultural cleavages we also have the classic left–right ideological dualism that has carved out two very contradictory yet totally parallel representations and understandings of what European culture represents, signifies and inspires. Thus, European culture evokes references to liberalism, competition, individuality, and the pursuit of freedom for the ideologies on the political right. In its most recent form it is defined in EU parlance as 'market democracies', underlining a defining relationship between economic matters and the quality of democracy. With the same breath, 'Europe' evokes references to solidarity, community rights, social justice, cohesion and the existence of a protective and redistributive welfare state. A strong social dimension, sensitive to the more vulnerable groups is considered to be what distinguishes Europe from all other Western liberal market economies and their unfettered capitalism.

Lastly, debates on the existence and substance of a European culture encounter yet another dualism: religion versus secularism. On the one hand, Europe is associated with a culture of religiosity and, more specifically, with Christianity. Depending on regional geography this religiosity is defined by Protestantism, which has permeated social relations and aspects of the work ethos, or by Catholic or Orthodox social conservatism. On the other, Europe is tantamount to the principles of *laïcité*, drawing from the values of non-discrimination and equality of treatment, to link the concept of Europe to the protection of religious freedoms in the private sphere and the independence of the public sphere. This constitutes probably one of the most fascinating features of European culture, as until recently Europe's pattern of secularization was deemed the standard development of modernization. In the twentieth century, sociological studies suggested that modernization (the process of industrialization, urbanization, and rising levels of education and wealth) was weakening the influence of religious institutions in affluent societies, bringing lower rates of attendance at religious services, and making religion subjectively less important in people's lives. Progressive religious decline, which was consistent across the continent since the 1950s, was considered the norm and, as José Casanova has noted, the USA's persistence on religion was studied as the exception. More recently, the argument has been turned on its head with scholars attempting to explain European 'exceptionalism' and the drastic secularization of European societies (see Berger, 1999; Casanova, 2009). At the same time, secularization was also taking place in the parts of Europe that were under Soviet rule; here, however, it was forcibly pursued as part of state doctrine. The secularization thesis was challenged at the end of the twentieth century. The collapse of the Soviet Union was followed by a dynamic resurgence of Orthodoxy and Catholicism in Central and Eastern Europe. On the rest of the continent, although the decline of religiosity in some communities has been continuing, multiculturalism has been posing unprecedented cultural, political and legal challenges as we witness the assertion of 'religious-communal', especially Muslim, identities in countries whose governments and majority populations perceive themselves as largely secular.

The ways in which identity is framed and the extent to which it is tolerant of various forms of difference within are also expressed through culture. In their ideal archetypes, the existence of an ethno-cultural national identity tends to be opposed to the construction of a civic culture that is open to multiculturalism. The former exults the heritage and identity of the nation, deemed as homogenous, that needs to be protected from all things foreign and from internal dissent in order to keep it pure, united and strong. The latter praises cultural differences, seeks to protect and emancipate minority identities, and promotes coexistence and tolerance. These concepts are not new, typical of 'modern' super-diverse multicultural societies, though they find their limits tested even more today. They trace their roots to the origins of European civilization. The following classic excerpt from Thucydides' *History of the Peloponnesian War* in effect emphasizes the principles of democracy, justice and equality, rule of law and good governance, tolerance and non-discrimination, and the underlying notion of leading by example:

> Our form of government does not enter into rivalry with the institutions of others. Our government does not copy our neighbours', but is an example to them. It is true that we are called a democracy, for the administration is in the hands of the many and not of the few. But while there exists equal justice to all and alike in their private disputes, the claim of excellence is also recognized; and when a citizen is in any way distinguished, he is preferred to the public service, not as a matter of privilege, but as the reward of merit. Neither is poverty an obstacle, but a man may benefit his country whatever the obscurity of his condition. There is no exclusiveness in our public life, and in our private business we are not suspicious of one another, nor angry with our neighbour if he does what he likes; we do not put on sour looks at him which, though harmless, are not pleasant. While we are thus unconstrained in our private business, a spirit of reverence pervades our public acts; we are prevented from doing wrong by respect for the authorities and for the laws... (Pericles' Funeral Oration, Thucydides, *History of the Peloponnesian War*)

These contradictory ideological pairs outlined above are cross-cutting, often untidily mixed and matched. Their combinations have constructed what Europe and European culture has meant for different groups at different times as each one of these sets synthesizes the core values and ideals that form the building blocks of our perceptions and expectations of Europe.

The 'other' Europe

One of the most interesting facets of the cultural dimensions of Europe is in its 'alternative' visions. Any account of culture, just as any proposed vision of Europe, is ideologically motivated because both the role of culture and the meaning of 'Europe' are defined and reinterpreted each time according to contemporary needs. Alongside the dominant, or mainstream, cultural definitions of Europe, we find a wealth of alternative propositions about Europe. What is common among these is their normative ambition. A normative ambition to attain the values that are perceived as representing the ideal of Europe, and an ambition to establish a different sort of Europe from the one that appears to be the dominant, or hegemonic, one at a respective moment in time. In other words, an ambition to strengthen the 'other' vision of Europe, to replace the values that are in the mainstream with those considered to be more 'alternative' yet more 'authentic'. Visions about new political and cultural alternatives tend to generate enthusiastic responses mostly during critical junctures; in other words, at times of crisis when existing ideas about political order (and its ensuing socio-economic balances and values) are collectively challenged, sometimes delegitimized and certainly contested. Europe has had many such critical junctures, some of which we examine in Chapter 7 on Political Europe. During these critical junctures, political visions of Europe tend to be (re)defined through cultural framings and modes of expression.

At present, the dominant form of Europe is the European Union. Although the European Union has become the point of reference for European values, its origins lie in precisely this logic of creating the 'other' Europe; specifically, of replacing divisiveness and competition with cooperation and integration, of replacing protectionism with free movement, of replacing aggressive nationalisms with voluntarily pooled sovereignty, consensus and wealth redistribution, of replacing autarchy with interdependence, all under the cultural and political banner of 'Unity in Diversity'. In spite of its limitations and unmet expectations, the achievements of the process of European integration could suggest that the most successful attempt at representing Europe thus far has sprung from an avant-garde minority that grabbed the political opportunities that presented themselves in a series of critical junctures in the second half of the twentieth century. In spite of strong traditions that are resistant to change, there was a strong enough consensus among political and economic elites across Europe that the nation-state had to be separated from the excess of nationalism and that interdependence rather than autarchy would contribute to a durable peace, economic regrowth and security. The 'other' Europe that the pan-European idealists had envisaged was presented as the most rational approach, the one that made economic and security sense, and the one that corresponded to Europe's civilizational aspirations after the destruction of the two world wars. This transition from the 'other' to the 'mainstream' was done incrementally, functionally, and in an inclusive manner, incorporating the member states' cultural diversity and encouraging its representation and dissemination. It eventually came to dominate definitions of Europe, largely rendering most other propositions (that may have taken either the form of [Euro]sceptical opposition or alternative institutional arrangements such as EFTA) peripheral, parochial, reactionary, insular, cosmetic or complementary.

The EU institutions, and particularly the European Commission and the European Parliament, took an active role in constructing and developing the 'cultural glue' of this political project. 'A Community of Cultures' is one of the referents the EU has used to present its vision of Europe and of the role of culture. In a 2001 publication, the European Commission articulated the relationship between values and culture and how these constitute the foundations for European citizenship:

> This idea of European citizenship reflects the fundamental values that people throughout Europe share and on which European integration is based. Its strength lies in Europe's immense cultural heritage. Transcending all manner of

geographical, religious and political divides, artistic, scientific and philosophical currents have influenced and enriched one another over the centuries, laying down a common heritage for the many cultures of today's European Union. Different as they are, the peoples of Europe share a history which gives Europe its place in the world and which makes it so special.

The aims of the EU's cultural policy are to bring out the common aspects of Europe's heritage, enhance the feeling of belonging to one and the same community, while recognising and respecting cultural, national and regional diversity, and helping cultures to develop and become more widely known. (European Commission, 2001, p. 3)

A number of points need to be emphasized here. First is the acknowledgement of the national; the expression of respect for the national cultures evokes a sense of participation and representation in order to avoid any potential sense of threat emanating from the European culture. Second, is the accent placed on diversity, which constitutes Europe's common heritage, protected where necessary, encouraged to thrive and to be confidently expressed in the public sphere. Third, is the desire to have impact; impact on everyday life, on emotions of attachment and belonging, and impact at the global level. Combining its mercantile vocation with market-inspired principles, culture is defined as an 'important sector' qualifying for all kinds of funding in order to support public broadcast, regional television stations, independent cinematography, theatre festivals, music schools, museums and cultural associations, and cultural heritage conservation projects.

There are also other 'other' cultures of Europe. There are cultures that throughout history have been consistently poorly understood or dismissed, or that have to constantly make the case of their European credentials. Cultures that have had to be vigilant to avoid persecution, discrimination and accusations of being the threat from within, or that have quite simply been consistently excluded. The Orthodox communities of Eastern and South-East Europe, Europe's Jews, the Muslims of South-East Europe and the newer Muslim communities in Western Europe's urban centres, and particularly the Roma, are and have always been on the margins of all European societies. These peoples are constituent and autochthonous elements of Europe's civilization yet they have constantly been considered as elements of the 'other', of the Orient. Mainstream discourses that speak either in the public or private spheres of the need for tolerance and dialogue with these cultures tend to oscillate between a conservative paternalistic Orientalism and a rather sincere belief in the respect for diversity. Regardless of approach, the issues at stake are consistent. These cultures are persistently considered as representing the 'other' within Europe, thereby evoking emotions of curiosity and fear that translate into phobias in the public sphere at times of crises, and into exotic stereotyping of the 'ethnic' during times of social peace and prosperity. Second, they are regarded as having experienced alternative pathways and historical trajectories to Europe and, therefore, as mentioned in this chapter, as representing values and traditions that bring vestiges from the past directly into contemporary daily life, thus often raising tensions and challenging modernity. Third, their commonalities with peoples and countries beyond Europe are regularly noted, thereby conditioning interactions: for instance, they may be approached as 'agents' of foreign powers who instrumentalize them in order to intervene in European matters (a perception often associated with Russia's influence in South-East Europe through panslavism and the role of the Patriarchate of Moscow). Alternatively, they may be practically objectified as exemplifying the '*Clash of Civilizations*' predicament (particularly Europe's Muslims), or as representing a rich cultural capital that can serve as bridges and cultural mediators with other non-European cultures and countries with which they may have common linguistic, ethnic or religious traits.

For several decades during the twentieth century, there was also the bloc culture, which characterized the societies of Central and Eastern Europe. The common institutional framework of autocratic polity and command economy that were imposed from Moscow had resulted in a cultural response defined more by dependency than self-reliance, by all-embracing conformism over individualism, and by a commitment to the equalization of opportunities and outcomes, of rigidity in beliefs and of intolerance (Boje et al., 1999). This bloc culture was bound together with the local cultural traditions in these countries, some of which were more adaptable to democracy and capitalism than others. It was also permeable to some components of Western culture that were penetrating directly into the societies of the regon. This process has been labelled 'globalization theory' and it affected each country in different ways, rendering the post-communist 'transitions' across Central and Eastern Europe each as a challenge in their own way.

Post-Western Europe in the Global Age

The massive socio-political changes that took place in 1989 in Europe and globally provoked a number of major transformations of collective identity and political culture. They constituted a major cultural break. The unpredictable revolutions of 1989–1990 led to the emergence of a narrative of a 'post-Western Europe' (Delanty, 2013). This notion emphasizes the recognition of the cultural plurality and pluri-civilizational background of Europe. Essentially, it postulates that, while Western civilization is one of the foundational sources of Europe, 'Europe' is the result of encounters with other cultures and civilizations.

The demise of the Cold War and the process of EU enlargement meant the end of a formal East–West identity marker that had defined both sides of the Iron Curtain for half a century. It brought to the fore a variety of historical traditions that challenged a strictly Western reading of European culture. Thus, whereas for a long time Europe was often considered as the 'authentic core' of Western culture, at the end of the twentieth century we can observe a shift towards a US-dominated idea of the 'West'. Moreover, there was a political need to strengthen more distinctly European notions of European identity and culture (as different from the Western one, or West-European one) in order to support the eastern enlargement of the EU integration project and to reconcile the traditions of Western modernity with Slavic culture, Eastern Orthodoxy and the legacies of state socialism. At the same time, the resurgence of nationalism that occurred in parallel with the EU's widening and deepening led not to the construction of a supranational EU-based cultural identity but rather a pluralization of European culture. This pluralization of European culture has also been affected by the process of globalization resulting in what Balibar has defined as the notion of Europe as a borderland resulting from inter-societal interpenetration, which we will return to in Chapter 6.

Gerard Delanty has argued that we are witnessing a communicative conception of culture that is more fluid, and that has resulted in the emergence of a European cultural model in which Europe becomes a frame of reference that exists alongside national frames. The notion of a European cultural model, which he distiguishes from a shared collective identity, is marked by contradictions, ambivalences and paradoxes, which have contributed to the emergence of a highly pluralized post-national culture (Delanty, 2013, pp. 257–8). Delanty has drawn from the works of Alain Touraine (1977), Jurgen Habermas (1984, 1987) and Cornelius Castoriadis (1987), and proposes the notion of a cultural model for Europe that includes normative orientations and self-understandings, which offers ways to conceive of public culture as non-essentialistic, and avoids the dualism of thin versus thick conceptions of culture (which are generally associated with post-national narratives of culture). This cultural model provides the context within which the European cultural heritage can be framed.

Europe's path through modernity has left a legacy of social norms that include collective bargaining, trade unions, public social services and individual rights. Goran Therborn has argued that Europe has in fact asserted itself as a normative area with considerable social appeal (Boje et al., 1999). This leads our discussion to the European Union, which has offered the most concrete and tangible effort of a European cultural model, one attempting to represent Europe in its entirety and its diversity. The consolidation of the European Union has attributed to the notion of Europe with a new political meaning and a more tangible geopolitical frame. In order to push the process of European integration forward, both in deepening institutionally and in widening through its successive rounds of enlargement, EU politicians and policy-makers who have been supportive of the European integration project, 'tap into' imaginaries of a common European civilization and refer to the existence of a common European history and common European values. Democracy, peace, solidarity, social justice, human rights and respect for diversity are the backbone values of this discourse, while cultural initiatives that contribute to pluralizing public debates, the public sphere and national identities are considered core to the quality of democracy in Europe's multicultural societies. European culture is thus normatively motivated to disseminate specific values within contemporary societies as well as into the future, while protecting and guarding its shared heritage in order to trigger a sense of belonging among the continent's citizens. Basically, in order to have 'Europe' it is necessary to have 'Europeans'. Hence the emphasis on European citizenship and efforts to construct a European belonging since the 1970s (Dell'Olio, 2005), an issue that we explore in the next chapter.

In this globalized context, culture is also lived as more global and as more local and regional. The public space within which we live and interact in everyday life has gained in salience. Europe's cities and urban centres have been assertively defining their distinctive identity, which has become increasingly relevant for their citizens and residents. This assertive cultural policy has been facilitated by the emergence of the European Capital of Culture programme since the 1980s, by a trend towards administrative decentralization along the principles of subsidiarity, and by economic motivations. Reinhard Johler, an Austrian cultural anthropologist, has described this as a process through which the 'European' has been localized while at the same time the local has been 'Europeanized'. Cities have been encouraged to present themselves and their culture as part of the common European culture – to present the local as European, thereby emphasizing individuals' local or regional attachments while also permitting non-nationals to also feel attachment and cultural belonging.

Lastly, the digital and audiovisual sphere has been particularly targeted by the EU in its efforts to contribute towards a common European cultural space. Through programmes such as Culture, Media and Creative Europe, the EU has aimed at enhancing European cultural and linguistic diversity, promoting Europe's cultural heritage, and strengthening the competitiveness of the European cultural and creative sectors with a view to promoting smart, sustainable and inclusive growth (EU 1295/2013). The economic and commercial dimensions are certainly priority areas for the European Commission in these efforts; however, these initiatives are also part of a wider agenda of improving mutual knowledge among European peoples and increasing their consciousness about commonalities they share (Morley and Robins, 2002). In the wider post-modern geography and a communications environment of cable and satellite broadcasting, along with the explosion of the internet and social media, contemporary cultural identities and understandings of Europeans are dynamically challenged, shaped and reshaped in unprecedented ways.

Concluding remarks

Although the idea of Europe has its roots in antiquity, it emerged as a cultural model after the seventeenth century. It is the result of the modern age. Its meanings and relevance have been transformed throughout the different phases of its history and the narratives it has inspired have emphasized specific dimensions of Europe's legacies and heritages depending on the political project that was being pursued. The idea of Europe became particularly relevant after the Second World War in order to overcome the continent's legacy of fascism and totalitarianism although this was not essentially achieved before the 1990s and the collapse of the Soviet bloc.

There has since been a growing interest in the idea of Europe and its cultural dimensions and particularly in the themes of unity and pluralism. For some, the idea of Europe has been most meaningful as a socially constructed discourse, a historically variable construction (Delanty, 1995). Others have postulated that there is no single conception of Europe (nor 'a' European culture) akin to the West, thereby emphasizing the multiplicity of Europe(s). This multiplicity or plurality can be observed in three related ways. First, as we discussed in this chapter, Europe can be conceived as an 'intra-civilizational constellation' composed of a number of civilizations from the Greco-Roman to the Judeo-Christian, from the Byzantine to the Slavic and Orthodox traditions, and from the Jewish diasporic civilization to the Ottoman Empire and contemporary European Islam. Second, it may be defined to include a wider transcontinental dimension of inter-civilizational encounters. This approach highlights the influence of the non-European world on the construction of Europe and its cultural capital. From trade to violent exchanges, colonization, imperialism and travel there has been a deep mixing with significant mutual exchange and learning between European and Asian civilizations. Third, the high plurality of Europe's constitutive civilizations is acknowledged and underlined (Delanty, 2013, p. 41). The policy relevance of this latter dimension is particularly strong in terms of being able to propose a pluralized identity that is inclusive of the cultural specificities of Europe's historical minorities and newer populations that have resulted from decades of immigration.

The concept of the 'other' is so integral to 'Europe' and to its culture(s) that it becomes pointless to keep on emphasizing its distinctiveness; rather, it should be fully embraced as part of European culture, and not as an ethnic flair or a daunting public policy challenge.

Perceptions about culture and cultural identities have been shifting. Increasing communication, interconnection, travel and trade are impacting societies at multiple levels. The more intense and increasingly rapid communication of cultural ideas and products are leading to greater socio-cultural convergence yet also to greater socio-economic fragmentation in both prosperous and less prosperous democratic societies. New patterns of inter-action and mobility pathways that have been associated with globalization have triggered new complexities and created new kinds of diversities. As Kevin Robins has argued, the European cultural space consists of new cultural encounters, juxtapositions and mixings that are transnational and transcultural in nature (2006, p. 256). These interactions are provoking challenges and needs that increasingly require transnational approaches and transcultural perspectives. Is globalization able to stimulate the European imagination to promote new kinds of critical reflection on the cultural meaning of Europe? Globalization seems to be having a dualistic impact on European culture. It is perceived as both a cultural opportunity and a cultural threat, as having the capacity to both revitalize and dilute European culture.

The dimensions of culture that we have outlined in this chapter are of course just a snapshot of the rather dominant perceptions of culture in particular phases of the European continent's course. Perceptions carry with them vestiges of the past and common aspirations for the future; they are impregnated with notions of 'other' yet have associated diversity with the very definition of Europe itself. European culture is defined in terms of values, norms and institutionalized customs; it is about belonging. It is also about cultural choices that involve individual and group empowerment, creativity, exchange and interaction. It is about framing culture outside the national frame and it is about critically questioning and revisiting the real and imagined divides that define us.

Chapter 5

European Identity – European Identities

One of the most difficult aspects in understanding Europe in the present, but also in the past, has been the question of European identity. Does a European identity exist? Do the Europeans feel European? And if they do, how does a feeling of belonging to Europe relate to other important collective and political identities such as national identity or indeed ethnic or minority identity?

This set of questions needs to be further examined and taken apart. First of all, we need to discuss *what kind of identity is or would be a 'European' identity*. Should we expect it to be like national identity? Should it have a similar type of cultural content, notably a language, a set of customs and traditions, a common civic culture, links with a historical homeland and a current political territory, a single economy, and a wish to be politically autonomous if not outright politically independent? And if it is to be such a kind of primary political identity, do we see such a European identity taking shape, considering that Europe has been culturally and politically reconnected since the implosion of the communist regimes in Central Eastern Europe in 1989?

Or should European identity be understood as an 'umbrella' type of secondary political identity that brings together a range of national identities that have some similarities in common, notably links to a common geographical territory (the European continent), and a certain link with a common European culture (see also Chapter 4)? This kind of secondary and mediated type of collective identity – mediated, that is, through national belonging – appears to have been a predominant feature of European identity during recent times.

Nonetheless, we should not perhaps exclude an understanding of European identity as a 'civilizational' idea. European identity can also be conceptualized as merely a vague reference to a set of values, a cultural content, that distinguishes 'Europeans' from 'others' but that remains cultural in character and scope without

117

any political predicaments. In this case, it would be an elective identity, among other identities available to people in Europe. Indeed such a 'light' version of European identity appears to be more consonant with the post-industrial societies of Europe where there is increasing cultural diversity (related to international immigration as well as the assertion of rights of native minorities), but also increasing flexibility in the set of identities that each individual may embrace.

A second range of questions that is of concern with regard to European identity is the *relationship between European identity, cultural diversity and democratic inclusive politics.* Is European identity an 'open' identity that allows for the inclusion of migrants and minorities or is it a 'closed' one, like national identities often are? Can European identity help 'us', the 'Europeans', better understand ourselves and clarify our relations with our 'significant others', irrespective of whether these are minorities and immigrants within Europe or other nations, world regions, cultures and civilizations.

In order to discuss the above sets of questions, this chapter starts with some ontological and epistemological remarks on what identity is and how we can certify (or not) its existence, with a view to casting light to our inquiry on European identity. It then continues by looking at the different theoretical perspectives that have been developed with regard to the nature of European identity and its relationship with national identity. Third, this chapter focuses on the 'colour' or 'whiteness' of European identity and whether 'Europeanness' is defined in an inclusive way to embrace migrants and minorities. In this part of the chapter we concentrate on how minorities and migrants, particularly Muslims and Roma people, challenge the understanding of both national and European identities and bring to the fore the 'limits' of European identity. In the concluding section we consider whether we should still be preoccupied today with the question of whether European identity exists and/or how to construct or maintain it.

What is identity?

Identity is fundamentally about sameness and about difference or distinctiveness. Identity signals a certain level of internal coherence and similarity, a bounded-ness of the individual or of the group. But it also needs difference to become visible. A person needs to make sense of her/himself in relation to others. The other is fundamental in our awareness of ourselves (Jenkins, 1996). Similarly, the members of a group make sense of their common identity by distinguishing themselves from the non-members, or the members of other groups (Triandafyllidou and Wodak, 2003).

Identity has become a buzzword in the social sciences and even in the media or public discourse in the past 50 years in Europe. Identity is clearly a modern concept; a concept that has arisen in the last 200 years, at the same time as a self-reflexive under-standing of the individual and her/his community emerged in Europe. In the past, identity was not a matter of negotia-tion but rather of ascription: one was born into a certain class, ethnicity or religion. Compared to modern times, mobility was limited, both geographical and socio-economic. While pro-motion to become a Knight in medieval times or to become a Senator in ancient Rome was possible, it was rare. Even in clas-sical Greece or in ancient Rome with their sophisticated political philosophical thought, identity was not problematized but rather taken for granted.

Identity became important after the Enlightenment and with the making of modern Europe. As people woke-up to being members of a nation and citizens they started thinking of their identity. While identity started being questioned from the eight-eenth century onwards concomitantly with the industrialization process, the emancipation of science and politics from religion, and the questioning of the socio-political order, there was little scientific study on what identity was, beyond philosophy. Or, rather, great philosophers or sociologists like Max Weber, Emile Durkheim or Karl Marx discussed issues related to identity in a number of ways: for instance, the notion of status as pro-posed by Max Weber, or the Durkheimian concept of culture as a moral totality, but they were not concerned about identity as such. They did not even use the term.

Interesting examples of the conspicuous absence of identity as a concept is the distinction introduced by Karl Marx on 'a class in itself' and 'a class for itself'. Marx noted that a class in itself is a class because of its objective features (its relationship with the means of production), but its members are not aware of their belonging to that class nor of their common socio-economic predicament. By contrast, a class for itself is a class that becomes aware of its position in the system of production and starts fighting for its rights. Similarly, later on, Anthony Smith (1991) distinguished between an 'ethnie' and a nation: an 'ethnie' or ethnic group is a group that shares some common cultural or historical features but is not fully self-conscious of its constituting a distinct social group nor does it request political autonomy. By contrast, a nation not only shares some common cultural characteristics but its members are aware of their belonging to a distinct national group and demand their self-determination as a function of this.

While identity is a quintessential feature of human existence, and has attracted the interest of philosophers and political thinkers (the answer to the question who am I? or who are we, humans?), it has become a prominent subject of research in its own right in the post-war period. As Western European countries, and Western countries more generally, grew more affluent in the 1950s and 1960s, overcoming the destruction of the Second World War, identity became a matter of concern as people, freed from the anxiety of physical and physiological survival, had the luxury of soul searching.

Indeed, identity became a buzzword, a stock technical term in sociology and social psychology in the past 60 years, even though there is no agreement or clear understanding of its various meanings. In an early article, Snow and Anderson (1987) analysed how disadvantaged populations, such as the homeless, construct a positive self-identity through what Snow and Anderson called 'identity work'. Most importantly, what the two authors illustrated is that identity-related concerns are as important as physiological survival requisites. Contrary to Maslow's (1962) well-known hierarchy of needs, which holds that the satisfaction of physiological and safety needs is a necessary condition for the emergence and gratification of higher-level needs, such as the need for self-esteem and for a positive personal identity, Snow and Anderson (alongside other sociologists such as Goffman (1961) in his seminal work on mentally ill people) show that a sense of meaning and self-worth, a positive sense of self is an integral part of our humanity and it is as critical for survival as food or water.

From a social psychological or sociological perspective identity relates to social roles that the individual is ascribed to or internalizes as hers/his in order to form her/his sense of self. Indeed, in his *Birth and Death of Meaning*, Ernest Becker (1971) argues that our sense of self-worth depends in part on the social roles available to us. It is thus difficult to distinguish ontologically between a personal identity that is distinct from collective identity. All personal identities are social in their anchoring to specific social roles or reference groups, or in their distancing from such roles or groups. They are also social in that they have social consequences in our making sense of ourselves and of our social positioning.

Collective identity is different from personal or individual identity, even if it is also socially constructed, in the sense that it too is based on social interactions and the meaning we attribute to them. Collective identity is not the mere sum of individual or personal identities. It involves the idea that a group of people recognize themselves as such. They believe they are similar to one another and they feel solidarity among themselves (Thernborn, 1995).

It is worth noting that the individual identity of each person includes multiple collective identities. Such identities are not of equal importance for the construction of the personal identity nor are they equally salient in any given context. Thus, I may be a Greek, a European citizen, a woman, a teacher, a mother and a fan of rock music. I may belong to related cultural or social associations such as the teacher trade unions, a parents' group, a fan club of the Rolling Stones, and support the fight for women's rights through a donation. These various 'identities' are not all equally important to me but are still constituent parts of who I am. Being, for instance, a Greek citizen or an EU citizen determines many issues in my social, political and economic life, many more than being a fan of the Rolling Stones. Being a member of a trade union can be an important identity and determine my civic and political behaviour, so it may be more important than being a fan of rock music but less important than being a citizen of Greece and of the EU, and so on. Collective identities come in varying combinations, and are of different salience depending on their 'primacy' in a person's life. This primacy is determined by both objective elements (how important is this identity for one's social, political and economic life) and by subjective issues (how important a person feels this identity to be for him/herself).

Collective identity can be distinguished in three types; it can be social, cultural or political in character depending on the type of features it refers to and on the type of groups to which it is ascribed. A fundamental social identity feature that we all have is our gender and our understanding of our gender identity. Naturally, gender is not one's only social identity feature; family situation or profession is another one. Being a supporter of a given sports club is also a social identity. There is a range of identities that we call cultural that refer to specific cultural features or attributes that we share, such as speaking a certain language (that makes one a member of a specific linguistic community), following a set of traditions or customs (of one's village, or region of origin or of a given ethnic group), believing in a specific faith, or even having a specific way of dressing that may find its origins in one's specific culture. Last but not least, our collective identities include also political identities notably identities that have to do with the relationship between the individual and the state, the exercise of power and the governance of public life. Our most fundamental political identity is that of being a citizen of a given state. But other political identities may also be important such as being a supporter of a given political party. Overall, collective identities that refer to gender, nationality, ethnicity, religion or social class form the main basis of a person's identity and are central to an individual's life.

It follows also from the above that any type of collective identity is historically situated. Identity cannot be understood in a social or political vacuum. Identity refers to a specific society and in relation to the material and social conditions of that society. In addition, identities are always in flux. They are living organisms as they refer to living organisms. They adapt to changing circumstances and conditions in order to maintain their function, notably that of helping humans make sense of the world and of their position within it. Even the same kind of social identity, being a man or being a woman, has different attributes and different meanings in different societies and in different historical periods. All collective identities *are* historically constructed and situated.

It is important to distinguish between collective identity and the process of identification. Identification describes the social psychological process by which a person associates her/himself to a given social or political group. The notion of identity speaks of the set of attributes or features itself rather than the process.

Before turning to consider European identity, a last point that needs to be made is that identity cannot be studied as such. It cannot be observed. We study identity mostly through people's discourse. Through the ways in which people make sense of the world that surrounds them, how they orient themselves in the world, and talk about themselves. Indeed, this is what Snow and Anderson have called 'identity work' (1987).

In addition, social or political identities cannot be studied as such. They always have to be approached through the individual level. A researcher cannot conduct an interview or fill in a questionnaire with a collectivity – s/he can only ask the individuals who are members of that collectivity, of that group, of their views, opinions, feelings, of the ways in which they see themselves as part of a group.

What is it that we learn from the above ontological and epistemological observations though with regard to European identity? Indeed, what we learn is that European identity like all types of collective identity, including the national identity, can only be studied through discourses, uttered by citizens or lay people, produced in public speeches of leaders or elites or reproduced in the media. Identity can also be observed through the actions of the individuals albeit we can only infer whether these actions are an expression of a certain identity. We can only for instance infer whether a certain protest march of angry European citizens in Brussels protesting against austerity policies is an expression of their national or European identity. This can be assessed through indirect indices such as the slogans they shouted, the way they were dressed, the stakeholders that organized the protest march and so on.

Second, we learn that unavoidably 'European' can only be one of many collective identities that people have, and that it is constantly in flux. There is no essence of a European identity that has always existed and that remains immutable. Indeed, taking into account the different meanings of Europe outlined in Chapter 2 as well as the different visions of Europe supported in the past couple of centuries (see Chapter 3) it becomes clear that European identity is a multi-faceted and ever mutating concept.

Third, European identity is part of a multiple set of identity features that may form part of an individual's identity. Its importance though may vary among individuals but it may also vary within the same individual's perception of their identity depending on the context and situation.

Fourth, European identity like any type of collective identity must be more than the sum of the individual identities. It needs to have a group reality: a group of people that define themselves as Europeans and are ready to behave in specific ways in function of their 'Europeanness', and within an institutional framework that supports this identity.

Fifth, European identity has emerged as a subject of study in itself in the last 40–50 years as part of the overall emergence of identity and identity studies as a subject matter in sociology, political science, social psychology, or also contemporary history. Actually, the inquiry on European identity has been slow to emerge because more attention was given to what is Europe, who belongs to Europe, and on the differences and conflicts that characterize Europe rather than to the commonalities that bring Europeans together. The discussion over European identity has emerged forcefully in the public and political debate after the 1973 declaration of the then nine member states of the European Economic Communities about a European identity. Indeed, any discussion on European identity today is necessarily partly intertwined with the discussion over the process of European integration.

European identity and national identity

One of the most well-known theorists of nationalism today, Anthony D. Smith, wrote in 1995 that a European identity could not possibly emerge as it is national identity that dominates people's primary loyalties (Smith, 1995). Smith could not imagine, and perhaps quite rightly, that any European citizen would be willing to sacrifice her/his life in fighting for Europe in the way in which people had gone to war to defend their nation. For him, this was an ultimate test that European identity would fail. Smith actually appears to assume that a European identity would be of the same kind as a national identity.

This assumption points to an underlying problem in the conventional study of European identity: there is an implicit assumption that European identity is about political loyalty. This assumption has skewed the conceptualization of European identity and as a result the area of investigation has been largely restricted to the political dimension. In other words, the accumulation of research into European identity so far is now signalling a fundamental problem: the under-conceptualization of European identity and the lack of diversification when definitions of European identity are provided (Duchesne, 2008).

European identity vs national identity

Indeed, a first question to be asked in our view here is whether European identity is or *can be* like national identity. In order to provide an answer to this question we need to imagine what European identity should or could involve to be resemble a national identity.

National identities can be ethnic in their orientation, based on a belief in common ethnic descent, a common culture and set of myths and symbols, or they can be civic based on a common civic and political culture, a common set of values, a single economic and political system, a common territory. Usually, most national identities involve a combination of ethnic and civic elements but are characterized by a stronger presence of one set of elements over the other.

Taking the blueprint of the nation then as a prototype for studying European identity, we would envisage that there could be a cultural form of European identity. In other words, a European identity would have a cultural 'baggage' similar to that of national identity. Hence, links to a common cultural heritage, a common language, myths, symbols and emotional bonds with a territory imagined as the motherland. Indeed such an identity could emerge through a long historical process of the 'classical' nation building type as happened in many nation-states in the nineteenth century.

There could however also be a national type view of European identity that would emphasize civic elements like a set of civic and political values enshrined in a constitution (Weiler, 1999). It could also include the construction of a civic European identity through the gradual emergence of a European public sphere (Risse, 2010) and of a common communicative space where Europeans meet (virtually) and exchange their views. This last view draws from a perspective of Europe becoming, through the European integration process, a state-like entity (perhaps a federal state), and from the Habermas view of constitutional patriotism as the possible 'glue' that can hold a nation or indeed Europe together, beyond and in the absence of a common set of cultural traditions and ethnic bonds.

Indeed Habermas has questioned whether we should consider this kind of civic identity as identity at all and whether it should be better conceptualized as transnational civic solidarity among Europeans. Such a civic conception however of a European 'non-identity', Habermas recognized (2006, pp. 80–1), 'cannot be produced solely through the strong negative duties of a universalistic morality of justice' but through 'a self-propelling process of shared political opinion and will-formation on European issues' that develops above the national level. Thus, national cultural differences can become of secondary relevance and a different order of European collective identity can emerge.

In reality European identity involves both cultural and civic elements but is certainly not a primary political identity in the sense that national identity is, requiring and actually obtaining the primary loyalty of Europeans (as it happens with members of a nation). Anthony D. Smith argued already over 20 years ago (1992) that Europeans differ among themselves in many respects such as language, law, religion, territory, economic and political system just like they differ also from non-Europeans. However, he conceded that 'at one time or another all Europe's communities have participated in at least some of these traditions and heritages, in some degree' (Smith, 1992, p. 70). He however distinguished between families of culture that tend to 'come into being over long time-spans and are the product of particular historical circumstances, often unanticipated and unintentional. Such cultural realities' he argued, 'are no less potent for being so often inchoate and uninstitutionalized' (1992, p. 71).

It would be fair to say that there is a lot of truth in Smith's scepticism over the mere possibility and probability that a strong sense of European identity would emerge in Europe, not least because this cultural 'glue' of the nation is lacking. Indeed this reflection brings us to one of the main issues that has prompted the whole discussion about what European identity is or should be and notably what is the relationship between national and European identity.

There are competing views on this topic. Inglehart (1977) in his seminal study suggested that national and European

identities are competing and that people who feel more cosmopolitan would tend to identify less with the nation and more
with Europe. From this perspective, this is the reason why
European identity is today (still) very weak: because it is in
conflict with national identity (Carey, 2002; McLaren, 2006).
According to this line of argument, nations possess a strong
pulling power over their members for a number of reasons
including a set of powerful myths and symbols or the state's
capacity of coercion. The emerging European polity, however,
does not possess these qualities and as a result European identity remains weak. European identity needs to be promoted by
the creation of historical myths and political symbols so as to
prompt citizens' identification with it. Indeed, European cultural
policies such as the adoption of the flag and anthem, and to
some extent the introduction of the single currency may also be
seen as strategies aiming to foster a common European political
identity (Shore, 2000).

While indeed national identity is by definition competing
with other primary political identities as it requires the uncontested loyalty of the citizen to the nation, research has shown
that national and European identity are compatible and can
even be mutually reinforcing. They can better be conceptualized as nested identities (Herb and Kaplan, 1999). Medrano and
Gutierrez (2001) argue that European identity is nested in local
and regional identity and they are not seen by individuals as
competing but rather that a positive identification with Europe
can empower a local or regional identity. The reason is that
these are two different levels of collective political identity. The
lower level which is closer to the individual identity is stronger
but the higher level and larger group identity may further add a
layer and reinforce that of the smaller group. Indeed Spaniards
that were studied in the Diez Medrano and Gutierrez study, felt
that their European identities symbolized their being 'modern'
and 'democratic'. They thus reinforced the cultural content and
emotional strength of their local and regional Spanish identities.
A different but converging explanation of such mutual reinforcement of local, regional and European identities comes also from
their contextual character: European identities are activated
under different circumstances than regional or national ones. For
instance, I am a Spaniard when abroad, an Andalusian in Spain,
a Sevillian in Andalusia and so on (see also Risse, 2003).

Indeed, there is a growing group of scholars who reject this conflictive model in which national and European identities are understood to be in an antagonistic or zero-sum relationship. They also however reject the notion of an umbrella type of secondary identity. This is seen as too simplistic to account for the relationship between European and national identities. Some have put forward a marble cake metaphor in which both national and European identities in addition to other forms of identity are held to co-exist, influence and blend into one another (Risse, 2004, 2010). This means that national identification and attachment to Europe go together and blend into one another. Thus there are different national narratives of a European identity. Also Ichijo and Spohn (2005) have argued that national and European identities are entangled and there is now a European dimension in national identities like there are different national versions of the European identity.

Identity within regional nationalism

In the early 2010s, European identity takes another twist and becomes relevant for the emergence of regional nationalism of nations without states (Scotland and Catalonia for example) that assert their right to independence. Europeanness for these small nations is adopted as an anchor, against the multinational state (the United Kingdom or Spain) from which they want to secede. Their belonging to Europe (and particularly the European Union) appears to provide for a relevant reference point and is actually manipulated in political discourse. While appeals by nations without states about their Europeanness may remind one of the bloody conflict in Yugoslavia in the mid 1990s which also involved references to Europe, the situation today points to less violent and more sophisticated identity discourses whose focal point is a renewed relevance for European identity.

European identity may be conceptualized as a mainly instrumental political identity. Indeed one built on individual interest: a perception of potential gains or losses from membership in a given social group can influence people's identification with that group. This perspective suggests that the more the citizens perceive that they have a net benefit from participating in a group, the more they will identify with it. In addition, if citizens perceive that their own nation-state is doing poorly in terms of economic performance and democratic accountability, the more likely they are to identify with a higher level political identity and in this case with a European identity.

An earlier comparative study looked at whether European identity develops in ways similar to national identities and how it relates to them (Ruiz-Jiménez et al., 2004). The quantitative survey findings of the project suggested that European identity rests mainly on two instrumental features of the European integration project: the right to free movement and the common currency. More specifically, the study found that national and European identities are compatible mainly because national identities are largely cultural while identification with the European Union is primarily instrumental. The findings of the study, however, also showed that there is a sufficient common cultural ground for a European identity to emerge. The study confirmed that because national and European identities are different, the development of a European identity does not necessarily imply the transfer of loyalties from the national to the supranational level.

Is it a civilizational identity then?

The question of course remains whether European identity, beyond the specific European integration process today, should better be conceptualized as a wider notion of a civilizational identity. In other words whether it could be seen as a looser cultural category that points to an orientation of a wider set of values or to a set of historical events but does not have immediate political consequences. Such an understanding of European identity resembles what Smith has called 'families of culture'. While such a view has some historical validity and is concomitant to the notion that Europe is a historically constructed idea with different facets at different points in time (discussed in Chapter 2), it would today risk neglecting the increasing importance of European identity. Indeed European identity is salient in the past decades even if it were for the simple fact that it is contested and denied by many of Europe's residents. Research on the public attitudes of 'Europeans' on Europe shows that there is an increasing effect of political socialization into Europe through the European integration project (Risse, 2010), and that people build their national understandings and attitudes based on their perception of what Europe is (Medrano, 2003; Bruter, 2005).

Most recent studies (Duchesne et al., 2013) also show that the way in which we study the attitudes and reactions of citizens towards Europe and the European Union matter. Thus, Eurobarometre surveys asking people whether they feel more or less national or European are misleading as they constrain people's opinions and force them into boxes of national, European, first national and then European or first European and then national. Qualitative studies as the one conducted by Duchesne and her colleagues confirm the importance of national lenses for understanding European identity, and at the same time point to the fact that citizens make sense of social and political developments in complex and clever ways rather than adopting blanket type explanations or definitions.

Class and nation within European identity

Our discussion of how national identity fits with European identity would not however be complete if we did not consider the class factor. Indeed European identity is not class-neutral. Neil Fligstein in his recent book (2008) entitled *Euro-clash. The EU, European Identity and the Future of Europe*, argues that the possible emergence of a collective European identity depends very much on socio-economic issues. Eurobarometre data (cited by Fligstein, 2008, p. 156) show that only 12.7 per cent of the respondents think of themselves as European and 56 per cent of the total respondents sometimes think of themselves as European. By contrast, there is a significant percentage of people (44 per cent) that never think of themselves as European. Naturally this percentage is not evenly distributed among countries. For instance, in some countries, notably the UK, Finland, Sweden and Austria, a majority of people do not feel at all European but this is different in France, Italy, Greece or Poland.

Indeed a European identity project remains mainly an elite project that concerns mostly educated people and people with high status occupations. These 'Europeans' are part of the national elites but are also people who have opportunities to travel for work and for leisure. Their European identity resonates with a narrative of a modern and enlightened, culturally diverse Europe that brings peace and prosperity and leaves behind a past of violent nationalism, war and authoritarianism. These people however are part of an elite minority that have opportunities to learn foreign languages, travel and work or study abroad. They are among the 'winners' of the European integration project. Their cosmopolitan European identity may be nationally coloured by their specific national narratives of Europe but it is overall characterized by a close intertwining of a national-cum-European identity that are fully compatible with one another and civic in character.

By contrast, blue collar workers and people with lower levels of formal education are less attached to a sense of European identity not least because they have fewer opportunities to travel and interact with other Europeans outside their own communities but also because European integration has neither brought them better jobs nor better income and quality of life (Fligstein, 2008; Green, 2007). Their nationalist view of Europe resonates with visions of a Christian Europe but from their specific national perspective. Thus for instance for French people, European identity is a projection of French identity writ large while for Polish people holding such views European identity is the sum of national Christian identities (Risse, 2010).

In other words, at the private level, any understanding of European identity is shaped by both the socio-economic and national positionality of the subject that expresses it. At the public level, official narratives of European identity are similarly incorporating national historical narratives and national understandings of Europe. Such official narratives are politically tainted and may be pro- or anti-European. They may come from an elite perspective and reflect the view of the 'winners' of the European integration process or they may be popular and populist and reflect the view of the 'losers' or of anti-systemic forces. What is however important to note is that they can never be either class-free or colour-free or void of national connotations.

Diversity as identity

There is a concern that if European identity is like national identity it can breed conflict. Jacques Derrida wrote in 1992:

> Hope, fear and trembling are commensurate with the signs that are coming to us from everywhere in Europe, where, precisely in the name of identity, be it cultural or not, the worst violences,

those that can recognize all too well without yet having thought them through, the crimes of xenophobia, racism, anti-Semitism, religious or nationalist fanaticism, are being unleashed, mixed up, mixed up with each other, but also, and there is nothing fortuitous in this, mixed it with the breath, with the respiration, with the very 'spirit' of the promise. (Derrida, 1992, p. 6)

Derrida was writing at a time of political and social turmoil signalled by the revival of national identities in Central and Eastern Europe after the implosion of the communist regimes. The breakup of Yugoslavia was still on course even if the worst atrocities happened later and there was a widespread concern in Europe about the management of minorities in the newly emerging nation-states in Central-Eastern and South-Eastern Europe. Such concerns about the destructive forces of national identity and about the divisions within Europe are part and parcel of the historical baggage of a European identity.

Writing in the same period, Mary Fulbrook (1993) was contemplating a possible future scenario where national identities would be transformed into a common European identity. Although she emphasized the contingency of such historical processes, she also only considered this process as unidirectional, from the national to the European.

Indeed European identity is not only contested and fluid, linked to different national projects as we shall explain below, but it also risks symbolizing more a history of conflict and friction rather than a history of unity or similarity. There is an underlying tension between *European nationalism* understood as the sum of nationalisms of different European countries and at the same time a common historical process that may have taken place in slightly different periods in the different countries. This process has some common discernible features such as the emergence of a national consciousness and identity, the building of a nation-state. *European identity* was thus understood as a cosmopolitan attitude based on a belief in European cultural unity and also a European cultural superiority towards non-European populations. Indeed the tension between these two intellectual and political currents is visible in nineteenth and twentieth century Europe.

What is perhaps paradoxical is that the rise of 'national nationalism' gave rise to the first expression of European nationalism (D'Appollonia, 2002). It was precisely the division among

European nation-states, the wars among, them that bred a belief in European unity. The different versions of a 'European nationalism' as visions of a united Europe have been discussed in Chapter 4 so we will not repeat them here. However it is important to note this double meaning that European nationalism can have as the sum of national nationalisms or as a distinctive current towards the formation of a common European identity, and perhaps towards some sort of a united Europe project. This project of course took various forms in the nineteenth and twentieth centuries (see again here Chapter 4 for a more detailed discussion) but culminated in the EEC and later EU, pan-European institutions that are still evolving to this day.

The notion of European identity can be seen as loosely linked to the overall idea of Europe through the centuries and to this day (see also Chapter 2). However, the discussion of a European identity enters forcefully into the public discourse in the early 1970s when the then nine member states of the European Economic Communities signed the famous 'Declaration of European Identity' in Copenhagen in 1973. This document stated that:

> The Nine member countries of the European Communities have decided that the time has come to draw up a document on the European Identity. This will enable them to achieve a better definition of the relations with other countries and of their responsibilities and the place which they occupy in world affairs.

That declaration already made a reference to the notion that European identity is characterized by internal cultural diversity and that it rather refers the idea of a wider European civilization understood as a common heritage that involves converging attitudes and ways of life while respecting the needs of individuals, the principles of representative democracy, the rule of law, social justice, and respect for human rights. The declaration continues:

> The diversity of cultures within the framework of common European civilization, the attachment to common values and principles, the increasing convergence of attitudes to life, the awareness of having specific interests in common and the determination to take part in the construction of a united Europe, all give the European identity its originality and its own dynamism.

The introduction of the European identity discourse in the 1970s was a political action and any European identity was intended as a political one, even if its referents were cultural and rather vague. As Luisa Passerini (2002) and Robert Picht (1993) note, identity is like health: you become aware of it when it is threatened. Indeed, that initial identity declaration at the Copenhagen Summit of December 1973 was brought into discussion at one of the many critical phases of the European unification project in the last decades. The failure to agree on anything led to launching the European identity as a face-saving tool (Schulz-Forberg and Stråth, 2010, p. 41), an 'escape forward'. Strangely, those views may seem out of tune today and highly contested even if the economic and political process of European integration has since deepened, expanded and enlarged to 28 European countries.

The values referred to in the declaration were broad enough to be considered also as overall Western values and at the same time allowed for cultural variation within Europe. Thus they did not oppose a vision of European unity that was characterized still by the existence of nation-states with their separate and much deeper national identities. Rather, this view was further reiterated in many EEC and EU documents which pointed out that respect for national and regional diversity and the flowering of the different national cultures of Europe was part and parcel of the valorization of a common European cultural identity and heritage as mentioned in the Treaty of the European Union signed at Maastricht in 1992 (Commission of the European Communities, 1992).

Through the development of regional and related cultural policies of the EEC and EU in the 1980s and the 1990s (Sassatelli, 2002), the conciliation of an emerging European identity and of antagonistic national identities took a new turn. Internal diversity which embodied both migration related diversity and native minorities, as well as distinct national identities, hence a multi-levelled diversity with different civic or ethnic connotations in each European country, became the distinctive feature of European identity. The discussion was no longer about how to reconcile unity with diversity but rather that the recognition and celebration of this diversity of Europe was a formative part of its unity. This is probably the concept that is embodied in today's slogan of 'Unity in Diversity', launched in the late 1990s. This view of diversity as constitutive of the new European identity signals the fact that the latter is neither a pre-existing quality nor a historical given, but rather a process in the making, an identity to be achieved.

There are several elements that come out of the conception of European identity as 'Unity in Diversity'. First and foremost, this slogan and a related set of cultural policies recognizes and valorizes the existence of a plurality of collective identities within Europe. Such identities are not necessarily political nor only national in character. They can be local or regional and have culture as their main reference point. But they may also be ethnic and have seeds of political autonomy within them. The level of diversity that is implied is left purposefully vague and unlimited in terms of character and scope.

At the same time the slogan 'Unity in Diversity' implies a self-limitation for both unity and diversity. The unity is self-limited in that it can never acquire a higher level of similarity and osmosis to the extent that these separate and multiple identities are constitutive of the common identity, of the European unity-as-identity. At the same time diversity is self-limited as the slogan posits that none of these interlocking and integrated identities will challenge the very existence of a European unity-as-identity.

Indeed the 'Unity in Diversity' slogan seeks to achieve a middle ground between a federalist view of a united Europe with a quasi-national identity that resembles a national identity in its features and functions, and a universalistic view of European identity as a set of moral values that would however fall short of distinguishing Europeanness from a universalistic culture of human rights (Delanty and Rumford, 2005, pp. 63–4).

There are a few problematic points in this version of European identity that point neither to unity nor diversity but actually turn diversity into unity. First, this view risks reifying regional, ethnic or national identities by taking them as given and static. The contestation and amalgamation or tension is recognized only at the European level and the sub-European levels are taken for granted. However, this view overlooks important levels of collective identity contestation and transformation that take place at the national and sub-national levels (see also Spohn and Triandafyllidou, 2003). Such a vision of 'unity in diversity' elevates diversity to a constitutive element of identity (even if this sounds paradoxical), but at the same time makes this higher level of identity merely a reflection of the unity. This concurrently over-looks the capacity of the unity-in-diversity process to generate social change and further transform both European identity and the national, local or ethnic identities that are included within it.

A second risk that the 'unity in diversity' identity model involves is that it eventually completely loses its cultural content and remains an empty shell. It actually is a form of cultural communication and exchange or a way of engaging with cultural diversity but is void of any cultural essence. Such a view conforms to Habermas' idea of constitutional patriotism in that it signals a way of engaging with diversity through public critique and deliberation (according to Habermas). The risk arises that such a type of identity is too 'cold', too culturally 'naked', to matter for people. Hence, we run into the risk that European identity becomes irrelevant.

Third, it remains unclear how much diversity is included in the European diversity-as-identity notion. Ethnic minorities, people who may be citizens or long terms residents of Europe, having moved to Europe two or three generations ago (often as part of post-colonial migration waves), put the 'unity in diversity' perspective to the test. How much diversity is included in this unity? Is 'Europeanness' a civic and territorial identity that can be acquired by anyone or are there some ethnic or racial boundaries that cannot be crossed? And also what about minorities that are European for a 1000 years, like the Roma, but still considered as 'culturally deviant' to the modern European way of life. In the following section we try to deconstruct some of these notions and cast light as to the 'colour' of European identity.

The limits of cultural diversity within European identity

The well-known French philosopher Etienne Balibar argues that racism as a social phenomenon has preceded all biological ideologies and has actually also survived them. In an interview on 15 April 2014, on his book *Race, Nation, Class* (Balibar and Wallerstein, 2011) Balibar states:

> No civilisation has a monopoly on racism. And, besides, as the history of the uses of the word 'race' and related

words like caste or lineage in fact demonstrates, racism both preceded biological ideologies and has survived them. The anthropological red thread of which I am making use consists of studying the discriminatory uses and the metamorphoses of the 'genealogical schema', that is, the idea that generation after generation children inherit the 'qualities'– or, conversely, collective 'defects' – of their parents, be they physical, moral or intellectual... (2014)

While Balibar argues that racism as a structural ideology of inequality characterizes human society and somehow reproduces an inner belief in our genealogical continuity, he also points to the fact that racism can take different forms, more or less violent and more or less explicit, in different societies and different political systems (Balibar and Wallerstein, 2011).

Looking at the history of Europe, racism has been part of the presumed cradle of European civilization, notably classical Greece with its slavery system. While during the Roman times, slaves were often taken from the subjugated peoples. Indeed slavery has been again a strong feature in the Age of Discovery (1700s). While transatlantic slavery was abolished two centuries ago, it was only after the Holocaust that biological racism was repudiated in Europe.

Despite the spreading of the values of the Civil Rights movement in North America in the 1960s, post-colonial immigration brought the question of 'colour' dramatically to the fore in European political debates again in the 1960s and 1970s. In France, the question of racism and of the construction of 'blackness' was discussed critically already in the 1950s (Fanon, 1952; Genet, 1958). While in Britain the issue acquired prominence from the 1960s onwards and was very eloquently analysed by Paul Gilroy (1987) in his famous book *There ain't no black in the Union Jack* (where the Union Jack is the national flag).

More recent debates (Modood, 1992, 2010) point to how religion and particularly Islam has become the new 'racial marker' as ethnic minorities mobilize on the basis of ethnic and religious disadvantage rejecting an imposed 'black' political identity. While Modood's arguments are mainly informed by British society, they are applicable to other European countries too. Indeed religious discrimination was recognized officially as a mode of discrimination in the European Directive of 2000

(Council Directive 2000/43/EC, 26 June 2000). The principle of equality and protection against discrimination for grounds of religion and beliefs was further reinforced through the Equality Act of 2006. These changes reflect a growing concern about the phenomenon of Islamophobia or Muslimophobia that has been growing in several European countries during the last 20 years (Erdenir, 2012).

The negotiation of cultural diversity within national identity has become more complicated, perhaps paradoxically, as European identity has been evolving into a salient (even if contested) cultural and/or political category in the 1990s after the Maastricht Treaty which created a European citizenship. The introduction of EU citizenship came at the wake of the 1989 landslide geopolitical changes and the historical reconnection of Europe after the implosion of the communist regimes. Both the old member states of the European Union and the newly emerging nation-states in Central Eastern Europe had to adapt to the new conditions. They had to re-define their geopolitical and cultural positions within the enlarging European Union (Triandafyllidou and Spohn, 2003).

Since the 1990s, however, Europe has experienced increasing tensions between national majorities and ethnic or religious minorities, more particularly with marginalized Muslim communities as well as with intra-EU migrants of Roma ethnicity. Conflicts with migrants and ethnic Muslim minorities have included violent clashes in northern England between and among native British and Asian Muslim youth (2001); civil unrest amongst France's Muslim Maghreb communities (2005); and the Danish cartoon crisis in the same year following the publication of pictures of the prophet Muhammad in a Danish newspaper.

Muslim communities have also come under intense scrutiny in the wake of the terrorist events in the United States (2001), Spain (2004) and Britain (2005) which also contributed to growing scepticism amongst European governments with regard to the possible accession of Turkey into the EU, a country which is socio-culturally and religiously different from the present EU-28 (European Monitoring Centre on Racism and Xenophobia, 2006). The first decade of the twenty-first century has also been marked by local mosque building controversies in Italy, Greece, France, Germany and the Netherlands (Saint-Blancat and Schmidt di Friedberg, 2005) and the 2009 referendum in Switzerland which introduced a constitutional amendment banning the building of new minarets in the country.

Tensions have further risen after the tragic events in Norway in the summer of 2011 when an extreme right-wing supporter put a bomb in the centre of Oslo and then opened fire in a summer youth camp in the Norwegian island of Utoya, killing in total more than 80 people and injuring hundreds of others. It can be argued that the challenges that cultural and religious diversity pose in European societies have come full circle engaging both Muslim fundamentalists and right-wing extremists in violent actions expressing feelings of marginalization and alienation from a mainstream culture.

The Cartoons debate has become tragically topical again ten years later in 2015 with the killing of 17 people in Paris in early January 2015. The victims included nearly the entire line of editors and cartoonists of the French satirical magazine *Charlie Hebdo*, a French policeman (of Muslim religion), and four customers in a Jewish grocery shop. The perpetrators were three young and socio-economically disadvantaged French men of Muslim religion, self-proclaimed as jihadist fighters killing the *Charlie Hebdo* editorial team to vindicate the publication of cartoons and comments considered offensive to the Prophet. A similar incident took place in Copenhagen on 14 February 2015 where again a socio-economically marginalized Dane of Palestinian origin attacked a café and killed a film director and then a guard in a Jewish synagogue before being gunned down by Danish police officers. The links of such isolated albeit tragic incidents have fuelled debates about European Muslims and the tendency of a tiny but still important number of estranged youth among them to espouse a terrorist vision of Islam, inspired by developments in the Middle East and engaging in such violent acts.

Apart from these most recent events, during the last two decades, the European motto of 'united in diversity' has been put to the test by two processes. The first was the possible accession of Turkey into the European Union. Turkey has long been one of Europe's historical 'others' as an heir of the Ottoman empire (see also Chapter 2 on the Idea of Europe and Chapter 6 on the Boundaries of Europe), and the discussion over its accession struck a chord with those that have considered Europe as historically a Christian continent.

A member of the European Parliament put it eloquently:

Leaving aside the cost because they [Turkey] are very backwards... [it is] Christendom, the area where Christians roughly were during the Middle Ages... We all [identified with] the Church, whether we [went] or didn't. But Turkey is an Islamic country – it is entirely different... The real problem is that the differences between Christendom and Islam are quite big. (quoted in Lahav, 2004, p. 161)

The discussion on Turkey's 'Europeanness' was particularly centred on the fact that Turkish people are in their majority Muslims (even if Turkey is largely a secular state), and further contributed to showing that the cultural diversity that would be incorporated in a European identity had some limits, even if Muslims are to be found as native minorities in several European countries like Greece, Bulgaria or Albania.

While a large part of the public and the political debate on Turkey's 'belonging' to Europe may have been driven by political expediency (both for internal consumption by voters who might have opposed Turkey's accession and for external reasons, to negotiate power balances within the EU and beyond), there is certainly a cultural crux, as it puts to the test the assumption that Europe is a 'Christian continent' (see also Chapter 2). Certainly the Islamic turn in Turkish politics, that were hitherto predominantly secular, have not eased these debates and rather has indirectly contributed to strengthening the view that Turkey does not belong in Europe. In essence, the whole debate rather concerns the type of secularism that is practised in different European countries, ranging from the concept of *laïcité* in France which leaves no room for religion in public life and constrains the behaviour of people in public places, to the much softer versions of secularism practised in Britain, Italy or Germany where recognized religions have a public role to play and are supported by the state.

The view that Islam purports a more forceful presence of religion in politics or that the Muslim tradition propagates gender inequality, one that is contrary to both European and national legislation, has fuelled debates on whether and to what extent the claims of European Muslims can and should be accommodated. Even though there are neither easy answers nor one-size-fits-all policies to address such issues, these debates have paradoxically contributed to making a sense of European identity more distinctive for European secular or Christian majorities, thus leaving Muslim immigrant communities and also Muslim native populations in a rather disadvantaged position (Modood et al., 2006; Triandafyllidou et al., 2012).

Second, intra-European mobility and the related cultural diversity (and socio-economic challenges) that such mobility brings also put to the test the actual political and cultural meaning of the 'unity in diversity' perspective. Indeed, the most important cultural diversity challenge in Europe in the 2000s has been posed by the Roma people, particularly those who have been moving among different European countries in search of better life and work opportunities. Even though Roma are native to most European countries numbering from a few thousand in Nordic countries to several hundred thousand in South-Eastern Europe, and while in most of these countries special programmes are in place with a view of facilitating their socio-economic and cultural integration into the mainstream (albeit with questionable success in most cases) (Triandafyllidou, 2011), it was their mobility that made their 'difference' and the discrimination they suffer, particularly visible.

While concerns about the exercise of the right to free movement have been registered in several countries including Britain and the Netherlands, one of the harshest reactions targeting Roma people in particular came from the French government which repatriated thousands of Romanian and Bulgarian citizens of Roma ethnicity in 2009 and 2010. The issue attracted criticism not only by civil society organizations but also by the EU Commissioner on Justice, Viviane Redding, who asked for written explanations by the French Minister of Interior. The whole issue drew attention to the challenges that intra-European mobility creates as well as to the discrimination that Roma people experience in everyday life and their disadvantaged socio-economic situation across Central Eastern, Southern and Western Europe.

During the first decade of the twenty-first century, politicians and academics have been intensively debating the reasons underlying cultural and religious diversity tensions and how these could be integrated in national identities as well as in a common

European identity. The question that has been posed, sometimes in more and others in less politically correct terms, is how much or rather what kind of cultural diversity can be accommodated within a liberal, moderately secular and democratic European identity.

A number of thinkers and politicians have advanced the claim that it is almost impossible to accommodate certain minority groups, notably Muslims, because their cultural traditions and religious faith are incompatible with a secular and liberal notion of Europe. Others have argued that Muslims can be accommodated in the socio-political order of European societies provided they adhere to a set of civic values that lie at the heart of the European identity and that reflect the secular nature of society and politics in Europe. Others still have questioned the kind of secularism that underpins state institutions in Europe. Some writers have also argued that citizen attitudes towards religion in Europe are not secular but rather lean towards individualized forms of religiosity. Hence the tension with Muslims lies at the level of public or private expression of religious feelings rather than on religiosity as such.

The debate has been intensive in the media, in political forums as well as in scholarly circles. In policy terms, the main conclusion drawn from such debates has been that multicultural policies have failed and that a return to a civic assimilationist approach (emphasizing national culture and values) is desirable. The Netherlands for instance that has been a forerunner in multicultural policies since the 1980s has shifted, at least symbolically since the early 2000s, towards such an assimilationist view. As such, it has established integration courses for newcomers to the Netherlands and more recently a civic integration test to be undertaken by prospective migrants before departure from their country of origin.

In the face of mounting civil unrest among second-generation immigrant youth in the mid-2000s, the French government has reasserted its Republican civic integration model banning religious symbols from schools by law in 2004. Germany, home to one of the largest Muslim communities in Europe, is a somewhat ambivalent case. On the one hand, politicians officially acknowledged in the early 2000s that Germany is an immigration country and a multicultural society making integration the new adage; on the other, the restrictive implementation of the liberal citizenship law of 2000 led to a decrease in naturalizations. Nonetheless, the annual forum on integration promoted by the German government has been considered a step forward in the accommodation and recognition of ethnic and religious minorities and their place in German society (Miera, 2012).

Britain and Sweden are perhaps the only European countries that have maintained in practice (even if they changed the terminology used) a political multiculturalism approach (Modood, 2013). Concerns for cohesion, however, and an underlying need to retrieve an inclusive understanding of Britishness particularly in the aftermath of the July 2005 London bombings – led the former Labour government to introduce a 'Life in the United Kingdom test' (a civic integration test) and civic ceremonies for naturalization. More recently, David Cameron, the current UK Prime Minister, called for a need to re-assert a 'muscular' version of liberalism, which he defined as a liberalism that is confident of its own civic and political values and asserts them towards minorities who may contest them.

In short, European identity as experienced on the ground (EU-MIDIS, 2011) by citizens is neither ethnicity-blind nor religion-neutral. People of Roma ethnicity or Muslim religion, whether migrants or natives, whether residents or citizens, are often faced with a double exclusion from European and national identity, as aliens, as 'others within'. Many naturalized migrant residents (that are fully integrated in their country of residence) encounter discrimination and exclusion when moving to another European country or when travelling for business or leisure. French, Dutch, or Swedish, and/or European though they may feel, they are scorned by fellow citizens as not 'fully' or 'properly' European because of their darker skin or their phenotypic traits that do not conform to a white majority stereotype. Similarly, Roma citizens are also excluded from the European identity narrative, and see their national and European citizenship rights contested because of assumptions mainly based on their ethnicity and the negative stereotypes that go with it.

Indeed, when considering European identity, one needs to take into account the experiences of minorities, like the Muslims and Roma, and their own view of what European identity entails and what kind of diversity can fit into the 'unity-in-diversity' motto.

Concluding remarks

This chapter has aimed to provide answers to some apparently simple but in substance quite complicated questions such as whether European identity exists and if it does, what kind of identity it is.

We have argued that European identity is, like all collective identities, in the eye of the beholder. It is shaped by the socio-economic, national, both subjective and objective circumstances of the subject that expresses it. It can be enacted or simply expressed through discourses. It is one among many collective identities that people have and is in constant evolution. There is no essence of a European identity that has always existed and that remains immutable. European identity is part of a multiple set of identity features that may form part of an individual's identity and its salience varies not only among individuals but in line with a given context and situation.

We understand European identity as deeply intertwined with national identity and reject the conflictive model in which national and European identities are understood to be in an antagonistic or zero-sum relationship. The question of whether European identity is a primarily political or cultural one is something that can be answered only with reference to a specific historical moment. Thus, today European identity is predominantly cultural in character and not political. It goes hand in hand, sometimes in tension and other times in mutual support, with different national identities, but it is nowhere near substituting them. Actually it is the cultural connotations that make European identity today compatible with strong national identities.

To our set of questions on whether European identity is essentially open to diversity and inclusive, answers are more tentative. Dominant European identity narratives today turn diversity into a distinctive feature of European identity. While this view entails a risk of reifying sub-national and national identities and neglecting important processes of national and regional or ethnic identity transformations, it is also promising because it remains open to diversity. However, there is a risk here that European identity becomes an empty shell and loses completely its cultural vitality. It becomes too 'thin' to matter.

Last but not least, a more careful and critical sociological inquiry shows that the type of diversity that can be incorporated into European identity is less open-ended than one would think. Minorities and immigrants, Muslims and Roma people have a hard time identifying as Europeans or being accepted as such. Indeed racism and ethnic superiority are strong historical elements that have in the past constituted European identity. Today, they are officially discredited but often creep into the everyday encounters among Europeans as well as in political debates, especially those that centre around security.

Perhaps the most important conclusion to drawn from our discussion in this chapter is that identity, not only national but also European, is a *dispositif*, it is a device for social or political ends. Thus more than what European identity is, one should pay attention to what European identity does. While European identity has not been inimical to national identities and actually has buttressed, indirectly, the development of regional national identities in places like Catalonia or Scotland (which saw in European identity their immediate referent bypassing the straitjacket of the multinational Spanish or British state), its effects on immigrant populations and ethnic minorities are ambivalent. While on one hand, European institutions like the European Union or the Council of Europe have taken a leading role in developing international law instruments for the protection of 'old' ethnic (mainly linguistic and cultural) minorities in the post-1989 period (Triandafyllidou and Ulasiuk, 2014), the European identity construct has rather marginalized and excluded 'new' minorities like Muslims of different ethnic origins, and particularly disadvantaged groups like the Roma.

Chapter 6

The Borders and Boundaries of Europe

On the European continent, borders have been drawn and redrawn through wars, annexations and peace treaties. They have shifted countless times in some areas and have remained constant in others. They have come to symbolically represent the essence of a nation in certain cases, or a seemingly insurmountable cross-border conflict in others. The consolidation and militarization of frontiers has been accorded immense political and strategic value throughout the centuries. At the same time, alliances, cooperations and, in more recent decades efforts at regional integration, have reduced the significance of some borders to administrative formalities or zones rich with various forms and types of exchanges. Europe's history has thus been a combination of efforts aimed at maintaining borders and efforts aimed at transcending them.

According to Count Richard Coudenhove-Kalergi (1926), 'geographically, there is no European continent; there is only a European peninsula of the Eurasian continent'. All discussions around borders inescapably lead to a couple of seemingly straightforward questions with far from simple answers. Why do borders matter? And where does Europe end? Obviously, the answers depend on where you stand: on one side of a border or on the other. They also depend on who you are. Nationality, race, language, religion, ideology, interests and wealth all define the answers to both questions. They also depend on time, as borders and their relative importance change over time.

Europe's external borders, or boundaries that trace its periphery and limits, are not the only borders that matter; there are also borders within. These internal borders – whether functional, spatial, national, ethnic, religious, linguistic, ideological or socioeconomic – are just as defining in terms of creating identities and attributing substance to the concept of Europe. These internal borders, in many cases much more than the external ones,

146

have structured both the course of Europe's history and also perceptions of the rest of the world about Europe. Finally, there are borders that are not even situated at the borders at all, in the geographico-politico-administrative sense of the term (Balibar, 2002, p. 84). In effect, informal, cultural or ideational borders may exclude or marginalize some socio-economic groups from access to certain policies, privileges or rights.

Understanding Europe's internal and external borders is core to any attempt at defining what Europe is, what it represents, and what it aspires to. William Walters (2009) has argued that debates about the frontiers of Europe are necessary political interventions, which interject elements of fixture into the fluid; a diverse and ambiguous space that constitutes Europe. So, in this chapter we highlight the politics of power behind different configurations of Europe's borders and boundaries and reflect on how they have transformed and influenced what Europe represents, and how others perceive Europe.

We start with a discussion on borders and boundaries, on why they matter and how they contribute to the definition of Europe. We then look at the presence of borders in contemporary Europe and how the continent has been de-bordered and re-bordered. This leads us to the consequences that the process of European integration has had on Europe's borders. Finally, we discuss the main phenomenon that appears to be defining and challenging both the role of borders and perceptions of Europe today, the phenomenon of immigration.

Why do borders matter? And where does Europe end?

Borders and boundaries represent the outermost limits of a system, an organism or a legal entity. Borders demarcate space and as such set limits and represent the physical and functional end of political power, sovereignty and authority. They delineate the space within which a certain order exists and define areas within which certain activities take place. Borders carry meaning and symbolism and take on many different functions. In their most typical sense, borders are boundaries between countries or within states. They are geographic contours, all too often adjusted through violent means to unite, reunite or separate peoples. For some they have been fundamental in the creation and formation of identities; for others they have been hindrances to unity, freedom and peace. In some cases they have constituted a means of protection from external pressures and competition; in others they have represented obstacles to the operation of free market forces.

Etienne Balibar has noted that since Antiquity there have been 'borders' and 'marches' with different and changing functions (2002, p. 77). These have been lines, zones or strips of land that have served either as places of separation, confrontation and blockage, or areas of contact and passage. In the post-imperial age, nations and states have been defined by borders, and geography has been of the essence. In fact, for many political geographers up until the early twentieth century, natural borders (such as mountains, rivers or deserts) were considered as the only 'good' borders to be had from a military standpoint (Minghi, 1963). Analyses gradually shifted away from a naturalistic or organic view of borders, approaching borders more as 'man-made' than as natural divisions. Borders indeed reflect the cultural life of a society as much as its territorial boundaries (Delanty, 2006a). As such, borders acquired increased political, socio-economic and symbolic importance in terms of both how and why they become established. The explosion of border studies throughout the twentieth century indeed testifies to the various ways in which borders, borderlands and border regions are understood and conceptualized by institutionalist, functionalist, constructivist, structuralist, post-structuralist, post-modern and cosmopolitan perspectives.

Borders are simultaneously creators and outcomes of spatialities (Herrschel, 2011, p. 17). They reflect current and historical legacies and political and social processes at all levels, from the individual, to the collective, the societal and the international. When unbundled from their territorial and spatial dimension, borders are a normative idea. They represent a belief in the existence and continuity of a binding and differentiated power that becomes concrete and real through everyday social practices. They involve the constitution of power and its control over a specific space. Borders are socially (re)produced phenomena that are context-dependent as regards their meaning and their form. Borders have been defined as legal facts, which materialize in a set of connected practices (ranging from maps, to checkpoints, guard towers and landscape inscriptions) (Van Houtum and van Naerssen, 2002; Van Houtum and Strüver, 2002; Van Houtum et al., 2005). They have also been approached as political and economic resources that can be mobilized as they are opened or closed, they have been studied as institutions, and as limits that condition human behaviour.

If these are some of the aspects of *what* borders represent, the next challenge is to understand *why* and *when* they matter. Borders matter because of the importance and meaning individuals, groups and societies assign to them – either individually or collectively. At the risk of generalizing, we could argue that borders gain importance mainly in two situations. First, when they are pressured or contested from the outside by external forces and actors; and second, when the 'in-group' has the need to define (and often expand) its standing. In the former case, pressure may be exerted in both direct and indirect ways in order to render them more open to trade and commerce, to human mobility and exchange, and various forms of influence. This occurs mainly when what lies within the borders is of geopolitical or economic interest. In the latter case, definitions of borders are associated with identities, with aspirations and often with emotional narratives of glory long lost or never quite accomplished. Thus, borders matter because they frame meaning – both real and desired.

Borders and boundaries demarcate between those who are included and those who are excluded and they are traced in relation to the 'other' side. The combination of these dimensions explains why the bordering, and thereby also the ordering of space, in whatever form or shape, seems to be such a persistent, constitutive human and societal need. Liam O'Dowd eloquently synthesizes the various dimensions of borders as follows:

> Borders are integral to human behaviour – they are a product of the need for order, control and protection in human life and they reflect our contending desire for sameness and difference, for a marker between 'us' and 'them'. They are ubiquitous human constructions, an inevitable outcome of the range and limits of power and coercion, social organization, the division of labour and the promotion of collective identity within a bordered territory. Yet, all boundaries must be sufficiently fluid and permeable to accommodate survival and change

and permit cross-border exchange.... It may be taken as axiomatic, therefore, that boundary creation, maintenance and transcendence will be integral features of human behaviour for as long as human beings demand a measure of autonomy and self-direction. (Anderson et al., 2003, pp. 14–15)

The question of where do Europe's boundaries lie has significantly defined Europe's history and its identity. It has certainly defined the identities and history of certain countries that have effectively been 'borderlands' themselves between East and West. Poland, Ukraine and Turkey are Europe's most meaningful 'border countries' and their identity and historical parcours have been deeply influenced by where the limits of one or another vision of Europe was traced, and by the criteria that defined these visions.

The subject of Europe's borders has also certainly defined the most elaborate attempt at regional integration, namely the European Union. It has defined its nature, its processes, its institutions, the way it defines itself and the way others view it. We will return to these points in this chapter's subsequent sections.

As we have already discussed in previous chapters, geographic criteria become combined with cultural and subjective considerations. Thus, there are those who are considered Europeans but only marginally, or peripherally so, and then there are those who neighbour Europe further east. France's General De Gaulle famously spoke of Europe spanning from the Atlantic Ocean to the Ural mountain range, and indeed, the further east we go, the more boundaries become fuzzy in this common civilizational and geographical space that ties the Old Continent with Asia. As the limits of Europe become blurrier, so too the question of 'Where does Europe end?' becomes ever more complicated as culture becomes entwined with geographical and political considerations. For some, the limits of Europe are determined by the borders of the ancient Roman Empire, which define the boundaries of what is widely referred to as Western culture and civilization. For others, Europe's borders lie well outside the limits of the continent's Christian legacy. The map of Europe's boundaries is further confounded as we move south. There are those on the other side of the Mediterranean sea who in spite of their extreme proximity are separated from Europe by geography. Nonetheless, their ties to Europe are as tightly-knit as possible, considering that they have been significantly 'exposed' to one or another kind of Europe through a common history characterized by conquests, colonialism, power relations of dependency and migrations.

Although Europe has unavoidably been attributed a map-based definition, its geography has always posed a challenge. The colonial legacy has meant that jurisdictionally, 'Europe' and even the EC/EU have often existed well outside the continent. Overseas departments, territories and countries are scattered across the globe and include *inter alia* Anguilla, Bermuda, Gibraltar, the Falkland Islands, Turks and Caicos Islands, the Cayman Islands, Pitcairn Islands and Monserrat (Great Britain); Greenland (Denmark); Aruba and the Netherland Antilles (The Netherlands); Saint Martin, St. Pierre and Miquelon, Wallis and Futuna or the uninhabited French Southern and Antarctic Lands (France). As for the EC/EU, it too has previously included territories well outside the European continent such as Algeria, Greenland or Saint Barthélemy, which broke formal links with the EU when they gained independence from their ruling country.

Sea and ocean borders have conditioned Europe's boundaries to the West, as maritime borders overall tend to be easier to define than land ones. The English Channel, or *La Manche*, has served as a marker of the British Isles from 'continental' Europe. The history of the Atlantic Ocean has been more tumultuous as it has experienced the great discovery expeditions, the slave-trade, and waves of emigrants fleeing poverty and persection in Europe. Nonetheless, this oceanic boundary has never been a problematic border, even during times when either side tried to assert its independence from the other. Rather, it has been perceived as a pond, pooling together Americans and Europeans, their identities and values, their security and their economies, their past and their future, irrespective of rivalries and differences. Europe's western borders fuse into a wider geopolitical space that has consistently been approached as a community of common values. Europe thus blends into, and is a core constitutive element of, the Transatlantic community that merges the concepts of 'Europe' and of the 'West' with a borderless seam. Differences are consistently underlined in order to subtly differentiate identities but these, by and large, have not been perceived as posing existentialist challenges to the definition of Europe.

On the contrary, the subject that has undoubtedly triggered the most passionate and divisive debates on where Europe's borders lie and, by extension, what being European means, has been Turkey and where it lies vis-à-vis Europe's boundaries. Although in the early twentieth century the Ottoman Empire was referred to as the 'sick man of Europe', at the close of the century the prospect of Turkey's accession to the European Union was fuelling passionate debates on Europe's and Turkey's culture, values, governance and religious differences. The political sensitivities that have framed the debate of whether the boundaries of Europe lie on the western side of Turkey's borders or on the eastern side, or even vaguely somewhere in between along the planes of Anatolia, are revealing of the importance that cultural, or rather religious, borders continue to have in Europe today. This is in spite of the dominant rhetoric promoted through the EU of a division-free Europe celebrating the richness of its diversities (see 'Unity in Diversity' in chapter 5).

The debates provoked by the EU enlargement processes and the prospect of Turkey's accession constitute tangible expressions of the long-running questions that have been running through this book, namely 'Where does Europe begin?', or more aptly, 'Where is Europe's core?'

The rise and fall (and rise again) of borders

The establishment of territorially defined and mutually exclusive enclaves of legitimate domination is a creation of the modern world that developed from the Westphalian order (Ruggie, 1993). Although Westphalia did not aim at territorial sovereignty of unitary states, it essentially led contemporary international relations to:

> A system of territorially organized states operating in an anarchic environment. These states are constitutionally independent (sovereign) and have exclusive authority to rule within their own borders. They relate to the population within their borders as citizens (*Staatsangehoerige*, those belonging to the state) and to other states as legal equals. (Caporaso, 2000, p. 2)

Drawing from this, the territorial dimension of states is a core idea, thereby rendering borders as strategic lines to be legally protected and militarily defended or defied. From a realist perspective of international relations, state survival is based on the deterrent function of borders against military incursions by other states. As noted by Charles Tilly (1992), the relationship between borders, states and wars is rather clear-cut: states make war and wars make states and it is all defined through borders. In order to wage wars, rulers needed to be able to raise funds through taxation; to be able to tax effectively, it was necessary to delineate precise territorial borders incorporating resources, people and their activities. These territorially bound communities developed collective identities. This description by Tilly is probably also the simplest, yet most straightforward, description of Europe's contemporary history: one of a continent of wars, states and borders created, erected, dismantled and refortified. Some of the most symbolic European borders include Hadrian's Wall, the *Ligne Maginot* between France and Germany, the Berlin Wall and Checkpoint Charlie separating East from West, the Green Line in Cyprus, the Rock of Gibraltar, the region of Kaliningrad or the German–Polish border. Europe's history is rich with sensitive cross-border conflicts that have defined alliances, political and institutional developments, and the continent's cultural and ideological diversity. On many occasions, and for significant periods of time, borders have been zones of conflict, mutual suspicion and threat.

Most European borders were traced during the eighteenth and nineteenth centuries but it is only in the twentieth century that these were consolidated and refined into their present form. Michel Foucher (1998) has estimated that approximately 60 per cent of contemporary Europe's borders were established during the twentieth century, which witnessed the splintering of all European Empires (Ottoman, Austro-Hungarian, Russian, German, French, British, and eventually Soviet) into smaller nation-states. The most intense period of border creation and change is associated with the two world wars and the post-1989 collapse of the Soviet bloc. Territories were taken away from all defeated nations of both world wars, while treaties, peace conferences and agreements attempted to stabilize new frontiers and land exchanges.

The Paris Peace Conference after the First World War prepared the peace treaties between the Allies and the vanquished. The Treaty of Versailles, signed in 1919, left an enduring mark on the history and the historiography of Europe and the world. The aims of this peace treaty between the Allies and Germany did not only involve settling the material issues arising from the war, but also setting the groundwork for a stable (or as it turned out unstable) international system. This meant defining the border between Germany and Poland, preserving Germany but containing its ability to fight future wars, and establishing a ring of independent and viable states around the Reich (Boemeke et al., 1998, pp. 2, 328). Although the Treaty of Locarno a few years later (1925) signalled a spirit of conciliation between the European powers, it also signalled the fact that some of the post-First World War borders (especially to the east) were contested. It also proved insufficient to overcome the effects of Versailles, whose harsh indemnity provisions contributed to German revisionism, the economic crisis of the 1930s, and the rise of national-socialism.

Versailles was followed by the Treaty of Saint-Germain with Austria, the Treaty of Neuilly with Bulgaria, the Treaty of Trianon with Hungary, and the Treaty of Sèvres (followed by the Treaty of Lausanne) with the Ottoman Empire and then the Republic of Turkey. Also perceived as a *diktat*, Trianon essentially dismantled Hungary, reducing it to a third of its territory and half of its population. Just as Versailles fed German vindictiveness, Trianon fed Hungarian irredentism. When the terms of the Treaty became public, there was outrage in Hungary. The same happened in Bulgaria after Neuilly, while Saint-Germain and Sèvres dismantled the Austro-Hungarian and Ottoman Empires, provoking much anger and resentment, which contributed to the resurgence of massive violence across the continent and around the globe just two decades later. The Treaty of Lausanne with the Republic of Turkey went even further by specifying the conditions for compulsory exchanges of minority populations of Greece and Turkey. So, along with borders being redrawn, people were also forcibly shuffled on either side of the borders in order to 'unmix' them.

As regards the borders that resulted from the Second World War, it is the meeting in the Crimean city of Yalta in February 1945 that brought together Joseph Stalin, Winston Churchill and Franklin D. Roosevelt, that essentially carved up the postwar modern world. The Yalta conference, which was code-named Argonaut, together with the Potsdam Conference in

July–August 1945, defined post-war Europe. Germany and Berlin were divided in four zones of Allied occupation, Poland lost territory to the Soviet Union and received a large swath of German land in return, and millions of Germans were expelled from the disputed territories.

During the Cold War that followed, the salience of borders became even more magnified with national borders hardening more than ever before. Militarized, securitized and impenetrable, borders came to symbolize a harsh and tense ideological division of Europe between liberal and socialist democracies. Where national borders coincided with the divisions between the two ideological blocs they were 'overdetermined' to use the terminology of Balibar (2002). National borders within either of the two blocs, however, though concrete and definite, were weaker, softer, more permeable to political exchange, commerce, trade, human mobility and cultural interaction.

The Cold War border-era was marked by three exceptional events that illustrate the political and symbolic significance of borders, and that are characteristic of the visions and identities of Europe. The first event occurred on 23 October 1955, the second on 13 August 1961, and the third in 1989.

In the first case we have what Liam O'Dowd described as a rare example of popular democratic input in the designation of state borders (2002). The Saar was for long a region of contention between France and Germany. Detached from Germany after the Second World War, it was a French protectorate until 1955. Although a plan was agreed between France and West Germany in 1954 to establish an independent Saarland, when asked to decide in a plebiscite, the region's inhabitants rejected independence and voted for unification with West Germany. This was indeed concluded on 1 January 1957 in democratic, and above all peaceful, ways.

In the second instance, we have construction of a border of concrete and barbed wire that defined the latter half of the twentieth century as a period of division and suspicion, ideological confrontation and isolation. For the East German leaders, the Berlin Wall was the only way to stop the flight of East Germans to the West. For the West, though unwelcome, the wall that was erected by the East Germans, dividing Berlin in two, was seen as a stabilizer of a tense situation at a time when the threat of mutual nuclear annihilation seemed very real. Apparently, better a wall than another war. As a side note here it is worth mentioning that the borders separating Eastern from Western Europe were essentially patrolled and policed by Soviet forces. The 'eastern' borders and thus the limits of Western Europe were strictly defined by the Eastern bloc, meaning that for each side there was notable ignorance as to whatever lay on the other side of the Iron Curtain. As is the case with most obstacles to human mobility, the Berlin Wall proved to be a short-sighted solution that perpetuated and magnified rather than resolved insecurities and weaknesses. It barely lasted the length of the bipolar Cold War. And indeed, as soon as the Soviet Union started to change, the wall tumbled down on 9 November 1989.

This leads us to the third exceptional border-related event of Europe's twentieth-century history. The fall of the Berlin wall served as the symbol of a new era for Europe and for international relations (Dalby, 1993; Bort, 1998; Donnan and Wilson, 1999). The end of the Cold War and the collapse of the Soviet Union and its influence over the Eastern bloc, were followed by the intensification of the processes of globalization and regional integration. This led to two completely opposite trends. On the one hand, these developments challenged traditional notions of borders, often rendering them less significant than ever, and on the other, they rendered previously 'inactive' borders relevant again. Let us briefly turn to each of these trends.

Volumes have been written over the past decades about the globalization of all aspects of human activity, ranging from culture to economics and politics. The associated time–space compressions have not rendered borders redundant by any means, but they have permeabilized and perforated them to movement, exchange and communication. As many scholars of international relations and politics have argued, global interconnectivity has resulted in major transformations in the strength and resilience of the nation-state, and in a variety of social, political and economic processes long thought to be the sole or principal domain of the state. As communication and exchange, formal and informal, legal and illegal, across national borders has become increasingly dense, the political importance of these national borders has been tested, while the concept of sovereignty has become ever more differentiated. The globalist understanding of borders stresses the benign, pacifying effects of interdependence, which involves a process of 'de-bordering' or 'unbundling' of the relationship between territory and the state, with authority simultaneously relocated upward toward supranational entities, horizontally toward transnational organizations and social movements, and downward toward subnational groups and communities and local levels of government (see Ruggie, 1993; Blatter, 2001).

At the close of the twentieth century there was a lot of public talk and euphoria about the prospects of a borderless world (Ohmae, 1990, 1995; Allen and Hamnett, 1995; Newman, 2006). Many hoped that Europe's borders in particular would wither away and gradually become irrelevant as the relationship between territory and governance was changing in innovative ways (Anderson and O'Dowd, 1999; Van Houtum, 2000; O'Dowd, 2003; Perkmann, 2003; Ansell and di Palma, 2004). But political developments were unravelling a different story with borders once again occupying centre-stage. The end of the bipolar system brought the revival of nationalism in Eastern Europe, that in turn led to the disintegration of Yugoslavia, the reconstitution of the Baltic states and the 'velvet divorce' of Czechoslovakia (O'Loughlin and Van der Wusten, 1993; Bort, 1998). Along with an impressive number of new states declaring their independence or waging war to achieve it, 8000 miles of new international borders were erected across Central and Eastern Europe during this timeframe (Anderson and Bort, 1998; Donnan and Wilson, 1999). The disintegration of the socialist system created a proliferation of borders and a new political geography that radically redrew Europe, geographically, politically, socially, culturally and economically.

Borders in post-Socialist Europe have undergone fascinating changes in recent decades. This area includes countries that were an integral part of the USSR or satellite states serving as 'border-lands' between the Soviet Union's borders. With the 1989 collapse of the Eastern bloc, fundamental changes were provoked to the borders, politics and identities of these countries of 'Central', 'Eastern' or 'South-East' Europe. The most radical transformation occurred in the case of East Germany and the Baltic states. In the case of the former, previously non-existent borders that had been traced by the Allies at the end of the Second World War were erased with Germany's reunification in 1990. To be exact, they were erased in administrative and military terms but they have persisted in socio-economic and cultural terms as almost three decades of cohesion and redistribution policies have still not eliminated the markers and institutional and cultural vestiges of the Soviet legacy. In the case of the latter, the Baltic countries went from republics in the USSR to member states of the European Union and NATO. This transformed borders that were an administrative formality to probably some of the most reinforced international borders on the European continent (Geddes, 2000; Herrschel, 2011).

Overall, the geopolitical changes affected all borders in the region, replacing previous dividing lines with new ones. These new dividing lines are the result of a number of very politically sensitive processes that have occurred since 1989. First, for the newly independent states of Central, Eastern and South-East Europe, asserting their borders and rendering them visible was an important way through which to assert their nationhood (Herrschel, 2011, p. 21). This was crucial both symbolically and substantially in order to make the break from the oppression that either Sovietization or the Yugoslav identity was felt to have had on their national identity. The second dimension also associated borders with power relations as the new dividing lines reflect various degrees of 'Europeanization' and 'Westernization', which also translated into different degrees of structural adjustment, political reform and economic development. The change in the importance of each border was voluntarily pursued by the countries in the post-Soviet space that wanted EU membership in addition to NATO membership, thereby transforming their new national borders into potential EU borders. This effectively meant once again sharing and giving up some of their very recently acquired territorial sovereignty and independence. Actually, as Milada Anna Vachudova explained, 'demonstrating that they could control their borders became a way for Poland, Hungary, Slovakia, Slovenia, and the Czech Republic to prove their "Western character" and stay in [the] good graces of EU governments' (2000, p. 153). They consequently guarded their borders vigilantly and adopted EU visa lists often at the expense of their historical ties with their own eastern neighbours. During this period, the borders within Europe that became the most politically important ones are those of the European Union. They became the dominant markers across the continent; the most important dividers, the core reference in any discussion about borders.

Thus, some borders were 'raised' into EU external borders and others were 'lowered' into intra-EU crossings. In both cases, the costs have not been insignificant. Where borders have been 'raised' or 'hardened', this has come at a cost as long established flows and patterns of mobility and societal ties were unavoidably hindered. The border between Poland and Ukraine is perhaps the most illustrative of this. Where borders have been 'lowered' this too has been difficult as the structural adjustments and reforms that have been demanded have been felt hard by some citizens and socio-economic groups of the newer member states, who have suffered the costs associated with transition, liberalization, privatization and globalization. This has also been felt at a psychological level, as border-change through EU accession has at times been pursued in a rather paternalistic manner by the EU institutions and its member states. The reforms and transformations that were expected on behalf of the Central and Eastern European countries were based on an underlying approach that they would totally adjust and 'slot into' existing policies, practices and ways of doing politics and business. The so-called reunification of Europe was effectively to be undertaken through a one-sided transformation. So, as Herrschel (2011, p. 13) noted, 'it is not surprising that border policies were expected to originate in the European Union and "reach out" to those outside, who would comply as a matter of course'.

These dimensions underline the power relations that may be associated with borders. Although their existence depends on the mutually accepted territorial delineation of the limits of each side's sovereignty, power and authority, nevertheless, the meaning that is attributed to borders and the ways through which cross-border communication and exchange is undertaken are the result of power relations between the two sides. When a relative balance between the parties on either side of the borders exists, then cross-border exchange does indeed lead to a constructive and mutually appreciated interdependence. Indeed, this does lead to border regions as zones vivid with cultural exchange and rich commercial activities. When the balance tips towards one side, then the overall power dependencies and asymmetries that characterize the political and economic dimensions of inter-state relations are reflected in the way common borders are managed and perceived. They are opened or lowered selectively, based on the more dominant side's interests and security concerns, and they are regulated in accordance with the more dominant side's system of governance. Naturally, this has not always been easily or happily 'digested' by many on the more 'eastern' sides of the EU's new internal borders.

So, as is often noted, Europe has not become border-free; it has been bounded, unbounded and rebounded in powerful ways. Developments at the onset of the twenty-first century complicated the picture further. The importance of borders in geopolitical and security terms has remained as pertinent as ever. The secession of South Ossetia from Georgia with the military support of Moscow in 2008, along with the Russian formal recognition of Abkhazia, demonstrated the importance that geostrategic territorial influence still holds. The Russian annexation of Crimea in 2014 and its military intervention in eastern Ukraine and mainly in the Donbass have further proved the unfaltering strategic and symbolic importance of territorial boundaries.

To this reality we can add a number of newer challenges to Europe's borders. Acute socio-economic inequalities, security threats ranging from one or another form of fundamentalism, challenges related to climate change, weapons proliferation and new trends in international migration have affected the roles, functions and appearances of borders in multiple ways. In the post 9/11 world, technological advances led to 'smart border' initiatives as a result of domestic security concerns, while the geopolitics of access to energy resources ensured that despite globalization's pervasive nature, borders are as important and relevant as ever. In effect, borders pertain and increasingly appear to be reclaiming their relevance as societies, states and regional organizations continue to try to find the right balance between openness and attempts to make borders more impermeable to threats both real and perceived. As Ricard Zapata-Barrero (2010) has correctly noted, the 'others' are no longer nations understood as geopolitical security threats. 'It is not the collective defence of the EU from Russia, Turkey, or Morocco as military powers or national movements which is at stake. Instead, the supposed security threat takes the form of human movement a host of transnational, social and identity threats' (2010, p. 7). This concern with human mobility and Europe's borders is explored in this chapter's last section.

Changing Europe and its borders

In the beginning of the twenty-first century, borders between most European countries have been altered significantly as a result of various initiatives of regional cooperation ranging from the Council of Europe to the OSCE and EFTA, and culminating in the EEC/EU experience of increased integration, pooled sovereignty and managed interdependence. The EU experience has been the most far reaching in this respect and the uniqueness of this experiment makes it particularly interesting to examine further. We focus here therefore, on the transformations that have occurred on borders and boundaries as a result of European integration. Cross-border, or transnational cooperation in the EU has been premised on growth, stability and security, as well as a limited but notable degree of solidarity and redistribution in order to achieve greater socio-economic cohesion within the member states and across the Union. The EU integration process has also affected the borders of non-EU member states such as Switzerland, Iceland, Liechtenstein or Norway, through their associations with the EU, for instance through participation in the Schengen Area.

The EU's underlying normative vision has been that borders should be more about defining the territorial limits of particular redistribution policies, rather than about sovereign control exercised by the nation-state (Zielonka, 2006). As such, Europe's 'internal' borders have been subjected to a process of denaturalization; that is, decoupling the connection between borders and nation-states (Walters, 2009). During this same period, Europe's external borders appear to have become more tangible, although certainly not more definite. As the EEC/EU has enlarged and has pretty much reached the imagined historic confines of Europe, it has gradually come to stand for Europe. Thus, the borders of its member states have increasingly defined contemporary 'in' and 'out-groups' and Europe's borders. With each enlargement, however, a number of parallel and often contradictory and even confusing processes seem to have been happening, rendering some borders harder than others, or more aptly, rendering borders 'harder' in some cases and 'softer' in others.

First, and probably most importantly, each enlargement has essentially been a geographic movement, a shifting of borders, and it has involved a substantial change in the nature of each acceding country's borders. These changes have in all instances occurred voluntarily, willingly and in some occasions with the explicit assent of the population through a referendum. This in itself is rather exceptional considering that most border changes throughout history and across the globe have occurred through violence and coercion. Furthermore, each enlargement has been presented as a (re)unification of Europe and as a historic accomplishment in overcoming one or another cross-border conflict that has stigmatized Europe's history. Initially, it was centred on Franco-German reconciliation; more recently it was about overcoming the Iron Curtain and even contributing towards improving Greek–Turkish or Cypriot–Turkish relations.

Building from this, each enlargement has also been a confirmation of each acceding member state's 'European' nature and has thereby been a normative step closer towards consolidating the Continent and Europe's core. Each country that applied for EU membership stressed its nation's quintessential 'European' values and history (Walters in Rumford, 2009, p. 493). As such, through a loaded civilizational discourse, 'old' historic borders regained importance as cultural markers in a new and very different geopolitical context and became instrumentalized to justify a series of policies associated with enlargement on the one side and transition and accession on the other. Thus, treaty changes, economic liberalization, privatizations, political, judicial and administrative reforms, redistribution policies, constitutional reforms and changes in citizenship legislation were all rationalized by the idea of 'return to Europe' and a shift of EU borders to coincide with Europe's borders.

Fourth, while each enlargement has shifted and delineated the EU's external borders southwards, northwards and eastwards in clearer terms, it has also always been accompanied by a promise towards the new neighbouring states for more privileged relations. For instance, the future potential of membership has been offered, though with reservations as in the case of the Western Balkans. In the case of the neighbours to the East (Ukraine, Moldova, Georgia and Belarus) or to the South (Middle East and North Africa), it has been more confusing, with long debates eventually leading to elaborate declarations of 'Neighbourhood Policies' and agreements limited in substance. Thus, Europe's borders may have become more tangible but they have also become more temporary, in anticipation either of the next EU enlargement round or of policies aimed at rendering them more permeable through visa or trade facilitation schemes, for instance. This temporary nature has affected the permeability and nature of the borders of the Union and its neighbours in a number of ways. The geographic expansion of EU borders was accompanied by an expansion of the Community's authority, extending it beyond the Union's physical borders. Through its external economic and political relations, EU policies and influence reach out further across and beyond borders. For one, accession and applicant countries focus their efforts on adopting, implementing and digesting the Copenhagen criteria and the *acquis communautaire* throughout the pre-accession procedure. Moreover, programmes such as INTERREG have stimulated regional cross-border networking through funding along both internal and external EU borders. Lastly, the functional nature of EU integration permits non-member states to participate in certain policies, thereby clearly leading to a situation where Community competence and outreach goes well beyond the Union's formal territorial limits. The customs union with Turkey is one such example, the inclusion of the EFTA countries and Israel in the EU's programmes of student exchange and academic mobility such as ERASMUS, LEONARDO or the Marie Skłodowska-Curie Fellowships are others. The influence and impact of EU policies and directives has trickled down through the borders into different economic and policy sectors of neighbouring regions. Even in cases where the prospect of future integration and membership is not a factor at play, countries that are recipients of EU technical assistance or development cooperation are held to political and economic conditionality criteria that may not be as determining as many would like them to be but that are certainly not negligible either (as in the case of the 'European Neighbourhood Policy'). Elements of the EU's common foreign policy and its security concerns also extend the EU's authority and competence across its external borders and into its neighbouring states' territories. The case of South-Eastern Europe is particularly illustrative of this, with the EU's involvement in Kosovo and Bosnia-Herzegovina, for instance. Thus, EU policies, values and governance methods have gone well beyond its external 'hard' borders.

Fifth, each enlargement has also been accompanied by a desire to harden Europe's external borders in order to protect the Union *inter alia* from the negative effects of globalization, unwanted and irregular migration, or informal and asymmetric threats. And, while all types of border controls have decreased among member states, they have substantially increased at these external borders, separating Europeans in two different categories (EU and non-EU citizens) and distinguishing Europeans from 'others'. As DeBardeleben (2005) has concluded, enlargement is not only about including EU members, it is also a new delineation of outsiders.

There is no doubt that EU integration intensified cross-border activity and cooperation in all sectors of social, economic and political life among its member states, its associated and candidate countries, and its neighbouring countries. The political project of constructing the European Union has focused on attempting to reduce the importance of borders through making them increasingly permeable. It has concentrated on bridging elements of civil society, of politics and of the economy, and linking them at the supranational level in order to transcend nationalistic or ethnically driven anxieties. The drivers have been security and prosperity. The EU has evolved based on the premise that the functional spill-over effects of trans-border cooperation and integration are the foundations for dynamic economic development. This has in turn been associated with a normative aspiration of consolidating a democratic peace and a stable and secure regional community of like-minded states with common interests and values. On the European continent at the beginning of the twenty-first century, the concept of security and of what constitutes national interest for a liberal democracy was re-defined on the basis of economic liberalism, inter-dependence, cooperation, integration and pooled sovereignty. Over the past decades, national security was gradually re-defined to no longer be solely associated with the military protection of geographically defined borders and the population within them. Rather, as the process of EU integration intensified, national security came to be increasingly associated with good neighbourly relations based on deeper cooperation through cross-border tackling of common problems and challenges, attachment to common values and principles, and inter-dependency, with common borders acting as a protective filter to the negative effects of globalization. As such, borders have been approached as impediments to the free movement of goods, services, information and ideas and most EU policies have been founded on strategies aimed at 'overcoming' borders (Van Houtum, 2000).

The EU's borders have been considered fuzzy because 'they produce interfaces or intermediate spaces between the inside and the outside of the polity. ... Fuzzy borders are moving zones and they can easily be crossed by persons, goods, capital and ideas' (Christiansen et al., 2000, p. 393). By no means does this diffused notion of borders imply that they are vanishing or losing their salience. Rather, it is argued that the continuous spill-over process and the intentional political project on behalf of the European political and economic elites have fostered conditions conducive to moving away from an inclusion-exclusion or inside-outside dichotomy and altering the concept of borders. It is certainly true that some of Europe's borders have become fuzzy, vague and even invisible. It is typically noted that driving from one Benelux country to another, one can barely notice where the border crossing lies, and even the French–German border crossing that was at the heart of the twentieth century's two world wars is today almost unnoticeable. The 1986 Single European Act had a remarkable impact on Europe's borders because it facilitated and encouraged the free movement of capital, goods, services and labour in order to create the Single European Market. And while in some cases borders appear to have disappeared from the visible geography, at others, even though they remain very vivid, cross border activity is denser, easier and probably also friendlier than it had been in a long time. The Greek–Bulgarian border would be one such example, the Gulf of Finland another. In these cases, the premise of EU integration and of the EU's enlargement strategy overall has been based on the aim not of necessarily doing away with borders, but transforming them into 'good fences' or areas of 'joint responsibility' as these may be able to facilitate the process of making 'good neighbours' (DeBardeleben, 2005; Walters, 2009).

Etienne Balibar (2002) has noted the *polysemic* nature of borders, meaning that borders neither function equally for all, nor are they all experienced in the same way by different people belonging to different social groups. This is truer than ever as regards the EU's borders. Balibar's analysis of Europe's borders as borderlands rather than rigid lines of division is perhaps the most suited to the continent's contemporary reality. Balibar has described borderlands as blurred zones of interchange and spaces of cultural mixing and ambiguous affiliation as much as fixed identity. Inspired by this definition, William Walters synthesizes the essence of the relationship between space, the notion of Europe, politics and the role of borders:

> To describe Europe as a space of borderlands is to insist on its multiple spatiality and its irreducibly plural social constitution. It is to understand Europe as an open space of intersection and overlapping borderlands. For instance, there is a Euro-Atlantic space, but also a Euro-Mediterranean space. Each borderland exceeds Europe, revealing how the world is folded into Europe and vice versa. Since each can provide the basis for a claim to be the authentic heartland, then the foundational character of such centres and peripheries is made relative, and Europe is decentred. (2009, p. 493)

These references to open spaces and out-reaching borderlands are suitable when Europe is defined in universalistic, cosmopolitan and humanistic terms. They are suited with the dominant rhetoric of aiming to reunify the continent and overcome inequalities, divisions and conflicts that have been consistently declared on the part of the EU and its member states. This is of course not the entire picture, nor is it the only dominant narrative regarding the notion of Europe and the role of borders. Borders as physical frontiers may have faded across most of the western and northern parts of the continent, but the importance of the territorial state has not. Indeed, not everyone has been convinced of the benefits of this approach to borders. In effect, along with apprehension about the fate of the nation-state (Milward, 1992), so too has the fate of Europe's borders continued to trigger much concern, anxiety, expectation, enthusiasm and trepidation. Must the EU's borders be lowered and further dismantled or should they be rescued and refortified? Are the borders of the EU member states withering away, or are they standing strong like fortress walls, withstanding attacks that are launched against them from within and without? Are they becoming irrelevant in some areas and extremely important in others? Do we want the Union's borders to shift further east, and if not why not? So it is not only a matter of where Europe's physical frontiers are settled, it is also a matter of what kind of borders will these be.

Unavoidably, geopolitical realities render some borders 'harder' than others and cultural differences may also render some borders more hostile, forbidding or difficult than others. The EU's external borders have indeed hardened in some locations more than in others, and in some spheres and public policy areas and not in others. To complicate matters further, the same external borders may be hard towards some countries and policies soft towards others. Thus, the border between Italy and Switzerland is softer than the one between Greece and Turkey, just as all of the EU's borders are open to goods from the African, Caribbean and Pacific (ACP) countries but increasingly closed to migrants from the very same countries of origin. This diversity has made border studies a rich field for research while also triggering passionate political debates on the need to open or close, and liberalize or securitize, the Union's borders. This leads us to the next core dimension of Europe and its borders that we explore in the next section, namely its response to human mobility.

Europe as fortress, with gateways and migrants

> The 126-mile border between Turkey, which is not in the European Union, and Greece, which is, has become the back door to the European Union, making member countries ever more resentful as a tide of immigrants from the Middle East, South Asia and Africa continues to grow. Frontex, the European Union's border policing agency, estimated that a vast majority of the crossings in 2011 occurred at the Greece-Turkey border.
>
> The flow has raised tensions throughout Europe, to the point where the top French official responsible for immigration seriously suggested that a wall be built along the entire border. In Greece, one person in 20 is estimated to be here illegally, at a time when the country is sinking in debt, the far right is making political gains and instances of knife-wielding vigilantes taking out their frustrations on immigrants are becoming increasingly common. (Kennedy, 2012)

This is a familiar account that can be read in most international and European newspapers. Migrants, without legal documents, some smuggled and others trafficked, make their way across land and sea borders from South-East Asia, from Asia's heartland, from Sub-Saharan Africa, from North Africa and the

Middle East into Europe in spite of persistently refortified and more restrictive external frontiers regimes. Many of the passages through which irregular migrants try to access the EU are dangerous and risky. Once they cross an EU external border, their adventures continue across less dangerous, but not less risky, intra-EU borders as they tend to aim for the EU's northern economies where employment and settlement prospects continue to be perceived as more attractive than the EU's more southern regions. If apprehended by the authorities, undocumented migrants or migrants with 'irregular' documents, asylum seekers and refugees often have to back-track to their border crossings to be sent back to the EU state that was their 'first point of entry'.

Greece, Italy and Spain top the ranks of 'first points of entry'. The Mediterranean Sea borders are patrolled more strictly than they have been in decades through operations such as the Italian Mare Nostrum, while the high-tech fences of Ceuta and Melilla and the 10.5km fence along the Evros River on the Greek–Turkish border aim to stem the flows of hundreds of illegal crossings daily. And though these border controls work imperfectly, ineffectively and provoke much contention, they do contribute to the image of Europe as a 'fortress'.

As Andreas and Snyder noted back in 2000, the popularity of walls persists in the West,

[B]ut the nature of these walls and the threats they are built to repel have changed. The new walls are designed not to keep people in or to keep militaries out, but to deter a perceived invasion of 'undesirables' – with unwanted immigrants leading the list of state concerns. Nowhere is this more evident than along the geographic fault line dividing rich and poor regions: most notably the…eastern and southern borders of the European Union. (Andreas and Snyder, 2000, p. 1)

Over a decade later, this description stands even stronger, with Europe's border controls being ever tighter and stricter.

It is usually contended that the EU lowered its internal borders at the expense of strengthening or raising its external ones (see for instance Stolcke, 1995; O'Dowd and Wilson, 1996; Bort, 1998; Foucher, 1998; Andreas and Snyder, 2000; Bialasiewicz and O'Loughlin, 2002; Lavenex, 2005; Neuwahl, 2005). Concerns have been particularly expressed with regard to the development of a protectionist internal market, or with regard to its asylum and immigration policies and the classic reference to 'Fortress Europe' (Geddes, 2000). The development of the European Area of Freedom, Justice and Security has been at the core of this discussion. In order to achieve a border-free zone and facilitate internal mobility and freedom for EU citizens and legal residents (including through the Schengen Agreement), the other two constitutive pillars have been security and justice. For the EU, this essentially translates into stricter control of external borders and intra-EU police cooperation in order to protect it from organized crime, illegal migration, terrorism and trafficking of people and drugs. It was also an effort at harmonizing immigration policies and achieving common standards in the treatment of asylum seekers and refugees (through a number of additional multilateral agreements such as the Dublin Convention, the London Resolutions, the Treaties of Amsterdam and Lisbon).

The 9/11 attacks and the launch of the so-called War on Terror led to a further securitization of member states' external borders and with efforts shifting to heightened security concerns, most of Europe's borders have become tenser checkpoints. This has been compounded with mounting anxiety about irregular migration pressures, as well as trafficking, smuggling and other criminal cross-border activities. This anxiety has increased over the past decade and particularly since the outbreak of the 2008 global financial crisis and the unravelling Eurozone crisis (Van Houtum and Boedeltje, 2009), as well as the outbreak of the Arab spring, and the conflicts and rise in fundamentalism that followed thereafter. Thus, in spite of the rhetoric of the declared aim of reuniting Europe and erasing dividing lines, EU integration and enlargement have essentially drawn new dividing lines, replacing the Iron Curtain with a 'Eurocurtain' (Bialasiewicz and O'Loughlin, 2002). As Foucher has concluded, far from having a Europe without borders, we have an EU that is based on a logic of 'frontierisation' (1998, p. 237). While the military function may have declined along most European borders and economic liberalization and globalization have lessened the role of the border as a site of customs inspection and foreign exchange control, this is not the case as regards human mobility. The function of policing Europe's sea and land borders, and also Europe's main city-centres, which have become gateways for legal and irregular migration mainly because of the role of airports and ports, has become central to the concept of the border. And it is this function specifically that is responsible for the 'hardening' of Europe's borders.

This hardening of Europe's edges is criticized for a number of reasons. It is criticized for having a destabilizing impact on the internal politics of its neighbours, especially towards those to which the promise of membership is not (yet) extended (Amato and Batt, 1998; Brusis, 1999; Batt, 2001, 2002, 2003; Batt and Wolczuk, 2002; Keating and Hughes, 2003). It is also condemned for the outrageous toll it has on human lives. As control has increased at Europe's external borders, smuggling and trafficking networks have intensified their activities, bringing migrants into the EU from the most precarious and dangerous crossings and routes. Europe's sea borders have claimed thousands of lives as boats have capsized or sank while being 'pushed back', and many other 'undocumented' migrants have perished in transit or in detention centres. The deaths of these 'undocumented' migrants, can neither be legally punished nor memorialized through rituals (Davison and Muppidi, 2009), thereby attributing a darker side to Europe's borders that is in antithesis with the sort of Union and global, normative actor that the EU presents itself as. Liz Fekete (2003) has described Europe's external borders as a space of suffering and death and the Mediterranean full of 'nautical graveyards' of 'dehumanized' desperate migrants, while Roland Freudenstein (2000) has referred to them as a new frontier of poverty. Lastly, the EU has been condemned for creating a 'Huntingdonian' border, a marker between civilizations, separating cultures and societies and laying the foundations for new divisions in the twenty-first century (Freudenstein, 2000). It has also been accused of creating a dividing line based on wealth and opportunity, thereby creating a 'golden curtain of wealth' (Dalby, 1993), a 'new Schengen wall' (Lowenhardt et al., 2001) or a 'Schengen divide' (Anderson et al., 2000).

Although some borders and passages have historically been tighter and more restrictive, Europe's borders have been seen in a uniform manner as 'Fortress Walls' only recently. Until the 1960s, Commonwealth subjects from South Asia or the Caribbean could travel to the United Kingdom without restrictions. Moreover, economic growth coupled with demographic stagnation led many Western European countries to formulate migration policies that welcomed significant numbers of migrant workers from Southern Europe, North Africa and beyond during the 1950s and 1960s. The oil crises of the 1970s and the challenges of urbanization, however, led European capitals to perceive immigration with apprehension, particularly as immigration influxes continued as a result of family reunification policies, in spite of the restrictive migration policies that had been adopted. As migration became entangled with security and identity issues in the latter half of the twentieth century, European borders became increasingly difficult sites for non-EU citizens. The effects of these developments on Europe's borders have not just been a challenging experience for individuals – whether migrants, refugees or asylum seekers. As mentioned in this chapter, they have also impacted countries adjacent to these borders that the EU has aimed at essentially transforming into a '*cordon sanitaire*', expecting them to adopt EU border control and visa policies in order to filter and limit migration and illegal cross-border movements of all sorts (Armstrong and Anderson, 2007).

Concluding remarks

On the European continent, establishing boundaries is not a nation-state affair solely. The EU has emerged as an influential actor in creating, relocating and dismissing borders, and in transforming national borders into 'European' ones. This transformation is deeply meaningful for all on both sides of the border, as it regulates, harmonizes and defines which borders are important for whom, when and where.

Access to financial means, access to rights, access to security and freedoms have changed in fundamental ways as national borders have become European (Rumford, 2009; Delanty, 2012). Ulrich Beck has framed the issue of borders from a cosmopolitan perspective emphasizing the range of possibilities and potential that may be offered when we approach borders as 'mobile patterns that facilite overlapping loyalties' (2000). This is largely what has been happening with Europe's borders and it has certainly contributed to the current definition of Europe in functional, spatial and identity terms.

Borders are integral to all visions of Europe. We consider that Europe's borders matter for those who are on the other side of the frontier when Europe is attractive, confident, inspiring, powerful and relevant. On the contrary, Europe's borders matter for those within when there is a perception of threat and peril that triggers protectionist and phobic impulses. They are hardened when the desire to keep out the 'undesirables' takes precedence. And they are indeed no longer just at the physical border of European nation-states because essentially, in this phase of European and global history, they are less about protecting territory and more, much more, about controlling and defining mobility – mobility of people, of goods, of services and perhaps also of ideas.

The hardening of the European Union's external borders seems to be increasingly following a modernist logic of (b)ordering. Van Houtum and Pijpers (2007) have described the EU as a gated community with what is increasingly resembling the colonial mind-set, one based on a divisive perception between what is on the inside of the borders as illuminated, enlightened, liberal and prosperous, and what is on the outside of the borders as threatening, invading and even culturally deviant. The current spatial imaginative bordering process of the European Union involves the colonization of neighbours and 'friends' as members or associated members, among whom common assets of knowledge and wealth are constructed and distributed. These must be separated by secure boundaries from 'the inhabitants of the imagined *terra incognita* surrounding the insulating Union [who] are the politically invoked new barbarians from a world outside who are undesirable, the imagined cause of many societal problems and hence, they are denied access' (Van Houtum and Pijpers, 2007, p. 298).

We thus see an absolute contradiction here between the principles upon which European culture is supposed to be based and the ways in which it is managing its territorial form and its boundaries. The gated community metaphor referred to above is particularly worrisome. Gated communities are clear-cut forms of socio-spatial *insolidarity*. By shutting the gates to the 'outside' world they attempt to purify space under the flag of privacy, control, comfort and security. They produce and reproduce segregation, by protecting and maintaining social homogeneity and wealth inequality.

This is neither a flattering nor a tenable state of affairs, and one that requires thoughtful reflection and policy attention for the ways in which Europe's borders and its boundaries are managed and defined, and the ways in which mobility across these is framed. It is fundamental to the quality of European democracy.

Chapter 7

Political Europe

> ...Europe will not be united unless it is able to form a
> common view of its history, recognises Nazism, Stalinism
> and fascist and Communist regimes as a common legacy
> and brings about an honest and thorough debate on
> their crimes in the past century...
>
> European Parliament Resolution of
> 2 April 2009 on European conscience
> and totalitarianism

As an adjective, the word 'political' refers to matters of the government or public affairs. It pertains to active engagement, to ideological alignment and, to power. In this chapter we delve into the political dimensions that have defined Europe. Europe's political map is rich with competing ideologies characterized by universalist aspirations and global resonance, political systems that range from the liberal to the illiberal, and from the democratic to the non-democratic. Europe has been crafted through the coexistence of a long legacy of nation-building and state-building, and of political projects aimed at improving democratic governance or imposing authoritarian rule. It has also been shaped by a history of tensions between the civil and the military centres of power and between the civil and religious centres of power.

Up until the thirteenth and fourteenth centuries, Europe's political landscape was characterized by a rather fluid territorial organization. Then, during the Late Middle Ages, the Church's hegemony was gradually challenged by powerful rulers, and the social structures of feudalism lay the ground for the political structures that established Europe's nation-states. This historical period saw the emergence of assemblies that are the roots of Europe's parliamentarism, and of a system of justice that enabled the systematic and organized record of judgements and administrative decisions. With the exception of the fluidity that continued to define South-Eastern Europe and the rise of the

173

Ottoman Empire in the east, the interstate system that began to emerge became characteristic of Europe and was then exported to the rest of the world, forming the basis of the organization of modern political life and the building blocks of international relations. This period of Europe's history also saw the emergence of capitalism, mainly in the urban centres of northern Italy and the Netherlands, which fundamentally shaped the socio-economic cleavages and ideological conflicts that characterized Europe's political systems over the next six centuries.

In these following sections we discuss the main political cleavages, currents and ideologies that form the background of contemporary European politics. We then examine Europe's authoritarian legacies of fascism and communism and the ways in which these remain part of the contemporary European political context. Certain countries (and particularly Germany) engaged in a collective self-examination, seeking to understand the conditions that led to the manifestation of fascism, nazism and communism, to purge their state apparatuses from these legacies, and move forward in their identity and policies without, however, denying these experiences from their national pasts. Others (such as Austria or Italy) treated their authoritarian experiences as unhappy interludes best forgotten quickly rather than criticized in discourse and through actual state policies. Obviously, most countries fall somewhere in between and some critical rethinking has gone hand-in-hand with a collective desire to forgive, forget and move forward (most notably in the cases of Spain, France, Belgium, Poland and Hungary). Against this background, it is interesting to consider the role that Europe may have played in becoming a moral and political vision that provided the vehicle for political change in national political discourses.

We concentrate on the left–right divisions in European politics among 'Western European' countries. Starting from the main tenets of the left–right wing cleavage in the 1980s, when the 'Iron Curtain' was still in place and the world was divided into 'good' and 'evil', 'Capitalists' and 'Communists', and corporativist models of mass production were still largely functioning in Western European countries. We then look at how the left–right dimension was re-considered in the post-1989 context. The demise of the Eastern bloc was so powerful that some thinkers announced that it heralded the 'end of ideologies' or even 'the end of history', as Francis Fukuyama (1992) famously put it. In the post-1989 context, the issue was initially mostly about how the left–right wing cleavage was reshaped and/or intertwined with the notions of 'Western' or 'Eastern' Europe. Very soon afterwards, however, as globalization and its impacts became more acute, the left–right cleavage morphed into a debate about what kind of reforms were necessary to address the consequences of globalization and the challenges these were posing, and what place, if any, did a 'united Europe' have in these efforts. Thus, in the concluding section, we follow up on the idea of a 'united Europe' explored in Chapter 3 and briefly trace some of its core dimensions in order to see whether we can witness the development of a distinct level of European politics – meaning here EU politics – that is more than the mere aggregate of national politics.

First, though, let us start from the building blocks of politics: values, cleavages, institutions and power.

On politics, political cleavages and political systems

To discuss political Europe, it is necessary to provide some definitions on politics, political cleavages, political systems and political thought in the European context.

Stricto sensus, politics is about competition for power. Individuals or groups seek power in order to further a specific set of interests or put into effect a political ideal. Politics are marked by divisions of interest between groups and individuals who compete for the resources of society. They are also marked by differences in doctrine and ideology (Keating, 1993, p. 39). To understand European politics it is necessary to understand the main social and political cleavages that cut across contemporary European societies and the core currents of modern European political thought.

Political cleavages are the manifestation of competing interests and values within each political system. Over the past five centuries in Europe, politics, or to be more specific, political conflicts, have been territorially framed. They have been framed within empires for a long time, within nation-states in more recent centuries, and over the past seven decades they have also been framed at the supra-national level (EEC/EU) as well as at the sub-national level (for instance, in the cases of Spain, the UK and Belgium). This territorial dimension has its origins in the Late Middle Ages, but it was during the Renaissaince that the principle of territorial sovereignty, that is, *raison d'état*, became consolidated. The rise of the nation-states in Europe was characterized by the establishment of absolutist monarchies and the decline of the influence of the Papacy, which in both cases basically meant armed conflict. Europe's political history has been defined by religious wars, by the Reformation of the Church and the need to find mechanisms of reconciliation (which formed the origins of Europe's tradition of consociationalism), and by the nature of the absolutist regimes that required a permanent state of war (against neighbours or countries in other continents) in order to consolidate their power.

In this context, social structural transformations that were triggered by large-scale processes such as nation-building or industrialization led to social conflicts that took the form of deep-seated 'cleavages'. These 'critical junctures' have subsequently been expressed through specific political parties and party families in each country. They consist of an empirical dimension (a socio-structural basis), a normative one (a specific set of political values and beliefs), and an institutional one (consisting of a particular political organization of social groups). Essentially, the way these critical junctures have been framed has largely shaped each country's political system in Western Europe (Lipset and Rokkan, 1967). For this reason, the Peace Treaties of Westphalia in 1648 are considered the foundations of the European interstate system and one of modern Europe's 'critical' political junctures. The French Revolution of 1789 is another such juncture, as it represents the final shift from the feudal world to the modern one. This shift was represented through the demands of the *Tiers Etat* (meaning the emerging bourgeoisie) for representation in relation to the nobility and clergy in the *Etats Generaux*. The democratic revolutions of 1848 constitute a third such juncture, marking the transition to mass politics.

Lipset and Rokkan attempted to identify the most important cleavage patterns for mobilization and politicization of collective action in modern societies and, in spite of the limitations of this analysis, their work has framed most comparative electoral and party research on Europe and is useful for understanding the patterns of opposition that we find across most of Europe's political systems.

Until the nineteenth century, European societies were characterized by two core cleavages: the centre–periphery cleavage and the religious cleavage, each affecting every country's political life in different ways. The centre–periphery cleavage was triggered by the conflict between the central nation-building culture and the resistance of the ethnically, linguistically or religiously distinct subject populations in the provinces and peripheries. The religious cleavage, for its part, developed from the conflict between the centralizing, standardizing and mobilizing nation-state and the historically established corporate privileges of the Church (Lipset and Rokkan, 1967). This division has taken two forms. Since the sixteenth century's Reformation, the divisions between Catholics and Protestants led to religious wars in which doctrinal differences were just as strong as power politics. And second, the Church–Lay division grew mainly during the nineteenth century as the anticlerical forces drew from the rational, secular traditions of the Enlightenment and the principles of the French Revolution to push back the established Church from public affairs, education and the economy. Although secularization theory had postulated the declining relevance of religion in the public sphere, in fact, the role of religion in Europe has been transformed in the beginning of the twenty-first century. The challenges arising from growing religious diversity within European societies resulting from decades of immigration from other continents have brought religion back into the discussion of what defines the quality of a democracy, the principles of the rule of law, human rights and non-discrimination and what institutional accommodations are necessary in order to achieve democratic, cohesive, mutually respectful and tolerant European societies.

Two further cleavages were produced in the nineteenth and early twentieth centuries; the sectoral and the class cleavages. The sectoral cleavage developed between the first and secondary sectors of the economy, opposing agricultural and industrial interests. As for the class cleavage, it fundamentally structured politics in every European country throughout the twentieth century and provided the ideological underpinning for regimes that separated the continent, and the world, into two distinct blocs for over 50 years (the 'West' and the Soviet bloc).

These four cleavages are considered to have structured political conflicts and coalitions in Western Europe since the nineteenth century. The long term alignments between social groups and political parties that framed each country's cleavages have been impressively durable, largely defining European politics and the public sphere. In more recent decades, however, class divisions in the traditional sense have become increasingly less pronounced, although the outbreak of the global financial crisis has revitalized political conflict on this cleavage in terms of 'haves' and 'have-nots' and the staggering wealth inequality between the famous 1 per cent and 99 per cent. Similarly, secularization reduced the importance of religious divisions in most European societies, so although class and religious motivated voting have manifested a declining trend, this does not mean that identity and social background have become irrelevant to electoral politics and attitudinal orientations. In addition, since the 1980s new value conflicts have been making their way onto the political agenda of Europe's advanced industrial democracies. 'Post-materialist' issues such as environmental protection and the extension of democratic rights over traditional materialist values, which emphasize physical and economic security have been brought into the political scene, mainly by the left and green parties. Ronald Inglehart and Christian Welzel (2005) described these socio-cultural shifts as a cultural transition that Europe has been undergoing from the survival values that were linked to industrial society, to the self-expressive values of the post-industrial society. Survival values emphasize collective discipline, group conformity and state authority. Self-expressive values include a postmaterialist emphasis on personal and political liberty, civilian protest activities, tolerance of the liberty of others and a sense of subjective well-being reflected in life satisfaction.

These changes have realigned the left–right cleavage but have not outright replaced it, as most of the mainstream parties have absorbed many of these post-materialist issues. Driven by the populist right and the parties of the new left, Kriesi et al. identified the emergence of a new value-based cleavage mobilizing voters 'along a protective-nationalist versus liberal-cosmopolitan divide' (2008, pp. 298–9). The end of the Cold War helped 'un-freeze' party alignments that had been consolidated in Western European countries under the blanket of the bipolar ideological opposition. Political coalitions across the political spectrum that were previously unthought of became possible. At the same time, the demise of the Soviet bloc completely altered the political realities and framings in Central and Eastern European countries where the class-cleavage had, in principle (though not in practice), ideologically overridden other cleavages. The cleavage approach to understanding the sociopolitical landscape in Europe is much less applicable to the countries of Central and Eastern Europe, where political parties originated in the state institutions and developed from there instead of following the trajectory common to the western parts of the continent, where political parties were firmly rooted in civil society.

More recently, Hanspeter Kriesi et al. (2012) argued that globalization, or 'denationalization', has transformed the basis of politics in Western Europe by giving rise to what they define as the 'integration – demarcation' cleavage between the winners and losers of globalization. The mobilization of the 'losers' by parties of the new populist right has been influencing the mainstream, established parties of the liberal and conservative right, thereby leading to changes in politics in Western Europe. This mobilization has taken place in response to their cultural anxieties more than economic interests, and has been as relevant for Western European politics as it has been for Southern, Central and Eastern European politics. Contemporary European polities are thus characterized by increased volatility and de/realignments, party fragmentation, a consolidated presence of populism and the rise of anti-establishment parties.

In order to gain a more complete understanding of Europe's political landscape it is also necessary to observe the sort of political systems that have been formed in each country. Political scientists have conducted extensive empirical analyses of the political processes and the underlying dynamics of governmental forms, and have yielded a rich base of data and an important body of comparative theory that classifies the continent's political systems in regional clusters. These categories of political systems have enabled us to highlight the differences that distinguish each country's political system and map the fascinating diversity that characterizes Europe's political realm. Studies focus on whether the state is unitary or federal, whether it has a presidential executive or a parliamentary one, or whether it has a party system that has been characterized by fragmentation or polarization, by multi-partism and a sequence of coalition governments, or by a two-party system resulting in durable single majority governments. Seminal studies of comparative politics have categorized European countries on the spectrum between the 'Westminster ideal' type (where Great Britain and its adversarial style of Parliamentary debate constitute the most representative example) and the 'Consensus' type (which involves far greater compromise and significant accommodation of minority rights, and is best represented by the cases of Switzerland, Belgium and actually even the EU). These studies have concentrated their analyses on explaining the different implications that majoritarian or consensual processes of politics have on the different democratic political traditions that can be identified across most of Western and Northern Europe.

What kind of democratic political traditions do we find in Europe's plural societies? Italy, France under the Third and Fourth Republic, and Weimar Germany have been classified as *centrifugal democracies* because of their fragmented political culture, immobilism and instability. Austria, Belgium, The Netherlands and Switzerland have been classified as *consociational* democracies as a result of the considerable stability they have achieved in spite of the fragmentation of their political cultures. Britain, Ireland, the Scandinavian countries and West Germany during the latter half of the twentieth century, have been described as *centripetal* democracies because of their homogenous political culture, characterized by a stability unthreatened by normal inter-party competition (Lijphart, 1969, p. 72).

The quality and stability of democratic governance have been the overriding concerns of most studies of Europe's different political cultures. As regards the political systems of Southern European countries, here too studies have emphasized the differences that set them apart from the Northern or Western European democracies even though their state institutions have been modelled on Western European prototypes. The entirely different way in which political and economic life was structured in the countries of Central and Eastern Europe during the latter half of the twentieth century left little scope for comparative analyses. In more recent decades, however, political studies have concentrated on the challenges of the transition from communist rule and the legacies of the Soviet era on the ways in which national politics and democratic governance are played out.

Politics are indeed mainly framed within the nation-state context. This does not mean, however, that political structures or political ideologies are nationally bound. The ways in which Europe's national political systems and cultures have developed are more intertwined than is commonly acknowledged. Institutions, constitutions, models and policies of one country have served as templates for others. Thus, the Belgian Constitution of 1830 was inspired by the French and the Dutch Constitution of 1815, which also served as a template for the constitutions of Denmark, Greece and various states in Germany. Or, for instance, when Romania and Bulgaria emerged as independent countries in the late nineteenth century they adopted the British two-party system. Furthermore, fundamentally similar ideas and ideologies have formed and framed similar political cleavages across countries, and they have acquired transnational momentum and cross-border relevance. Thus, tensions between authoritarian and libertarian values and between individualism and collectivism have structured the political systems of all European countries. This essentially implies that Europe's historical context has produced similar kinds of political parties in all countries, with remarkably stable patterns of political behaviour over a long period of time (since the nineteenth century), based on similar types of constituencies (see Bartolini and Mair, 1990).

Values, ideologies and main political currents

Politics is also about ideology and values. Ideologies try to explain, shape and direct social change. As such they consist of a comprehensive set of ideas that (subjectively) explain and evaluate social conditions. They offer a normative understanding of the way society functions, or rather how it ought to function and the individual's place in it. They also propose a programme for social and political action (Ball and Dagger, 2009a, 2009b). It would not be too much of an exaggeration to say that Europe is the birthplace of the most influential and defining political ideologies, and that the main political currents that have developed in Europe have had a unique unrivalled global resonance and applicability in societies that are extremely different from around the world.

The European political map has been defined by two core value axes that interact in complex ways. First, there exists a historic opposition between authoritarian and libertarian values. This has been most distinctively expressed in the nineteenth century by attitudes to the French Revolution and the liberal and democratic movements that followed it across the continent. Second, there exists a value cleavage between individualism and collectivism, where the former is wary of big government and strong social institutions, whereas the latter stresses the need for cooperation and collective institutions that further common interests. Michael Keating has convincingly argued that the ways in which these two axes have interacted across three issues have essentially framed European politics (Keating, 1993). These three issues involve the role of the state in managing the economy and the means of production, in managing societal differences and inequalities, and in setting the framework within which different identities can be expressed and can coexist.

As regards the role of the state in managing the economy, the core challenge has been to ascertain whether and in which ways the state should indeed interfere in economic life. It has also been about the form that government policies ought to take in order to nurture economic growth. In the post-Second World War era, in Central and Eastern Europe, the state defined economic needs, controlled the means of production, and planned all aspects of economic policy. During this same time, however, across Western Europe there was a consensus in favour of mixed economies based on a Keynesian logic and with substantial roles for the public and private sectors. In the 1980s this was challenged by neoliberal economic thought, which pushed the state back in favour of de-regulation and privatization. The global economic crisis in 2008 and the subsequent eurocrisis in principle demonstrated all the flaws of neoliberal governance; yet seven years after the crisis, the paradigm shift away from deregulation and privatization does not seem to be taking place.

As regards the role of the state on matters of wealth distribution, the issue that European governments have had to respond to was how to manage differences in wealth, income and opportunity between social groups, classes, regions and generations. The different ways in which the welfare state has developed across Europe testify to this challenge, which is suffuse with ideology and value choices as Chapter 8 argues. Class structures that developed in the period of industrialization were transformed in the post-industrial era. With the working class declining or becoming more affluent, societal tensions shifted, and as the processes of globalization led to new tensions between winners and losers, haves and have-nots, the challenges of how to deal with exclusion or whether to pursue policies of inclusion has led to new social questions of how to deal with inequalities or diversities.

Finally, in all political systems across Europe, governments have had to balance the need for societal (or national) cohesion with respect for diversity, democracy, equality and justice. The expectation that mass consumer society and democracy would lead to assimilation and uniformity, making questions of identity less relevant, has not materialized. Rather the contrary would seem to hold true today. Similarly, shifts towards non-material values, such as respect for the environment, culture, leisure and quality of life that are associated with the post-material reality of the late twentieth century, have not rendered traditional identity cleavages less relevant or less politically salient across Europe.

Against this background, seven political currents have developed in Europe: liberalism, socialism and social democracy, communism, conservatism, Christian Democracy, the extreme right, and the Greens (draws from Keating, 1993). Although it is not the aim of this chapter to thoroughly review these political currents, it is necessary to highlight the core principles of each because they have defined the political conflicts throughout Europe's history and continue to define Europe's political nature. Moreover, the universalist aspirations that are inherent to each one of these political currents have global resonance and have become relevant or influential in the political life of political systems in every corner of the planet.

Turning to Liberalism first, it has its origins in the eighteenth-century Enlightenment. It grew to become one of the dominant political forces of the nineteenth century through its opposition to the absolutism of Europe's monarchs and the Church, and its support for constitutional government with clear checks and balances and division of powers. Liberalism has taken a variety of forms, from the more radical, to the republican or democratic, but essentially it has advanced political claims that emphasize individual liberty, a set of economic doctrines based on private property, the market economy and free trade. In some countries of the continent, such as Spain and France, protracted conflict with the Church infused it with anticlerical sentiments, whereas English (and American) liberalism was largely devoid of hostility towards the Church or religion in general. Considering that the wider political context within which liberalism developed was that of nationalism and nation-building, liberals also supported collective claims of self-determination. As a largely middle-class movement that reflected social change, industrialism and the rise of entrepreuneurial and professional groups, liberalism challenged traditional social hierarchies on the basis of rationalist, materialist and individualistic principles. One of the most challenging aspects of the liberal movement is that it has been characterized with a wide, and often opposing, range of views on important political issues. For instance, some liberals favoured universal suffrage as a means to advance democracy, others saw mass democracy as a threat to the values of individualism and constitutionalism. Similarly, while some supported the development of an active welfare state as a means to create an equal citizenship, others concentrated on the need to limit the outreach of the state and public expenditure. Liberals were also divided as regards Europe's colonialism. Whereas, for some, colonial expansion offered new commercial outlets, others opposed this military expansion either on pacifist or libertarian grounds, or because of its burden on public expenditure. In the twentieth century, with most of their demands concerning constitutionalism, national self-determination, secularization and the market economy met, liberals lost most of their political relevance and have been largely limited to small political parties in the political centre, often participating in coalitions while remaining by far among the strongest supporters of European integration.

As regards Socialism, it emerged in the nineteenth century in response to the social and economic inequalities produced by the rise of industrial capitalism. Driven by a strong morality and the belief in a more egalitarian society, socialism has urged a more collectivist, socially conscious mode of government. European socialism's different shades of 'left' cover a wide range of strands from those who favour a revolutionary overthrow of the existing order and the establishment of Marx's proletariat rule, to those who considered that the advance of democracy meant that socialism could be achieved through constitutional means (mainly in the UK and Germany). The different strands essentially coalesced around two poles: the communists who aligned themselves with the Bolshevik Revolution in Russia and took a pro-Soviet stand, preaching the overthrow of the state and capitalism, and the moderate ones who became the socialist or social democrat parties across Europe and who sought gradual improvement from within the system. This division was maintained throughout the Cold War until the demise of the Soviet model, which in part discredited the applicability of the social ideal. However, during the four decades that followed the end of the Second World War, social democracy was particularly influential in building Europe's welfare states, each country's public services, particularly as regards health care and free education, Europe's mixed economies where public and private ownership coexisted, and an elaborate taxation policy driven by ideals of social equalization and redistribution of wealth and opportunities. Social democracy was challenged by the economic crises of the 1970s and the slowdown in growth rates across Europe, the changing realities of the global economy that shifted towards privatization, monetarism and reliance on market self-regulation. From the shift away from the old statist model by the German Social Democratic Party in the 1950s to Britain's New Labour in the late 1990s, in order to remain relevant, social democracy repositioned itself as a socially and environmentally conscious form of liberalism.

As regards the communist strand, it was suppressed and persecuted in the inter-war period, especially in the countries that experienced authoritarian and fascist rule, and formed much of the basis of the resistance during the Second World War. It governed Central and Eastern Europe after the Second World War and was largely a political outcast in most of Western and Southern Europe during this same period as a result of its faithful support of Moscow's policies. Its undemocratic nature made it a marginal political force in most of Western Europe, while it remained important in France and Italy and was respected in Spain as part of the anti-Franco resistance. The reformist tendencies within Western European communist parties, which argued that radical change could be achieved through peaceful parliamentary means and which recognized national differences and that the Soviet model could not be applied to Western Europe, came to be known as 'Eurocommunism'. In spite of these changes, the communist parties experienced severe declines in their electoral bases as a result of social change, the shrinking blue-collar working class and, after the 1980s, the demise of the Soviet bloc.

At the opposite end of the spectrum, the doctrine most resistant to change has been Conservatism. Its origins can be traced to the opposition on behalf of the ruling classes to the Enlightenment and the French Revolution. Traditional conservatism highlights the importance of hierarchy, order and the prerogatives of traditional authority in the state, church and family. Intertwined with nationalism, Europe's conservatives often endorsed militarism and the continent's imperialist aspirations. In the inter-war period, the conservative segments of Europe's societies became the support base of the rise of fascism. This led to conservatism being discredited by the experience of the extreme right just as moderate socialism was later discredited by the experience of communism in Eastern Europe. This did not last for long, as conservative movements increasingly became proponents of privatizations, pure market economics and the roll-back of the state on all matters except security, law and order. The adoption of a neo-liberal or neo-right school discourse enabled them to return to power, while in more recent decades their tougher talk on immigration policy has also enlarged their support base.

One of the most influential varieties of Europe's Conservatism has been Christian Democracy. Driven by the goal to reconcile Christian values with industrialism, class division and the democratic demands of the liberals, Christian democratic movements spread across Europe, mainly in Italy, Germany and France. Between the two world wars, along with the papacy, which aligned itself with Benito Mussolini's and Franco's fascist dictatorships, many Christian democratic movements also sided with the authoritarian, reactionary regimes that swept across Europe. However, a strong Christian democratic tradition opposed the dictatorships and then became one of the most powerful political forces in post-Second World War mainland Europe. In Germany, in fact, it brought together Catholics and Protestants and the Christian democrats played a key role in pushing democracy forward at all levels, and proposing policies aimed at reconciling class conflict, improving the socio-economic conditions and political participation of the working class, and developing a welfare state with an expansive social programme. The

Christian democratic tradition was also particularly instrumental in favouring the development of a strong and vibrant civil society of voluntary associations from trade unions to youth organizations and sport clubs, and to humanitarian organizations. Inspired by the principle of subsidiarity, according to which matters ought to be regulated at the closest, smallest level possible before being turned over to larger institutions, Christian democrats favoured corporatist principles for the representation of professional groups and the virtues of intermediate associations between the citizen and the state. These principles have defined to a large extent the development of civil society in Europe and the contintent's corporatist tradition. They have also served as the blueprint for the construction of the European Union (according to the principle of subsidiarity, for instance) and its policies both within the member states and in its external relations (for instance in the vast grass roots democracy building projects that it has funded for decades in its development cooperation policies in the ACP partner countries).

At the far right of Europe's Conservatism lies one of its darkest political legacies. The various expressions of Europe's extreme right have deeply stigmatized the continent's history, with implications reaching far beyond Europe's boundaries, not only through the impact of pseudo-scientific theories of racial superiority but also as a result of the global consequences of the Second World War. Since the nineteenth century, rejection of the Enlightenment (also known as the Counter-Enlightenment) and the principles of the French Revolution were associated with a preference for pre-democratic forms of governance. Drawing strength from Monarchists and absolutists, and from nationalistic impulses, the far right adapted to the advent of the modern age through the new fascist movements of the early twentieth century. Fascism perceived itself as a cultural and revolutionary movement (Mosse, 1999). It aimed at the restoration of authority through its distorted view of popular sovereignty; it violently rejected parliamentary democracy, the principles of liberalism and all elements of an independent civil society. While fascism took its most extreme form in Adolf Hitler's regime of national-socialism in Germany, revolutionary fascism swept across all of Europe in the 1930s, feeding on Europe's legacy of racism and anti-Semitism. Europe thus introduced this openly totalitarian ideology to the world. An ideology that expressed contempt both for the liberal emphasis on the individual and for the socialist emphasis on contending social classes, and instead proposed a world view in which individuals and classes would be absorbed in an all-encompassing mighty nation under the control of a single party and a supreme leader. The scars of the atrocities of the Second World War delegitimized the far right in the immediate post-War period, although not for long as far right parties eventually reappeared across Europe and even in France, Germany and Italy. Since the 1980s, the far right appeared in the political arena with an increasingly explicit anti-immigration discourse, playing on the fears and insecurities caused by the pressures of globalization, competition and growing unemployment rates. The most evident illustration has been the consolidation of Le Pen's Front National in French politics, though the importance of the far right in the Netherlands, Austria, Italy, Hungary, Poland, in Scandinavian countries and more recently in Greece is just as noteworthy. The far right has also expressed the claims of perceived superiority of minority nationalists and separatist movements as the cases of the Belgian Flanders region and the Italian Lega Nord have long illustrated. Europe's far right appeals to nationalism and racism and has in the past inspired regimes in other continents, such as Peron's Argentina or South Africa's Apartheid policy, illustrating yet again the global outreach of ideologies that have been constructed in European settings and as part of Europe's historical development.

Finally, the last, and also more recent, political ideology that has its roots in Europe and has influenced political life across the continent, while also inspiring similar movements around the world, are Green politics. Green parties find their origins in the 1970s environmental or ecological movements that built on the social movements and student protest movements of the 1960s and the libertarian left. The prospect of total annihilation resulting from the Super Power's Nuclear Balance of Terror during the Cold War, along with the fear of massive ecological and humanitarian disasters from potential accidents in nuclear energy power plants, and increasing scientific evidence of human-induced environmental degradation and ecological destruction brought together Europe's long pacifist tradition with a newer 'green' awareness. What started as protest movements aimed at raising environmental awareness and driven by what many analysts have defined as 'post-materialist' values, eventually took the form of Green parties in Western Europe in the 1980s. These developed much later in Southern Europe (1990s) and later still in Central and Eastern Europe. Situated on the left arm of the political spectrum, the Greens promote principled positions on environmentally friendly growth, ecologically conscious consumption, ethical trading with the developing countries (fair trade), participatory democracy and decentralization. They have had their largest electoral successes in elections for the European Parliament but have also managed to join government coalitions, as in the case of Germany.

This very brief overview of Europe's main political doctrines did not aim to thoroughly describe these families of political thought. Nor did it aim to cover, even succinctly, European political thought that is quite simply vast. Rather, the aim of this section has been two-fold. First, to highlight some of the core features that have indeed defined political life, and the bases on which political conflicts have been battled out in European countries. And second, to identify the key elements and dimensions within these doctrines that have made European political thought relevant, influential and even defining in framing the political systems, cleavages and conflicts across Europe but also around the globe, however different and however distant.

The political legacies of Europe

Liberal democracy and authoritarianism/totalitarianism have defined Europe's political landscape and have had a global influence as we have mentioned in the previous section. In this section we review these legacies not so much to study their historical evolution but rather to see to what extent they continue to be part of the contemporary European political context.

What is perhaps most interesting to highlight is not the benign nature of democracy and the malignant forces of totalitarianism, but rather how these seemingly opposing legacies have in fact interacted in modern European history. One of their most powerful interactions was during the tail end of the French Revolution, when Modern Europe experienced totalitarian democracy during the radicalization of the French Revolution under Maximilien de Robespierre, also known as the 'reign of terror'. This period of totalitarian democracy, characterized by the dominance of a self-proclaimed elite that claimed to represent the 'absolute truth', abused its powers in order to eradicate alternatives. It controlled the population through intimidation and the extreme use of force, and defended an ideological commitment to a model of society (the Republican model) while eliminating all other symbols of power (such as Christian symbols) and replacing them with symbols related to the principles of Deism and the Enlightenment. This approach has been compared to the methods adopted by the early twentieth century's totalitarian movements, namely national socialism, fascism and communism, whose vestiges continue to frame current European politics (Magone, 2011). We do not endorse legacy theories suggesting that the power of the past defines subsequent eras, but legacies are meaningful in the way they frame the narratives and understandings of national identity and the relationship between people and polity.

So, let us first turn to Europe's tradition of liberal democracy. Far from having developed in a uniform manner, it came about through two paths: through gradual (largely peaceful) reforms, and through revolutions.

Nordic Europe and the United Kingdom share certain common experiences, as a series of reforms undertaken from the seventeenth century resulted in a strengthened role of their parliaments on matters of taxation and the army, and a gradually elaborate system of checks and balances over the powers of the Monarchies. In parallel, the institutionalization of political parties and formalization of the representation of organized interests resulted in the incremental expansion of voting rights to ever greater parts of the populations throughout the nineteenth century, even though male universal suffrage was only introduced in 1907 in Sweden (1917 for women) and in 1918 in Britain (and in 1928 for women).

The democratic trajectories across the rest of the continent were, however, more revolutionary. In some cases the revolutions were smoother, in others more interrupted. Belgium declared its independence from the Netherlands while establishing one of the most sophisticated constitutions in Europe, which later served as a template for many countries of Central and Eastern Europe. In Italy, Germany and Hungary, democratic ideals were closely linked with the nationalist movements and the push towards unification as elites and social groups that were excluded from the existing power structures wanted political liberalization and democracy in order to emancipate themselves. As for the Baltic States, the February and Bolshevik October Revolutions in 1917 in Russia offered the opportunity to establish independent, though short-lived, democracies in the period 1918–1920.

The evolution of democracy in the Iberian peninsula was repeatedly interrupted by military coups and periods of authoritarian rule throughout the nineteenth century, which continued well into the latter half of the twentieth century with the military dictatorships of Franco and Salazar. As for South-Eastern Europe, democracy also arrived there through the struggles of independence from the Ottoman Empire. This late or incomplete experience of state-building unavoidably affected the way democracy developed resulting often in weak political institutions and even weaker civil societies.

The early twentieth century presented a rather confusing political reality. On the one hand, democratic governance had been established in a growing number of countries and universal suffrage had become the norm across much of Europe. On the other hand, emerging democratization was accompanied with political and economic instability and particularly in Southern and South-East Europe with manipulated electoral systems. These conditions were propitious to the rise of authoritarian dictatorships. The 1929 crash of the New York Stock Exchange and the economic depression that followed had shattering consequences for Europe's newer and inexperienced democracies. As an alternative to the instability of liberal democracy and in response to the threat of a communist revolution, authoritarian regimes multiplied across the continent.

This leads us to the political legacy that lies at the opposite side of liberal democracy, that of authoritarianism and specifically its manifestations in the twentieth century. Italian fascism derived its ideology from Italian nationalism of the pre-war period and drew its revolutionary politics from the socialist parties. It fed off the discontent of the liberal democratic political system and proposed an authoritarian state based on a new corporatist organization of the economy that would restore social order as well as the glory of the Roman Empire. The establishment of fascist squads, *Fasci di Combattimento*, aimed at intimidating the left and scaring local government epitomized their use of scare tactics. Fascism's corporatism presented itself as an alternative to the extremes of capitalism's competition and communism's planned economy that would restore an idealized balance of power between labour and employers' associations. Benito Mussolini's regime succeeded in establishing a semi-totalitarian state, whereas the German version of national socialism led to the establishment of a fullfledged totalitarian dictatorship and the Second World War. Adolf Hitler used similar scare tactics and political violence to come to power in Germany in 1933 and then pursued militaristic ideological indoctrination and an aggressively expansionist *Lebensraumpolitik* to establish a prototypical totalitarianism and one of the most sophisticated regimes of mass politics.

Regimes emulating fascism that were established in Central and Eastern Europe collapsed during the Second World War, while those in Portugal and Spain survived until the mid 1970s. While very few countries were able to resist the temptation of authoritarianism in the 1930s and 1940s, the collapse of the Third Reich created the conditions for a more democratic Europe. The end of the Second World War thus constituted another significant critical juncture for European politics. After the atrocities and scars of the Second World War, although the European far right did not disappear, it seemed that far right parties would not be able to become a significant presence in European politics again. The post-war constitutions of Italy and Germany outlawed fascism and Nazism, while Germany embarked on widespread denazification (with the Allied Powers playing an often controversial role). Facing what happened during the Third Reich and emphasizing the importance of remembering the Holocaust and learning the lessons that had to be learnt from the crimes of Nazism has been an on-going process in Gemany, both during the post war period of division and after reunification.

And yet, only a couple of decades after the end of the Second World War, right-wing parties adopting an increasingly populist discourse started gaining in strength. By the 1990s they had visibly emerged as legitimate political actors in many contexts. The rise of Gianfranco Fini's 'post-fascist' National Alliance, Jorg Haider's Freedom Party in Austria, Jean-Marie Le Pen's *Front National*, Pim Fortuyn's and later Geert Wilders' PVV in the Netherlands, and more recently the rise of Jobbik in Hungary or the neo-nazi Golden Dawn in Greece, all confirm that the extreme right is a fixture rather than a fissure on the European political map. The legacy of the extreme right remains relevant in the current political landscape of both Western Europe, which has experienced seven decades of stable liberal democracy and economic prosperity, and of Eastern Europe, which experienced half a century of socialist rule. Though it may not benefit from a consistent loyalty on behalf of its electorate it does manage to capture the vote of once again growing segments of the population who are feeling insecure, threatened by globalization and European integration, increasingly xenophobic towards non-Western immigrants and racist towards Roma, and that are disenchanted and 'distrustful' of mainstream politicians.

The other major manifestation of authoritarianism/totalitarianism in Europe was expressed in the form of communism. In the second half of the nineteenth century the dire social conditions of the working class led to the emergence of new political forces that wanted reforms. Friederich Engels' critique of the unregulated labour conditions, the exploitation of workers including child labour, debt dependency and poverty of capitalism in Manchester was accompanied by proposals for social reforms that would improve the situation of the working class. In the *Communist Manifesto* that he then published with Karl Marx during the revolutionary period of 1848, they lay the foundations for social democracy and communism that were to fundamentally change Europe's politics both conceptually and in practice. Marxism became the foundation of social-democratic parties in Western Europe that pursued a reformist approach to improving the conditions of the working class. It also provoked a set of pre-emptive measures on the part of conservative governments (such as German Chancellor Otto Bismark) that aimed at creating a welfare state that would provide social protection to the working class and hence neutralize the revolutionary potential of the social question. Finally, it inspired the Bolshevik revolution under Ivan Illitsch Lenin, which completely altered Russia's political life, Europe's political life, and the international political system.

Under the rule of Joseph Stalin, the first communist state in the history of humanity, the Soviet Union, eventually developed into a totalitarian regime based on a centrally planned economy, forced collectivization of the agricultural sector, single party politics and blurring between the party and the state apparatus, and massive ideological indoctrination. Although efforts were focused on building communism in the USSR, Stalin supported the establishment of communist parties across Europe. In Southern, Central and Eastern Europe, these communist movements were at the centre of the resistance against the emerging fascist/authoritarian regimes. The Second World War threw Stalin into an alliance with the UK and the USA in spite of their ideological differences, thereby consolidating the USSR as a global power that replaced the Russian Empire. The Allied Victory in 1945 enabled Moscow to carve a *cordon sanitaire* separating it from its capitalist neighbours by establishing people's democracies in Central and Eastern Europe and controlling East Berlin, and to roll-out a sphere of influence with global outreach. The Cold War and the division of Europe that followed the end of the Second World War meant that each bloc followed a different trajectory for the subsequent half century with limited exchanges and influences between the political systems of either side.

Half a century of communist rule left significant imprints on the countries of Central and Eastern Europe in all spheres of societal and state life. Gabor Toka identified at least four mechanisms that had defined the political realities and attitudes of people in these countries and which subsequently affected their (often difficult) experience of transition from communism to liberal democracy after the demise of the Soviet bloc. The first dimension involved indoctrination in the fields of economic policy and egalitarianism, leading to an emphasis on industrial progress (even at the expense of the environment) and the easier acceptance of the role of women in the workplace. The second involved repression. Freedom of expression was curtailed while criticism of party political choices was suppressed, often violently, thereby limiting public deliberation and experience with public debate. Third, radical social change was rendered familiar and even perceived as mainstream. This did not only involve nationalizing the means of production, for instance; it also meant dynamically establishing compulsory education for all, thereby achieving unprecedented levels of literacy in all countries of Central and Eastern Europe. Finally, the demise of communist rule left a number of vacuums in these societies with dramatic and traumatic results. One of the most widespread phenomena that followed the fall of the Berlin Wall and the USSR was the backlash against communist rule, or what has been termed post-communism.

As these former communist countries of Central and Eastern Europe embarked upon their transition from communism, they had to come to terms with their communist past. Each state adopted a different approach in dealing with this reality. In some cases they banned communist parties (a ban later lifted), in others they replaced monuments of the old regime with new monuments in honour of democracy. In other cases still, they encouraged the opening of secret police files, lustration and restitution (Nodia, 2000; Appel, 2005). Lustration was the process of screening groups of people for previous acts of collaboration under the communist regime. For instance, the Czech Republic passed laws in 1991 prohibiting members of certain groups (mainly the secret police) from entering high public office for five years. Restitution, for its part, was a programme that sought to return 'illegally confiscated property' to misappropriated owners and heirs.

The 'Return to Europe' of these countries essentially meant that all political institutions had to be restructured and reestablished. Thus, institutions were modelled on their Western European counterparts, the EU *acquis* was imported and automatically transposed into national legislation, national identity and sovereingty were rediscovered, the economy had to be modernized, privatized and deregulated, and civil society had to become plural, active and democratic from below. These dramatic changes meant that during this period, in Central and Eastern Europe, one of Europe's defining political cleavages between left and right took on a different dimension. In fact, Francis Fukuyama (1992) argued that the end of the ideological opposition that had come with the end of the Soviet Empire meant that the political cleavages that had divided populations across industrial societies were henceforth anachronistic. The argument was that if the end of the Cold War meant the absence of an alternative method of organizing modern society, then this convergence of values and ideologies around the principles of liberal democracy had rendered Europe's political cleavages irrelevant.

Many expected that communism had 'flattened' the social and ideological landscape (by atomizing social relationships, disaggregating social classes, destroying or inhibiting the formation of voluntarily organized civil society, causing citizens to retreat from the public to the private domain) to the extent that no political cleavages would or could appear, at least without significant long-term social reconstruction. It was even argued that communist rule had removed the capacity of East Europeans to locate themselves on a left–right spectrum and had caused them to distrust politics. Peter Mair's work (1997) suggested that decades of communism had led to a pronounced lack of social stratification in Central and Eastern Europe, which was reflected in the fact that post-communist electorates were volatile and that a crystallization of socio-political identities was unlikely to consolidate for quite some time. Thus, party formation was based more on politicized attitudinal differences concerning the desirability, degree and direction of regime change than the result of politicized social stratification. Herbert Kitschelt (1992, 1995) posited that during the period of their transition to market democracies, post-communist societies were divided in a distinctive manner along a single liberal-authoritarian axis of political competition. As regards the positioning of citizens on this cleavage, those best suited to market conditions and globalization – the young, the educated, men, those with transferable skills, or even those who had privileges within the old communist system that they could privatize to their benefit in the new order – were likely to be found in the promarket/libertarian quadrant. On the contrary, those likely to be most adversely affected by change, or cognitively least able to deal flexibly with social flux – the old, the less educated, industrial workers, and so on – would support anti-market/authoritarian ideologies. Furthermore, he argued that the higher the degree of the country's economic development, the more market liberals it would contain. A more diverse reading of the post-communist political landscape of Central and Eastern Europe was put forward by Stephen Whitefield (2002). He argued that political cleavages emerged in each state across the region, reflecting the country's historical inheritances as well as its post-communist economic and social experiences. He made the case that communist rule did not destroy social identities of class, religion, region and ethnicity, which were to prove immediate sources of division; rather the contrary, he argued, it probably maintained them and even stimulated them.

Studies of Europe's post-communist democracies have emphasized the lack of institutionalization of patterns of government and opposition (characteristic of Western Europe) and the fragmentation of their political systems. However, recent studies have exposed a significant confluence between East and West to a much wider degree than previously expected (Albertazzi and Mueller, 2013; Best, 2013; Casal Bertoa, 2013; van Biezen and Wallace, 2013).

European politics transformed

Examining the political dimensions that define or contribute to our understanding of what Europe is essentially requires one to navigate between continuity and change. The twentieth century has been a period of deep transformation that has culminated in the present reality of a Union of 28 member states that by and large represent the long-aspired-to ideals of peace, unity and democracy. These accomplishments may at present be severely challenged by the euro crisis and its consequences, but in order to better understand today's undercurrents of political change within and across Europe it is useful to take a closer look at the transformations that occurred during the twentieth century on the European political landscape.

First, many analysts have argued that in the course of the twentieth century there has been a transition from modern to post-modern politics. Although the nation-state remains at the core of all political action and identification, nonetheless, the processes of de-territorialization, de-nationalization, internationalization and increasingly transnationalization have deeply transformed national politics. This is closely connected with the transformation (for some even the decline) of the concept of state sovereignty that has been taking place in the late twentieth century. This has been happening through the process of European integration and member states' decisions to pool together sovereignty at the EU level in order to allow for more leverage and influence in policy areas ranging from economic matters to trade, justice and home affairs. It has also been happening through pressures from below and the moves towards devolution. As a result, since the 1980s there has been a clear move towards decentralized subnational government, as the examples of the UK, Belgium, Spain, Italy, Poland, the Czech Republic and Slovakia illustrate.

Second, European politics have been transformed through large-scale immigration since the 1950s, which has diversified societies to an unprecedented degree. 'Multicultural' societies and 'super diverse' cities from a religious, ethnic, cultural and racial perspective have emerged, and in spite of decades of integration policies in some countries, some segments of society are still finding difficulties in adjusting to the new societal realities. Integration policies have been underpinned by very different conceptions of national identity or of how to manage and accommodate difference in the public space both in older host countries, such as the United Kingdom, France, Belgium, the Netherlands, Denmark and Germany, or in newer migration-receiving states, such as Ireland, Spain, Italy and Greece. In spite of the recognized benefits of immigration, either with regards to Europe's demographic decline or actual economic needs, there has been increasing resistance towards further immigration, which has provided a growing electoral base to populist and far-right parties and has also increasingly influenced the discourse of mainstream political parties in more restrictive directions. The political context has also been affected by the coming of age of the second and third generations, that is, individuals of migrant origin born and/or raised in the European countries of destination, who may or may not have naturalized (depending on citizenship policies), and who have been increasingly stating their claims in the public space, seeking rights, recognition and acceptance. They have been defending their participation in the receiving society and the need to pluralize conceptions of national identity, revisit the nation's historical narratives in order to accord greater attention to the country's migration history, and open public institutions to different religious practices.

Third, changes in the post-War global economy combined with the gradual decline of Europe's industrial sector and the increasing importance of its services sector have provoked far-reaching transformations on the European political scene. In post-War Europe, the welfare state developed as a fundamental pillar of each country's political identity. In the East, it was essentially at the heart of the Soviet Union's ideological project. In the West, Keynesian economics enabled the rebuilding of Europe's economic prosperity, which permitted upward socio-economic mobility, societal democratization and an improvement in living and working conditions for the post-War generations. The stagflation-stagnation of the 1970s challenged both East and West and the state became increasingly inefficient as a result of increasing welfare costs. Efforts to reduce welfare costs were met unavoidably with very strong resistance from trade unions and employee associations. The retreat of the state from the economy was most successfully championed by Margaret Thatcher, who also managed to change the nature of interest intermediation in economic and social policy, but even in the UK this took a long time and was rather restricted. Thatcherism had limited resonance in the rest of Europe and the reform of the welfare state in Western, Northern and Southern Europe was resisted until the end of the twentieth century. In Central and Eastern Europe, the welfare state simply collapsed with the demise of the Soviet bloc. The pressures of competition from globalization and persistently high levels of (particularly youth) unemployment led to an approach defined as 'flexicurity' on the eve of the new millennium. Devised in Denmark initially and spreading first to the Scandinavian countries before serving as a model for the rest of Europe, 'flexicurity' aimed at increasing labour market flexibility while maintaining a strong welfare system that would assist people to return to work with new qualifications. The global and financial crisis that unravelled after 2008 challenged the welfare state even further across Europe, making it increasingly evident that the welfare state as we knew it was no longer a viable possibility. The socio-political, and even cultural, repercussions of the shift from a 'welfare' to a 'workfare' state have been far-reaching, not only in the countries more hard hit by the crisis. The socio-economic groups that have been feeling most threatened by the pressures of globalization and immigration have been voicing their insecurity through protest voting and have shifted to the extremes of the political spectrum and towards populist and even anti-systemic parties. These electoral shifts towards populist and, particularly, far-right parties in recent years have been challenging the political balances of power that had been worked out between centre-right and centre-left parties in the post-Cold War era of European politics. And, one of the core issues that is being challenged at present involves the political nature of the EU, and the accepted role that it should play in national affairs.

European integration and the establishment of an Economic and Monetary Union have deeply transformed Europe's politics. The Single European Market programme essentially pushed an agenda of liberalization, privatization and deregulation in all member states, while the introduction of the euro in 2002 reduced the powers of national governments and magnified the interdependence between the European economies and consequently between Europe's political systems. The *sui generis* political system of multilevel governance that developed through the process of European integration, and the fact that the member state national governments have voluntarily assigned sovereignty to supranational institutions, has affected Europe's political systems and its political cleavages. The formal and informal structures, decision-making processes and coordination mechanisms have led to vertical and horizontal EUropeanization of national politics.

The EU remains one of the least well-understood political systems in the world and has been elite-driven for decades, benefiting from the continent's economic growth and a widespread permissive consensus. The nature of its politics and its institutional complexity are at the same time its strength and its weakness. On the one hand it has facilitated the most successful exercise of interstate cooperation in the history of the continent, and the world. On the other hand, it has limited its potential, frustrated Euro-enthusiasts and offered ample room for further criticism to Eurosceptics. Euroscepticism has been an increasingly prominent force since the Maastricht Treaty. Political parties in the EU member states have positioned themselves in favour or in opposition to the EU project and to their country's participation, suggesting the emergence of an increasingly potent socio-political cleavage with particularly strong relevance for the UK, Denmark, Poland, Hungary, France and the Czech Republic.

Across Europe's national political systems, in the post-Cold War era, there has been a notable convergence towards more accountable, transparent and participatory democratic governance, towards an increasingly consolidated institutional and regulatory framework that defends principles of equal opportunity, non-discrimination and fundamental human rights and freedoms, and towards regional integration. There has also been the widespread phenomenon of the 'disappearing voter' (Patterson, 2002): plummeting electoral participation rates that often lead to unpredictable electoral results (mainly benefiting fringe, extremist and populist parties). High rates of abstention along with increasing propensity to fluctuate between parties has been characteristic of current European politics, suggesting not so much the 'end of ideology', but rather what Gianfranco Pasquino described as the end of ideological commitment. This has coincided with the 'Americanization' of European parties and party systems, which means that elections are polarized around two main parties or party coalitions where clusters of specific issues are emphasized rather than ideology (Magone, 2005). Europe's party systems have been changing; they are more volatile and are witnessing a gradual erosion of their electoral base. They have also become increasingly characterized by a growing de-ideologization and pragmatism as politics have become increasingly mediatized.

This increasing pragmatism is indeed a sign of the times as the rising complexities in global politics have been pushing for improved technical capacity and skills to meet common challenges through shared means, policies and instruments. The process of European integration has thus transformed European politics towards a system of multi-level governance, linking even closer together the national politics of the 28 member states, and linking national politics with supranational European and global politics. William Wallace thus defined the Euro-polity as 'governance without statehood' and European governance as the 'post-sovereign state', characterized by extremely high levels of interdependence and elaborate regimes of cooperation, spilling across boundaries and penetrating into what were previously domestic aspects of national politics and administration. European integration has thus challenged what used to be a core principle that defined inter-state behaviour: the principle of non-interference in each other's domestic affairs. The European political system no longer allows this non-interference and its multi-level governence system has presented itself as a model for world politics.

However, the case in favour of further European integration has been increasingly challenged as the European political landscape has been witnessing new forms of opposition and contestation. Alongside the electoral growth of populist parties on the left and right we have also seen an emergence of anti-establishment parties that are generally extremely critical of, if not outright opposed to, 'Europe' and to deepening integration. Since the 1990s in effect, populist parties have been rapidly spreading across Europe, constituting at present 'an important undercurrent in many European polities, if not a predominance in some' (van Biezen and Wallace, 2013, p. 294).

Populism has been defined as an ideology that splits society into two antagonistic camps, pitting the virtuous people against the corrupt establishment, manifesting itself in discursive patterns that identify foes. Populism has also of course been a political strategy pursued by personalistic leaders to win power (Laclau, 1977; Weyland, 2001; Mudde, 2004; Jansen, 2011; Pappas, 2014). The rise of populism has been a long-term process in Western Europe, largely nurtured by the malfunctioning of representative democracy. In short, mainstream political parties have been less and less able to mobilize voters and to respond to the new or changing societal demands. In effect, party membership and party identification have been long declining as has voter turnout, and while volatility of voting has increased, what has also become amply obvious is the declining share of voters who choose mainstream parties. This erosion of the mainstream parties' representation function has been attributed to the increasing tension between 'responsibility' and 'responsiveness', that is, the tension between their role as representatives of the national citizen publics, and their role as governments responsible to a range of domestic, inter- and supranational stakeholders (Mair, 2009). The lack of responsiveness of established parties to the plight of the 'globalization losers' offered the grounds from which the new populist right was able to mobilize, thereby largely transforming the basis of politics in Western Europe and giving rise to the 'integration-demarcation' cleavage (i.e. the processes of increasing economic, cultural and political competition linked to globalization have created latent structural potentials of globalization 'winners' and 'losers') (Kriesi et al., 2006, 2008, 2012; Pappas, 2014). The success of the populist challengers has been mainly a result of their appeal to the cultural anxieties of the 'losers', which, given the 'losers' heterogeneous economic interests, provided the least common denominator for their mobilization. Moreover, considering that populism distinguishes between the 'pure people' and the 'corrupt elite' and pits them against one another it is often perceived as a threat to the very principles of liberal democracies. The current opportunity structures across Europe appear to have been conducive to a consolidation of populism, or what Cas Mudde (2004) has even referred to as a populist *Zeitgeist*. In Western Europe, populism finds its roots in post-industrialization, globalization, the changing nature of the nation-state, the transformation of political parties and party systems, and the consequences of the economic crisis. In Central and Eastern Europe, populism has been nurtured by the frustrations emanating from the combined effects of the transition to and consolidation of liberal democracy, the implementation of a market economy and apprehensions concerning European integration (Zaslove, 2008). The low level of institutionalization of the party systems along with citizens' disenchantment with democratic politics, distrust in the political elites and perceptions of corruption have facilitated the rise of new populist challengers here too.

The ongoing economic crisis and austerity policies have further fuelled right- and left-wing populism across Europe, and have even further fuelled debates about the merits of European integration.

Concluding remarks

Political cleavages, ideologies and political processes have shaped Europe's current political landcsape. This landscape is marked by both continuity and change. In the post-materialist, post-communist and until recently often proclaimed post-national era, to what extent are pasts and presents reliable guides for the future of Europe's politics?

The European political landscape has been recast a number of times over the past century by changes triggered from a number of different dimensions. The most influential among these include:

> the transformation of the European state through progressive European integration; the redrawing of the boundaries between public and private (nationalisation and, later, privatisation), as well as the readjustment of territorial boundaries through decentralisation, regionalisation and federalisation; changes in patters of democratic participation, protest, elections and political communication; the changing character of political parties and changing patterns of party competition; the new challenges faced the European welfare states; and changes in the organization and style of executive government. (Goetz et al., 2008, p. 40)

Europe has changed for a number of reasons because there has been a pervasive decline in traditional industrial and agricultural employment and an emergence of a new post-industrial occupational structure, which poses an entirely new set of issues and challenges. Europe has also changed because there has been a wide shift towards democracy that has included a set of new or reborn countries from Central and Eastern Europe.

These changes have altered the character of Europe, as well as our understanding of it. Today, any discussion of European politics or of politics in Europe, is overshadowed by the European Union. Since the 1980s, researchers have been examining the effects of the EU on democratic politics within and across the member states. One of the core concerns was whether European integration could remain a broadly consensual elite project detached from domestic political competition. Another was how could the democratic deficit that characterized the EU be addressed in order to protect the quality of democracy within the nation-states. In essence, these issues raised the overarching question of whether European integration might constitute a new political cleavage, one pitting the winners of globalization against the losers (Hooghe and Marks, 2008).

Stefano Bartolini argued in 2005 that European integration was undermining national boundaries without replacing them with a meaningful European boundary. On the positive side this meant that individuals who had the resources to be mobile were no longer constrained by national borders and could therefore take advantage of the processes of EU integration and globalization and thrive. Those who did not were trapped in weakened national states that were increasingly unable to provide the necessary economic security. We are vividly living the consequences of this dichotomy a decade later with the eurozone crisis having nurtured an unprecedented rise of populist parties, of anti-establishment parties and of far-right and far-left parties openly Eurosceptical and explicitly calling for a roll back of EU integration. Hanspeter Kriesi and colleagues (2008, 2012) detected this powerful dimension of conflict resulting from EU integration and globalization, which has given rise to three kinds of competition that have in turn generated new sets of winners and losers: competition between sheltered and unsheltered economic sectors; cultural competition between natives and immigrants; and competition between defenders of national institutions and proponents of supranational governance. Political actors that propose to demarcate their society against external competition and to push back the powers of supranational and international institutions in order to reclaim national sovereignty thereby attract the 'losers' of globalization and EU integration. Given that the traditional left–right cleavage and the respective mainstream political parties are not able to respond to this discontent in a meaningful manner, partisan realignment and a rise in radical right populism is the result.

Current political developments across Europe but particularly in the countries hardest hit by the economic crisis have indeed confirmed the powerful impact that European integration has had on the structure of political conflict in Europe. In the present conjuncture, it appears that we can attribute a very politicized meaning to the term 'Political Europe'. What will be interesting ahead will be to see how the EU integration cleavage will be managed by the political actors at the EU and domestic levels and whether the current eurozone crisis will indeed eventually be identified as another 'critical juncture' in the political history of Europe.

Chapter 8

The Social Dimension of Europe

> we have a vision of the good society and a more egalitarian economy that will create a secure, green and fair future. But to achieve it capitalism must now become accountable to democracy; and democracy will need to be renewed and deepened so that it is fit for the task. A good society cannot be built from the top down, but can only come from a movement made by and for the people. Creating the good society will be the greatest challenge of our time and it will shape the lives of generations to come. (Tony Blair and Gerhard Schroeder, Press release of the Third Way/Neue Mitte, 19 June 1999)

Introduction

Europe has long been known and distinguished from other parts of the world for its social dimension, notably for its social policies that aim at taking care of the most vulnerable populations in society, on the basis of a shared notion of social solidarity. Even if the exact breadth and depth of this social solidarity may differ among European countries and the welfare systems that each supports may vary, there is a view that European countries have put great emphasis on their systems of social protection in the post-war era in particular. A distinct European model (or indeed a set of European models) has thereby been created with some common characteristics and is certainly distinctive from what happens in other parts of the Western world (such as North America or Australia). Indeed this emphasis on both synchronic (within the same generation) and diachronic (inter-generational) solidarity is seen as an identifiable feature of European societies and European nation-states as well as of the European Union as a regional system of government today.

206

However, this research hypothesis, or indeec
about the existence of a European social model ne〈
examination in order to unravel its complexities. Fi,
similarity between the national models of social prc   ‸‸
exist in Europe and the related national understandin₅₃ ot values
such as community, solidarity and social justice has to be examined in relative rather than absolute terms. In other words, their
similarity in *absolute* terms is limited, and certainly, as we shall
argue in the second part of this chapter, there are regional clusters or families of European social models rather than a single
model for Europe. The question, however, that can be posed is
whether these models are *relatively* similar; that is, whether they
are more similar with one another than with the social protection models that exist in other countries outside Europe.

Second, this assumption of relative similarity with one another
tends to be Western Europe oriented and leaves out the distinctive experiences and policy models of Central and Eastern
Europe. Former communist countries have been through an
important transition in the last 25 years from a system of absolute, centrally imposed social solidarity and welfare, to a free
market capitalism with a rather limited net of social protection
for the citizen. Indeed the memory of the communist experience
and the cherishing of freedom and democracy sometimes lead
to opposite effects where citizens are left too much to their own
devices, in the name of freedom, democracy and the market. In
this chapter, we also reflect on these countries' experiences and
consider how their socio-economic transformation of the last
25 years has developed and how it is inscribed in a common
European matrix of social solidarity, if such a matrix exists.

Third, this generic assumption about the overall benign and
supportive role of social solidarity and the social protection
system in Europe tends to overlook the exclusionary aspects of
the system (and of the cultural values that underpin it). Thus,
solidarity as a value and practice, and welfare systems as institutions may be challenged when migrants and minorities come
into the picture. In other words, conceptions of social solidarity and social justice as well as welfare policies and institutions
have in-built assumptions about who deserves to benefit from
the system and who does not. Such assumptions interact with
considerations of who belongs and who does not, and hence
when it comes to ethnic minorities or migrant populations,

both the normative and political foundations of social solidarity conceptions may be drawn into question. In other words, solidarity is neither ethnicity- nor religion- nor gender-blind. Or it may be actually so myopic towards ethnicity, religion and gender dimensions that it becomes discriminatory. These are issues that need to be addressed in our consideration of social protection in European societies.

Fourth, the term 'European social model' has been used over the last two decades mainly to refer to the social model developing in the framework of the European Union. While the idea that the European Communities should have a social dimension may have been around since their very foundations and even since the Spaak Committee (1955–1956), the term was emphatically launched by Jacques Delors in the mid-1980s with a view to emphasizing the welfare dimension of European capitalism and designating it as an alternative to the North American form of pure market capitalism (Jepsen and Serrano Pascual, 2006, p. 25). This book engages critically with the term 'European social model', which it considers as a wider-than-EU but perhaps also more diffuse model, encompassing some values or features that are common among different social models identified in European countries rather than looking at social policies developing at the EU level.

This chapter starts with investigating what the 'social dimension' consists of, as the term is often used generically without clarifying what it includes. The social dimension is about conceptions of equality and inequality, solidarity and community, or indeed responsibility and autonomy; it is about rights and obligations of the citizens towards the state and of the state towards its citizens. The social dimension is fundamentally about what we consider a 'good' society and, it lies at the heart of the functioning of democracy and citizenship. Social protection enables all citizens to function as such and provides for the institutional links between the individual and her/his family, on the one hand, and the state and society, on the other.

Thus, the sections that follow concentrate on the political framework and cultural connotations of concepts such as community, solidarity and social cohesion. We argue that the current concept of social solidarity is strongly based on the concept of national citizenship that purports a high level of community cohesion and solidarity among fellow nationals. At the theoretical level this is translated into T.H. Marshall's well known elaboration of three types of citizenship rights: political, social and economic. At the policy level it has led to the development of the welfare state that provides for citizens when they face hardship, illness or vulnerability of any sort.

The situation has profoundly changed in Europe since when T.H. Marshall was elaborating his approach. First and foremost, we have witnessed the withering away of the Fordist system of production and its replacement by a post-Fordist world that is much more volatile; one where geographic and socio-economic mobility have intensified. Without underestimating the importance of south to north labour migrations in the post-war period, the range and complexity of labour migration flows today is on a higher scale. People move in multiple spatial and professional directions. Workers move among different countries and also change jobs and labour market sectors more often than before. Upwards or downwards socio-economic mobility is also faster and more volatile. There are few guarantees for a skilled worker who works in a large company, or in a small firm or shop, that at the end of her/his working life, s/he will have climbed a few steps up the professional and socio-economic ladder. On the contrary, we may witness both faster upwards socio-economic mobility (particularly among those who are university educated) as well as a rapid fall, as professions and sectors experience important market fluctuations.

Second, national societies, particularly in Europe, are more diverse than in the past. Such diversity has largely been the result of post-war migration in Western Europe, of post-1989 migration in Southern Europe and of the revival of nationalism and ethnicity in the post-1989 period in Central and Eastern Europe. Thus, the national cultural foundations of social solidarity and the welfare system have all been challenged by these fluctuations.

Third, the demographic parameters have changed. After the baby boom generation of the 1970s, Europe has been experiencing constant demographic decline. While the severity of this decline may not be as dramatic as originally envisaged, and varies among countries, it is still a fact that needs to be taken into account when considering the future of national or European level systems of social solidarity and social protection. In addition, in the case of Central Eastern European countries, the demographic decline has been absolutely steep, influenced by both a sudden drop in birth rates after the transition to democracy and free market capitalism, as well as by significant out-migration, especially of the younger generation.

Fourth, the implosion of the communist regimes in 1989 contributed to the rise of neo-liberalism as a dominant, if not hegemonic, paradigm for socio-economic relations. This temporary disruption of the ideological struggle among different conceptions of social solidarity and justice has transformed social justice struggles to technocratic debates about whether one system of welfare payments or entitlements is more effective than another. This has had important implications for the normative and political foundations of European welfare systems and the values and self-conceptions of European societies. Interestingly, today we are entering yet another phase, after the acute financial crisis that Europe has experienced in the late 2000s and early 2010s, where the hegemony of neo-liberalism is challenged, and the importance of social protection and social solidarity is being considered anew albeit in a completely different framework of employment relations compared to the late twentieth century.

After discussing the above issues and mapping how social protection has evolved in Europe in the post-war period, but also particularly during the last 25 years, the chapter proceeds with presenting the main features of the different European social models, outlining their normative and institutional foundations. Naturally, we take into account both the institutional apparatuses of social protection in each country but also the related cultural assumptions and political culture that buttresses those. Thus, the second part of the chapter discusses the distinction between the more family-oriented social models of southern and continental European countries, to the more rational, Protestant-ethic-based models of Northern European and Nordic countries, the Anglo-Saxon system as well as the emerging Central Eastern European social models.

There is a set of assumptions and norms that stand behind the social dimension in each society and the social model of each country and these need to be explicated before we consider what is the specifically European aspect of this social dimension or the specifically European social model. Thus, after discussing briefly the foundations and main features of these different welfare state models we discuss whether there are some common principles or features that are distinctively European and that mark these models as not only national but as pertaining to a wider European perspective towards social protection.

The historical cultural and socio-economic foundations of social protection

Before outlining how the notion of social solidarity and social protection emerged historically and what are its current dilemmas and contradictions, a word on the terminology is necessary. We use the term social protection in a slightly generic way to encompass a variety of terms used in different languages to refer to different types, modes and degrees of welfare policies, whether services in-kind or cash payments, that aim at providing a safety and support net for citizens and their families.

The term social protection is certainly imperfect but is probably the most current in different European languages (*protezione sociale, protecciòn social, κοινωνική προστασία*) and the less nationally loaded. Indeed, the terms welfare system and welfare state have a strong English connotation as the term welfare is difficult to translate and is actually used in some countries (such as Italy) with the English word (*politiche di 'welfare'*). Expressions such as *état providence* in French have an implicit religious connotation because of the use of the term 'providence' as in 'divine providence'. The term *Sozialraat* (in German) or *état social* (in French) is considered by some to be an exaggeration as it overestimates the role of the state (Barbier, 2013, p. 11). Back in the 1980s, the OECD had translated the term welfare state as *état protecteur* in French, although this translation overloaded the protective character of the state and perhaps downplayed the accent that welfare puts on the collective well-being. The term social security or also *securité sociale* is also more limited as it mainly refers to the institutions and the social security apparatus rather than a wider notion of social protection. Security is a narrower concept that brings to mind the notion of insurance rather than a wider concern of enabling people to live well and act as citizens.

The terms social solidarity and social justice carry a very high normative load; they are values that underpin the notion of social protection to the extent that social protection is the institutional expression of a solidarity feeling shared among members of the same community and their wish to live in a good, just society.

Below, we discuss the cultural and political framework of social solidarity as a value, and the historical context within which social protection as a set of institutions, policies and practices emerged and how it is transformed in twenty-first-century Europe.

While the question of community solidarity is probably as old as mankind, it is the advent of the nation-state that proposes it with a new emphasis. The nationalist doctrine asserts that each individual belongs to a nation, that all members of the nation are equal and that each nation has a right to self-government. These views implicitly create the basis of a notion of social solidarity that extends beyond the immediate local community, the community of fellow villagers or of the family clan as it existed in pre-modern times. Indeed, the possibility of a social solidarity system is born together with the notion of the nation as an 'imagined community'. As Benedict Anderson argued (1981), nations are imagined communities in the sense that all members of a nation imagine their fellow nationals but they will never get to meet them all. Still, this does not prevent them from feeling a sense of common belonging and solidarity with one another. According to Anderson's well-known analysis, this kind of national imagination was made possible by the advent of print capitalism, which transformed people's understanding of time and space, allowing news to be distributed quickly across different parts of large territories, providing the conditions for the necessary unification of the social, economic and political space that we find in the national state. As hardly any country in the world, let alone in Europe, is a nation-state in the proper sense of the term, meaning in the sense that its population all belongs to one single national group, we use the term national state instead of nation-state here. The term national state denotes that the country includes a large national majority that probably dominates the state apparatus and may think of the state as its 'property', and one or more minority groups that again may be autochthonous (that is established in that territory for several generations) or may be the result of recent migrations.

In addition to this, the advent of nationalism and of national states has created the normative and cultural basis for social solidarity to emerge among such large communities. Fellow members of the nation share a common culture and language and can thus communicate more easily among themselves and with the state institutions than happened previously in large empires or in feudal states that were politically and culturally fragmented. They are equal and they have to care for one another, or at least so the nationalist doctrine says. Their feeling of belonging to the nation, their mutual solidarity bonds and their rights and obligations as citizens of the nation-state are all tightly integrated into the modern concept of the nation-state and of national citizenship. This cultural assumption of solidarity among fellow nationals, that is inherent to the very conception of the national state, may be challenged by class differences and contrasted interests of different socio-economic strata. Nonetheless, the feeling of belonging to the nation forms the basis of the solidarity bond that links the citizens to the state.

Beyond the cultural framework provided by the nation and the nation-state for social solidarity as a norm and as a set of institutions and policies, it is important to understand the socioeconomic processes that brought about the notion of social protection and the welfare state. Following Polanyi (1957), we argue that the notion of social solidarity within a nation-state and the concept or institution of social protection are closely linked to the process of industrialization and the contradictions that this entailed. It was the advent of capitalism and economic liberalism that, perhaps paradoxically, brought with it the seeds of the social protection system. The development of a self-regulating market in capitalism found its counterpart in the development of a social protection regime (of different types in the different European countries) that would tame the forces of the market and provide security to workers and their families. It would thus solve the contradictions that arise between the inequalities produced by a market economy and the fundamental equality among citizens up on which democracy is postulated and finds its legitimacy.

Indeed, in order to achieve a deeper understanding of the role of the welfare system in contemporary European societies, we need to consider not simply its levels or sectors of social expenditure but most importantly how state activities are intertwined with the role of the family and the market in providing for social protection to the citizens. Industrialization and capitalism stripped society of the intermediate layers of community, kinship, family, the servant-and-patron relationship or the parish/church that in pre-capitalist societies would provide for social protection to those in need. The welfare state acquires a fundamental role in contemporary societies as farmers and other workers are drawn into the wage-earner status and societies become fundamentally wage-earner societies. In this new socio-economic order, work and the worker are commodified and the welfare state must intervene in order to de-commodify work by providing social rights. National social protection systems in Europe have different ways of providing for social protection, different levels and logics that we discuss in further detail later in this chapter. It is, however, important to note that the welfare state is today a structural feature of society; it organizes the relations between the individual, the market and the state in very important ways.

Social solidarity has become codified into a national system of social protection with the advent of the wage-earner society in the twentieth century and particularly after the Second World War and the traumatic experiences of the great recession of the 1930s. It is not by coincidence that T.H. Marshall (1950) developed his theory on citizenship rights and social welfare in the late 1940s and early 1950s. Marshall saw citizenship as developing cumulatively through a social struggle over rights. Civil rights were the first to be fought for in the seventeenth century by civil rights movements that demanded what have become commonly considered the most basic rights, such as individual freedom, freedom of speech, right to own property, liberty of the person and so on. Political rights, associated with representative democracy, were achieved in the eighteenth century as a result of the French Revolution and were further developed in the USA and the rest of Europe. They included universal (white) male suffrage, but also the right to organize in political parties, the right to assemble, to petition, to hold public office and so on. These rights were extended in the twentieth century (earlier or later) to include women as citizens, and also to include ethnic and religious minorities.

According to Marshall, the above two sets of rights, the civil and the political, helped individuals to organize democratically and demand socio-economic rights. These rights developed from the mid-twentieth century onwards to address the concern for the guarantee of minimum standards of housing, employment and health care, as well as insurance against unemployment or illness, and free collective bargaining over wages and working conditions.

In Marshall's conception, the state is the citizen's 'birth place, executive manager and guardian'. Citizenship and its three sets of rights (civil, political and socio-economic) thus formed the public realm, and the state was the enclosed territory where private interests and public issues met (Bauman, 2005, p. 13). The system was seen to serve well as it managed to counter-balance the opposed interests of the state, the corporation and the citizen. There have been several criticisms of Marshall's theory in that it failed to take sufficiently into account the exclusion of women, ethnic minorities or religious groups, thereby neglecting the related structural barriers that women and minority members experienced. A second criticism concerns the fact that Marshall failed to see that the relationship between the state and the market is not linear but cyclical: the national states that Marshall had in mind were capitalist states. They would thus periodically retreat, particularly in times of recession, with a view to opening more room for corporate growth (and worker exploitation). Thus the linear view of accretion of rights could not work. Third, a major criticism against Marshall's theory has been that it was based on the prototype of the waged workers as citizens rather than on membership in society (Murray, 2007).

The transition to the post-industrial phase in Europe

The emergence of national systems of social protection in the twentieth century, and particularly in the post-war period in Europe, finds its socio-economic and political foundations not only in industrialization and the class struggles that marked the first decades of the past century, but also in the pre-war depression, the protectionist policies that ensued and the war itself, which left European economies relatively autarkic compared with the period before the First World War. Keynesian policies and Fordist production methods encouraged the development of national planning and investment with concomitant systems of social protection gradually emerging in the most industrialized countries of the European continent (see Jordan et al., 2003).

The 1950s and 1960s were a period of high growth and increasing demand for workers. Thus, those decades were also characterized by substantial recruitment of foreign workers. Migration flows followed post-colonial as well as intra-European pathways:

the UK recruited from Ireland and the new Commonwealth countries, France from Spain, Portugal and North Africa, Germany from Italy, Greece, Yugoslavia and Turkey, and so on. Native and migrant workers all contributed to national welfare systems, which were managed through the 'holy trinity' of state, employers and trade unions/workers. This period has been known as the 'golden age' of European welfare state development.

However, the situation changed after the oil crisis of the early 1970s. Already economic growth was slower in Western Europe, the need for structural change in labour markets had become evident and unemployment was growing. Welfare state provisions came to be seen as untenable at the levels previously envisaged and started experiencing both decline and reorganization. Perhaps the most obvious case is that of Margaret Thatcher's Britain where changes to the British welfare state had already begun under the Labour government. But reforms took effect also in France, Germany and other continental European countries. During this same period, migration within Western Europe declined because the northern countries put a stop to their recruitment policies but also because the Southern European countries, like Greece, Portugal or Spain, joined the EEC and enjoyed a certain level of industrial development accompanied by a wide expansion of the service sector. These developments helped to keep Southern European citizens at home.

The 1990s and the beginning of the twenty-first century have been characterized by deeper integration of the world economy, further affecting the employment and social protection landscapes, which were still organized mainly at the national level. Barriers to free trade have been removed across the world, global trade has increased exponentially, and regional and megaregional schemes like TTIP (Transatlantic Trade and Investment Partnership) are today further promoting international trade in goods, services and foreign investment. As the mobility of the factors of production and trade has increased, welfare states have been faced with hard choices. Embracing global market forces entailed the risk of exposing citizens to poverty and insecurity, and reducing protection for those outside the labour market, for the sake of 'flexible' adaptability. Resisting such forces, however, did not appear a feasible solution either. The transfer of production sites to developing countries where salaries and welfare costs were low and labour protection policy lax has made goods produced in European countries often too expensive and hence less competitive in an integrated global trade environment. Thus, it was thought that to resist the *flexibilization* trend would create unemployment and at the same time undermine the very foundations of national welfare systems. The collapse of socialism in Eastern Europe served as a warning to the latter approach. Neither the more 'flexible', pro-globalization regimes of the UK and Ireland, nor the more social protectionist regimes of France, Germany, the Netherlands or Denmark have been able or willing to do much about this, while the governments of Southern Europe have been quite unprepared for it.

The very preconditions of national social protection systems have been fundamentally altered in the last 25 years. Not only was industrial society transformed into an information society and a society engaging more with consumption and the production of 'goods' related to status, but it was also the organization of the labour market that underwent a radical transformation. In the old order, capital investments in factories lasted over decades and were as easy to control as the labour that worked there. In the new order, capital became much more transient and much less tied to physical investments and the exchange value of goods.

Today, and as we have seen in the recent global financial crisis, portfolios replaced machines and investment ignored borders in a way that factories never could. The labour force became much less substitutable and much more specialized, less homogeneous and less hierarchically organized, with growing segmentation in labour markets. Trade unions lost their control over the supply of labour and governments lost much of their control of capital. Both the ideological and the technical means for sustaining desired economic behaviour changed in line with these shifts. First, stemming from the USA, came an emphasis on citizens as self-responsible actors in the market place, and hence as active agents who could make their own choices in issues of both employment and welfare. This in turn justified state regimes that sought to 'activate' and bring back to employment those who claimed benefits by virtue of unemployment, as European governments attempted to adapt to the new global economic environment, including new patterns of working lives, new household and family structures and new demographic balances (Hemerijck, 2001, p. 159). Changes in tax and benefits regimes aimed to improve incentives for low-paid employment, to promote part-time and temporary employment, and to reconcile work with family life. All this involved the transformation of ideas of social rights (Cox, 1999), an emphasis on the responsibility of the government to avoid burdening the taxpayer, and a new approach to the implementation of enforcement (Jordan, 1998) – all for the sake of 'flexibility'.

These new regimes were developed in Northern Europe – in the Netherlands, Denmark and Ireland as well as the UK. Although ideas such as 'activation' have different meanings in Southern European member states with respect to Northern ones, there were common patterns between them. In either case, *mobility* played a key role in the search for better incentives and a more flexible workforce. The problem was partly one of getting workers who were socialized into expectations of security, fixed hours and stable working conditions from the Fordist era to accept more fragmented and changeable patterns of work, less reliable (and often lower) earnings, and the need to retrain and move between different professions or labour market sectors.

In Northern countries, welfare benefits discouraged unemployed workers from getting jobs in the new flexible labour markets. In Southern countries, where benefits were too low or non-existent, the family provided the safety-net for unemployed workers, and youth in particular, which discouraged them from being mobile or accepting flexible forms of labour. In the 1990s, governments across Europe were forced to recognize the limits to flexibility among indigenous populations. New regimes, policies and practices could not shift stubborn concentrations of unemployment, poverty and deprivation, either by bringing employment to the suburbs or to former industrial districts now in decline, or by moving people out to occupy vacancies elsewhere. In these respects, international immigration has come to play a key role in offering a plentiful, flexible and cheap labour force to meet temporary or seasonal demand and to fill the shortages in specific labour market sectors both in the lower and high skilled ends.

Mobility is, of course, intrinsic to globalization. Transnational firms move staff around the world, and employees in these firms travel incessantly to create contracts, pursue production opportunities and market products. Accelerated border crossings for the sake of business, governance, tourism and study are the very stuff of the new integrated world economy. Governments, competing for investment by such companies, seek to facilitate these movements of people – to be 'business-friendly' is to be mobility-friendly. In this universe, national systems of social protection rooted in a bounded membership appear to be obsolete, impossible to sustain at the same level and perhaps also less useful, as they cannot take into account the new levels and types of inequality.

The challenge has been both an economic and socio-political one for European countries, as welfare reform has been called upon to address new forms of labour, new types of employment relations, but also a much more individualized labour force, internally divided not by its relation to the means of production but by a more complex matrix of inequality, which includes socio-economic status and skills as well as gender, ethnicity and religion.

Social protection and complex inequality

Before delving into the national particularities of social protection concepts, cultures and systems in Europe, it is important to discuss some new features that characterize European societies in the late twentieth and early twenty-first centuries, which have implications for the concept and practice of social protection. Part of the flexibilization shock in European labour markets has been absorbed by increasing international immigration, which had to do both with the changing needs and structures of the labour market and the international division of labour, and with the declining demographics of Europe. The European migration landscape has been radically altered after the end of the Cold War with the implosion of the communist regimes and the opening up of borders with Central Eastern Europe. Indeed, the East to West migratory flows have particularly characterized the 1990s and 2000s. Southern European countries were converted to immigration hosts nearly overnight, while Northern and Western European countries started receiving new large flows of both skilled and unskilled workers from Central and Eastern Europe that came to fill shortages in the 3-D jobs (dirty, dangerous and demanding), particularly in the 4-C sectors (care, cleaning, catering and construction).

At the same time, increasing global inequality, political instability and ethnic or religious strife in Africa, Central Asia or former Yugoslavia contributed to increasing, as well as diversifying, the new migration flows of the last 25 years. These flows were facilitated by improved access to intercontinental transport and the development of communication services. The new flows presented themselves to the authorities in the form of steeply rising applications for asylum, and in undocumented immigrant workers occupying niches in European labour markets at a time when unemployment stood at a post-war high. In the 1990s, EU member states overhauled their asylum regimes, adopting more deterrent and restrictive, and less welfare-orientated, systems, as well as tightening external border controls at the periphery of 'Fortress Europe' (King et al., 2000). But even these measures are now recognized as inadequate, because they do not address economic globalization and the international division of labour.

These new flows have contributed to making virtually all European societies culturally diverse. With the exception of Central Eastern European countries that are yet to face significantly large immigration flows, all other European countries, whether north, west, south or centre of the continent, whether more or less industrialized, whether more or less open to diversity, received significant numbers of migrant workers. Indeed, migrants account for more than 5 per cent of the population in countries like Britain, France, Germany, Austria, Denmark and Sweden, but also Greece, Spain, Italy and Cyprus but their participation in the labour force is even higher as most migrants are in the working age bracket.

This new workers' cohort has come to boost contributions to European welfare systems but it has also profoundly shaken the assumption that social solidarity is circumscribed culturally within the nation. In addition, and in line with the post Fordist world of fluidity, mobility and flexibility, some of these migrant workers came undocumented. Their cultural or religious difference, their frequent arrival outside labour recruitment schemes or bilateral agreements, the initially undocumented status of many immigrant workers and/or their work in the informal labour market, all these are elements that made their integration into the national welfare systems challenging. Their legitimacy as beneficiaries of national protection schemes has been questioned as they were meant to be there temporarily, they had not been 'invited' by the host society, and often are considered to be culturally alien and not able to assimilate, holding values that are incompatible with the dominant culture and work ethic.

An additional layer of this cultural and ethnic diversity of the workforce comes from the increased participation of women in international migration and the effect that this has for receiving societies in Europe. The ties between female migration and social protection are multiple and influence in important ways the restructuring of welfare regimes in Europe today. Migrant women from Central Eastern Europe and the former Soviet republics have been pushed to migrate, not least because of the implosion of the communist regimes and their social protection and employment systems, but because they became unemployed and had no safety net on which to fall back.

At the same time, there has been a strong 'pull' effect in Western and Southern European societies, where care work needs have increased. Such care work was traditionally performed by women (in Southern Europe) and to a certain extent by welfare services (in Northern and Western Europe). But as European societies have been rapidly ageing and the demand for caring and cleaning services has boomed, welfare services have been increasingly reduced or monetarized. Thus, a whole market for social services has emerged, particularly in countries such as Britain or in Southern Europe (Triandafyllidou and Marchetti, 2014). But the allowances paid to the families were too low to enable them to hire a local worker and local skilled social workers were probably not prepared to work for private homes on an unstable and flexible work contract. Thus, migrant women have come to fill important gaps and to actually substitute for services that are not there, while at the same time enabling native women to take up paid work outside the home. The current economic crisis and the further restructuring of welfare systems and reduction of both services and cash allowances (most acute in Southern Europe and Ireland, but also felt in Northern and Western European countries) make the need for an affordable domestic care labour force all the more necessary and sought after, especially as life expectancy is prolonged and the European population is increasingly ageing.

The tensions that cultural diversity brings to social equality have been described by Banting and Kymlicka (2006) as the 'progressive dilemma'; notably, it concerns the renegotiation of principles for economic redistribution with the recognition of diversity. The present economic and financial crisis in Europe has further exacerbated these debates as it has put under a magnifying lens the already stark contradiction between nationally framed welfare regimes (and the related fundamental principles of citizenship, democracy and social solidarity) and post-national social and economic conditions.

In today's context of individualized, ethnicized and flexible labour – indeed what Anton Hemerijck has labelled 'a nearly full part-time employment' (Hemerijck, 2001, p. 158) – there is a growing emphasis on the individual's autonomy and responsibility as a worker and as a citizen and a decreasing attention to social solidarity, as a norm or as an institution. While the concept of social class in its Marxist version may have lost some of its meaning as it is no longer the relationship with the means of production that is important, the notion of social inequality and social stratification acquires new emphasis as the distance between the winners and the losers of globalization and Europeanization becomes greater.

Indeed, the increased freedom and mobility of post-industrial and post-Fordist societies, the present time of 'fluid modernity', has melted 'the bonds which interlock individual choices in collective projects and actions – the patterns of communication and coordination between individually conducted life policies on the one hand and political actions of human collectivities on the other' (Bauman, 2000, p. 6). The very emancipation of the individual from the forces of nature or religious belief achieved in modernity has gone into a new phase, a 'stage B' of modernity. Thus, while free individuals in modernity were to use their freedom to find the appropriate niche in which to settle, and adapt to the rules and modes of conduct identified as appropriate for that location, argues Bauman, free individuals today have lost their stable orientation points. Citizens no longer have pre-allocated reference groups (such as those provided by class, kinship, ethnicity, religion and locality). Their point of reference is universal comparison. There are too many patterns and configurations available to the individual. The responsibility of the pattern-weaving is left entirely on the individual's shoulders, while patterns of dependency, interaction, cooperation or solidarity have become too volatile for one to rely on them.

This new freedom of fluid modernity has happened, however, in a context where the economic logic has taken precedence over any other political, ethical or cultural entanglement (Bauman, 2000). The new order is defined in purely economic terms. Economic, and hence instrumental, rationality is immune to non-economic challenges and concerns. The new order was legitimized by the desire of individuals to be free agents, argued Bauman (2000). However, this desire for individual freedom has released too many demons; it has led to excesses of deregulation, liberalization and flexibilization, leading to the entrenchment of the community and the welfare state, and creating human agents that are radically disengaged – they bypass one another rather than meeting with one another (Sennett, 1996).

The liquidity of modernity and the 'individualization' of the citizen is, however, not total. There are actually new configurations of class and inequality that are emerging today through the processes of both globalization and Europeanization. Indeed, old 'solidities' may still be important as individuals may still experience disadvantage in the labour market because of racial discrimination (see for instance the case of racialized labour in Bonacich et al., 2008), or an old 'solid' factor such as religion may remain as a source of community and solidarity, and an anchor in migrants' transnational lives (as in the study of immigration and religion in the USA by Peggy Levitt, 2007). There are also new solidities, new inequalities and privileges, new social classes that are being reconfigured in this age of globalization. Thus, migrants and other under-privileged groups who are forced to be mobile (the 'vagabonds' in Bauman's metaphor) are faced with new solidities of economic exploitation and socio-cultural marginalization. Under these conditions, these people may seek anchor in old community bonds or in the formation of new networks (Lee, 2011).

These complex processes of social change have contrasting impacts on citizens' feelings of social solidarity within the national state: citizens are both in need of some solidity to hold on to (whether it be the health service, or unemployment aid, or indeed family allowances); and at the same time they are increasingly questioning what is the scope of social solidarity, when one has trouble identifying with one's (national) community and when social stratification is determined no longer by national factors (the state, the stakeholders, the national market) but by transnational forces (international trade, global value chains, global competition, Europeanization of social and economic policies, international mobility of goods, capital and people).

European social model(s)

From a historical perspective, different European countries have developed their understandings of social solidarity and their social protection systems in different ways. Thus, for instance, while in Germany it was the question of poverty and the need for social protection by the state that arose in the 1870s under Bismarck, with an emphasis on the workers' question, in France it was more related to the enfranchisement of all male citizens above the age of 21 and, hence, with the political role of the people and the working class. Similarly, the most controversial issues in relation to social protection and welfare differ among European countries. In Britain the quintessential institution seen to represent the British welfare system has been the National Health Service (NHS), while in Germany it is more related to unemployment insurance and assistance, and in Italy it has more to do with pensions and the same was true in Denmark, while in France it related strongly to both pensions and benefits such as unemployment allowances (Barbier, 2013, pp. 24–5).

Indeed, social protection is nationally rooted in many functional ways. First, national protection is physically rooted to the related infrastructure (buildings, administration systems, documents, health cards or ID cards); it speaks the national majority language, and is regulated primarily by national law. It is national law that guarantees institutionalized solidarity and trust among people who do not know each other and will never know each other. In addition, clear-cut definitions and rules are necessary to manage beneficiaries and expenditures and to ensure that the system functions. In addition to these practical issues, social protection systems and notions of social solidarity are rooted in specific national political and administrative cultures.

This national framing of social protection contrasts with the efforts taken at the EU level to construct a set of European social policies. Indeed, there are two ways in which we can speak of a European social model(s). One is a comparative approach that looks at national social policies, compares welfare state institutions, public expenditure levels and labour market regimes, seeking to identify the special factors that have led to the formation of each specific national welfare system. A second line of research treats Europe as a whole and looks at common socio-economic and political processes as well as common trends among the different countries; it investigates their interdependencies as well as mutual influence. While acknowledging that welfare systems are national, it pays more attention to the emergence of an EU social policy and seeks to identify what sort of capitalism is European welfare capitalism, conceiving it as a whole that is more than the sum of its parts (Hay and Wincott, 2012).

In this section, we combine both perspectives. We first review the relevant literature on the different social models present in Europe, as these have been identified in the seminal work of Gosta Esping-Andersen (1990) and were later developed and modified, in line with wider socio-economic and political changes, as well as extended to include social reform in Central Eastern Europe. We then consider whether there is such a thing as a European social model or whether a European type of capitalism exists that is distinctive.

In our approach we pay particular attention to the weight of political culture as one factor that shapes principles such as social solidarity and related welfare regimes and practices (Barbier, 2013). Indeed it is not simply a question of institutions, or of organized class interests and their mobilizations. The configuration of each national social protection system has largely to do with the overall relationship between the state and the citizen as much as it has to do with the relationship between the state and the market. Historical experiences and processes of state formation are largely enshrined in current social protection regimes and play an important part in social policy reform.

Social policy theorists have identified five ideal-typical social models: the Southern rudimentary social model, the continental Romano-Germanic, the Nordic social democratic model, the Anglo-Saxon liberal-individualist, and the Central Eastern European model, which probably resembles mostly that of the Southern European countries (see also Adnett and Hardy, 2005). These ideal models differ from one another not only in the different types and degrees of social protection that they provide but also in their effect, in the type of social stratification that they actually (re)produce (Esping-Andersen, 1990, p. 23).

The liberal Anglo-Saxon model

The liberal individualist social model is also known as the Anglo-Saxon welfare regime. In Europe it is to be found mainly in the UK and Ireland (but is also the model that prevails in the USA, Canada and Australia). This model adopts a view of the welfare state as a residual institution that covers what cannot be addressed by the self-regulation of the market. While the welfare state covers all major areas, notably health care, unemployment and retirement benefits, family and disability support, its level of provision is relatively low. There is a strong concern within this model that people should not transfer responsibility for their own welfare to the (welfare) state. Welfare dependency should be discouraged: for instance, recipients of unemployment benefits have to show that they are actively seeking work. The Anglo-Saxon model privileges a notion of individual autonomy and responsibility, which goes hand in hand with economic (neo-) liberalism and is meant to support a flexible labour market. It guarantees a minimal level of livelihood for all, but it predominantly caters for the needs and desires of the middle strata, who are invited to satisfy their demand for superior welfare services through the private sector (Esping-Andersen, 1990, p. 26).

In Europe, the typical example of the Anglo-Saxon model is found in the British case. The classical period of the welfare state in Britain lasted between 1945 and the 1980s when Margaret Thatcher came to power. During the Thatcher years, several public institutions were privatized and a more *laissez faire* approach to social protection became dominant. The Thatcherite turn took Britain out of the orbit of a social democratic approach (with universal flat rate benefits, national health care and high levels of employment) into significantly reduced public spending, means-testing, and a two tier system of public-cum-private in many areas of social welfare. Remaining within a logic of personal responsibility for one's welfare, the New Labour period of the late 1990s and early 2000s increased public spending on welfare (and sought to improve the quality of services provided to users). At the same time, it encouraged the capacity of the individual to overcome their problems by themselves (see, for instance, the activation schemes for unemployed or underemployed people) (Taylor-Gooby, 2013). However, the liberal features of the Anglo-Saxon model took a new turn with the austerity that followed the financial crisis of 2008–2009. 'Big society' (Cameron, 2010) has been called upon to make up for the severe cuts in public welfare spending, while the 'undeserving poor' have been further stigmatized.

While such a system of flexible work, moderate social protection and strong incentives for self-regulating one's own level of social protection and assistance might seem to fit the globalization context best, the fragmented character of labour, the decline of trade unions and the individualization of employment patterns has brought to the fore two fundamental weaknesses. It fails to 'de-commodify' labour, if we are to use Esping-Andersen's terms. In other words, it fails to give the worker some degree of autonomy from labour market forces in a context where employment is increasingly precarious (see also McKay, 2013). Second, it inherently erodes the support of the middle classes for welfare expansion because these last see it as a system that benefits only the poor and the idle. It is also a system that provides minimal benefits that in any case would not satisfy the higher needs and expectations of the middle classes. In conditions of increased cultural diversity and intensified mobility, the system risks falling apart even if it is recast into a new label like Ed Miliband's 'One Nation' (Miliband, 2014) campaign.

The Continental Romano-Germanic model

The continental social model is characterized by a strong corporatist organization of work and welfare relations. The aim of the system is to guarantee a certain level of social rights and assistance to all citizens so that they can be relatively protected from the ups and downs of the economy and the labour market. The system is financially supported by relatively heavy indirect employment costs that are carried by both employers and workers.

The continental social model includes a universalistic coverage of all citizens, with, however, a modest level of coverage. The model generally does not involve means testing. But it includes a set of special schemes, programmes and measures of complementary pension funds or health services that cater for specific professional categories, notably civil servants but also the liberal professions and other privileged groups of workers. The continental model thus provides for a safety net but does not lead to a significant redistribution of income. It actually perpetuates status and class differences by providing further privileges through public channels to the middle strata and only minimal assistance to the poor.

The continental model leaves a lot of room for, or rather actually counts on, institutions other than the state to provide for citizens' welfare and social protection. These include primarily the family and wider kinship network, and the (Catholic) church and its social support services. Thus, considering the overall relatively low level of social assistance, day care for children, and health care for the sick and the elderly is either provided by relatives or actually bought (through the state cash for care allowances) in a segmented labour market of care, where mostly migrant workers are employed (Triandafyllidou and Marchetti, 2014). This model has important gendered effects as overall it discourages young mothers, or generally women, to take up paid employment as they have increased responsibilities for care of both the elderly and the younger members of the family within the home.

Of course, this is an ideal-typical model and there are important variations within the countries that are seen to conform to it. Thus, France, for instance, is characterized by a high level of social assistance to families and a wide network of child-care services, which promote women's participation in the labour market and socialize the costs of family-hood. Germany and Italy, by contrast, offer means-tested and rather low family allowances. In addition, public childcare facilities are very limited. Dual wage families have, thus, to rely on the support of grandparents or other relatives or turn to the market (whether to private childcare facilities or to migrant women carers, if they can afford either) to cater for their family needs.

The continental model, with its wide safety net and its corporatist structure, is probably the archetypical welfare regime that comes to mind to many people when one speaks of a 'European social model', not least because it is the system prevailing in the major European continental countries such as France, Germany and Italy. In the past this model has offered a high level of de-commodification of work by giving the state a central role in guaranteeing social protection. As such, it has been contrasted to the laissez faire policy of the Anglo-Saxon model, which gave primacy to market forces and individualism. Indeed, the continental model was a good fit for European nation-states: it reinforced a sense of national belonging, as the welfare regime contributed to the legitimacy of the state. In addition, its corporatist structure and the role of trade unions and professional associations also guaranteed that demands and protests would be challenged through these formal channels and be absorbed by the system. Indeed, security and stability were the main goals but also the main advantages that this system has offered in the postwar period. But all this seems to be changing in early twenty-first-century Europe.

The centralized public character of the continental model, its corporatist perspective and its in-built gender bias in favour of male breadwinners are elements that do not address the new realities of flexible work and fragmented labour markets. As high levels of coverage become increasingly difficult to afford (as global competition and international trade intensify, wages and welfare benefits are pushed downwards), welfare state provisions tend to decrease. In addition, the ageing of European societies puts the system at risk of implosion as contributors are not numerous enough to support the beneficiaries. At the same time, as new economic and political forces arise because of economic restructuring and social discontent, the privileges of some professional categories and groups are either scrapped because they are too expensive or contested because they are no longer legitimate. The rigidity of the system provides incentives for people to take up informal employment to evade tax contributions and employment legislation, while women are faced with a trade-off between work and family, eventually postponing family formation (Esping-Andersen, 1996, p. 82). In short, the main weakness of the continental system is probably its difficulty in keeping up with current socio-economic transformation processes and effectively addressing them.

The Southern European social model

The Southern European model may be considered a variant of the Continental Romano-Germanic social model presented in the previous sub-section. It is characterized by a rudimentary level of intervention by the state to regulate labour market behaviour and redistribute income and wealth. It is, rather, the family, the church and the local community that mitigate the effect of market forces on workers and provide for a safety net in case of ill health, unemployment or assistance in old age. Indeed, the system as initially developed in Southern European countries was characterized also by a large agricultural sector, and a low level of industrialization.

As Southern European countries (Greece, Spain, Portugal) developed socio-economically into a modest level of industrialization and created a stronger service economy, passing on to the post-industrial phase, their welfare systems developed characteristics similar to those of continental European countries and Italy. They thus applied higher levels of social assistance and social protection (higher unemployment benefits, expansion of family allowances, better pensions) even if these remained modest and were not means tested (for instance a family with two children might not receive any type of child support even if it lived in poverty). These countries, however, remained profoundly marked by a clientelistic type of politics that operated underneath the formal level of welfare entitlements to carve benefits for specific categories of workers or pensioners. Thus, there has been a wide disparity at the level of pensions or social assistance that different categories of workers received, let alone the fact that pensions or other types of benefits were occasionally distributed as 'favours' accorded to citizens by MPs or other members of the political elites, often to people that were not entitled to them.

In line with the continental social model, the Southern European one is also pervasively characterized by two levels of protection, one that is universal and relatively weak and another that is much better developed but that is afforded only to special categories of workers such as civil servants, or certain professions that have their own privileged health and pension funds.

The system is shaped by a profound mistrust between the citizen and the state and an appropriation of state power, including welfare services, by governing elites as a mechanism for distributing favours and buying citizens' support for them personally and overall legitimacy for the political system. In other words, the system does not respond to a formal logic of impersonal redistribution of income and wealth but rather to a highly personalized access to privileges and services regulated through complex networks of clientelistic power. Thus, the effects of social transfers, for instance, on reducing poverty and inequality were minimal even if a relatively wide level of social assistance has been provided (up until before the current crisis) to citizens through, for instance, an extraordinarily extended system of public pensions that were secure even if quite low (see also Matsaganis, 2013; Petmesidou, 2013).

The social democratic Nordic model

The Nordic or social democratic model has a significantly different approach to social protection than the other European social models outlined in this section. This model is universalistic; it puts a lot of emphasis on providing social protection and social assistance to all and not only to vulnerable or disadvantaged groups. Everybody has to contribute to the system equally and everybody should profit from it as equally as possible. In other words, the model does not compensate the 'losers' and punish the 'winners' but rather aims at promoting an equality of the highest standard rather than of minimal coverage.

The universalistic and equally generous coverage for all is based on employment and relatively high levels of taxation, but in compensation it contributes to forging a strong sense of social solidarity. It emancipates the individual from both the market and the family network. In other words, the welfare state intervenes not when the family resources are exhausted, as would happen in the continental model, but pre-emptively by providing for the costs of raising children or caring for the sick and the elderly.

As Esping-Andersen describes, this model is based on:

A fusion of welfare and work. It is at once genuinely committed to a full employment guarantee and entirely dependent on its attainment. On the one side, the right to work has equal status to the right of income protection. On the other side, the enormous costs of maintaining a solidaristic, universalistic, and a de-commodifying welfare system means that it must minimise social problems and maximise revenue income. This is obviously best done with most people working and the fewest possible living off of social transfers. (Esping-Andersen, 1990, p. 28)

Thus, the model encourages labour market participation but in an entirely different way than happens in the liberal individualist model. It is based on a strong sense of social solidarity with an equally strong notion of individual independence, made possible through the guarantees of state-funded welfare. In other words, it presents a peculiar combination of liberalism/individualism with socialism/communitarianism.

This model was predominantly developed in the Scandinavian countries in the post-war era. However, like all other social models described in this chapter it has undergone certain transformations with a view to responding to the changing needs of society and the economy. Thus, the model has had to put major emphasis on not discouraging the market but rather simply taming its effects on the workers/citizens. The model distances itself clearly from state socialism and the Central European social model discussed in the next sub-section, but also from left-wing socialist models that aim at maximizing transfers from one social class to another (Rothstein and Steinmo, 2013).

The Nordic countries categorized as having a social democratic welfare model, like all other countries, have had to deal with the challenges of increasing cultural diversity and the needs of a post-industrial economy in different ways. This has led to discussions over, on the one hand, the need to introduce reforms that would benefit the middle classes (highly skilled workers, professionals, civil servants) and, on the other hand, to reduce benefits and assistance for newcomers, that is, immigrants. In addition, there have been discussions on gender equality, environmental sustainability and, of course, multiculturalism. These discourses created opportunities for new political forces, mainly on the populist right wing of the political spectrum, to gain influence and propose liberal individualistic visions of limited social solidarity. However, different Nordic countries reacted in different ways. Thus, while in Sweden social democracy has been upheld and the multiculturalism approach has been favoured as a basis for integrating newcomers, in Denmark these considerations led to a partial overhauling of the welfare system through which migrants were integrated in Danish society. In Sweden, the primacy of individual social rights over obligations was maintained, while in Denmark an obligation to contribute was given precedence over the right to social assistance (Meret and Siim, 2013).

One of the main advantages of the Nordic model is that it upholds and further reinforces social solidarity within society, emancipates the citizen and legitimizes the state. It does not require a national mono-cultural framework to function even if cultural diversity does raise tensions within this model too. For instance, the question of women's participation in work outside the home can be a thorny issue. However, the model has shown a significant capacity to adapt to the differentiated demands of people for individualized choices and life styles without sacrificing a strong sense of trust, solidarity and a high level of social cohesion. Supporters of the model argue that its secret of success lies in its high quality universal coverage, which actually transforms the meaning of the welfare state as a general social institution rather than an assistance mechanism for the poor. The question, of course, remains open whether the Nordic welfare model only functions in countries with relatively small populations, a high degree of political stability and consensual politics, and a specific type of political cultural tradition that buttresses a common concept of social solidarity (even in the face of increasing cultural diversity).

The transitional Central Eastern European model

Central and Eastern European countries have experienced a radical change in their social protection systems along with their overall socio-economic and political transition to democracy and free market capitalism. After several decades of communist rule with a universalistic, employment-related system of social protection, where full employment was the norm, they transferred nearly overnight to the world of residual, even if still universalistic, social protection and a partial privatization of welfare services.

During the Soviet period, both employment and welfare were highly regulated. Wages were very low, while social benefits were substantial. Even though there has never been a 'golden age' of social policy under the communist regimes, social benefits were secure and so was employment. There was a high and broad level of social security, and earning differentials were very modest. There was a monopolistic organization of production and employment as well as of distribution of social services. The collapse of the economic system that supported social policy in the communist countries led to a radical reorganization of their social protection system. First of all, the three major guarantees that the previous system offered to citizens were removed: guaranteed employment, social protection via subsidized prices, and enterprise-based social benefits. Indeed unemployment grew dramatically, but there was neither a Soviet-type nor a Western-type safety net on which to fall back. Thus, rampant unemployment led to widespread impoverishment and deprivation.

The effects and pace of the change differed among Central Eastern European countries, as, for instance, the Czech Republic showed considerable economic dynamism and experienced low levels of unemployment, while most of the other countries in the region, notably, Poland, Hungary, Slovakia, Romania, Bulgaria and the Baltic countries experienced high unemployment rates and impoverishment of their populations. All countries gradually introduced basic schemes of unemployment protection and a universalistic pension scheme, albeit with a high number of pensioners and very low levels of pensions. Pension age was gradually raised to meet Western European standards. What was harder to reform was health policy, as these countries had had a universalistic health care system for a long time.

These countries faced significant pressures from international financial institutions to introduce a two-tier system with minimal universal coverage for pensions and a third-tier voluntary pension, or of minimal public health service and additional commercial private clinics. In addition to these changes, social assistance benefits such as child or family allowances became means tested and entitlements were tightened. Under pressure for market liberalization and privatization by the European Union and the International Monetary Fund, most of the Central Eastern European countries adopted a Continental model approach, in the sense that they provided for minimal coverage for all and allowed for the development of corporatist status-preserving sets of privileged provisions (in the form of special health coverage or pension funds) for the middle classes. Social assistance schemes and unemployment benefits have been cut back significantly in these countries because of budgetary constraints. Variations exist of course within the countries; thus Nelson argues that Hungary and the Baltic states have been developing their social assistance schemes more than other countries such as Poland or the Czech Republic (Nelson, 2010).

The social dimension of Europe

> Long lines of the unemployed caused by economic crises are the core business of the welfare state....These are precisely the kinds of emergencies that welfare state programmes and institutions are designed to deal with, so that when a financial crisis turns up we have routine mechanisms...for coping with its consequences. (Castles, 2010, p. 96)

In the wage earner society, for example in a society where the vast majority of citizens work to make a living, social protection is a genuine social relation that brings together the family and the state. Indeed, looking at Eurostat data on public expenditure for functions that are related to social protection we realize that social expenditure in European countries, if we also include education and culture, exceeds two-thirds of all recurrent public spending. In other words, social protection has been one of the main functions of the modern democratic state in post-Second World War Europe. However, the socio-economic and political context within which the welfare state operates has important implications. In other words, it is not only the level of expenditure that counts but the direction and type of services and allowances that it provides, which in turn contribute to the legitimacy of social protection and social assistance schemes.

Europe has been going through several ups and downs in its social policy in the last 60 years. Starting from a 'golden age' of the welfare state, which evolved hesitantly in the 1950s but developed into a full-fledged system in the 1960s and 1970s, it went through a crisis in the early 1970s after the oil price shock that European economies experienced. The period that started then and lasted till the late 1980s has been labelled as the period of the 'Great Moderation' (Hay and Wincott, 2012, p. 30) as welfare systems sought to address structural change while guaranteeing stability in social protection if further development (as was happening in the 1960s) was no longer possible

The post-1989 period has been marked by a dominance of the neo-liberal model, understood as a process of further liberalization of the market and privatization of social assistance and protection. The evolution of this period within Europe was largely uneven as Southern European countries, for instance, experienced political stability and economic growth and thus expanded their welfare systems during the 1990s and early 2000s, while Central Eastern European countries went through a particularly harsh reform and significant reduction of their social services in the same period.

During this same period, however, we witnessed a significant development of a European set of social policies within the EU framework (see also Jepsen and Serrano Pascual, 2006; Barbier, 2013). These policies have promoted a levelling-up of protection in several areas and have institutionalized certain norms such as gender equality or anti-discrimination. Indeed, their impact through norm setting and harmonization and coordination of national social policies is far from negligible. They have intervened in areas such as health care, labour law, labour management negotiations, agricultural policy, educational and training curricula. Similarly, EU policies have had an impact on national social policies through, for instance, the Stability and Growth Pact or the recent programmes imposed on Southern European countries and Ireland to enable them to achieve fiscal consolidation. Thus we may witness contradictory influences emanating from EU social policies. What is more interesting is that the EU has created a set of not only political but also socio-economic rights for EU citizens that are valid wherever they settle in the EU. Despite these important direct and indirect influences of the EU level, the latter remains fully dependent on the national level for implementation (even if significant amounts of social funding have flown from the EU to the more disadvantaged regions of the European Union). This is indeed what explains the persistence of distinct regional social models in Europe despite the intensification of Europeanization during the last 20 years.

Perhaps what European countries share in common today is the common pressure that they face to find ways to preserve their social protection systems while adapting to the rapid pace of socio-economic change that characterizes the twenty-first century, and how they face important fiscal pressures (Sapir, 2006). Indeed, the greatest challenge is to ensure flexible labour markets and economies that can take advantage of the opportunities that the globalization of the economy offers while still upholding a relatively high level of social solidarity and social protection. The task is complex as ageing populations, declining birth rates, the weakening of families as welfare providers, technological change and the related outsourcing of production and services to third countries, and the rise of an unequal service economy within Europe all contribute to creating new types of inequality and new insider–outsider divides within the labour market. Thus, the lower skilled and immigrants are more at risk, while some privileged constituencies of welfare benefits find it hard to shed their entitlements, inherited from the good times of the welfare state (Rhodes, 2013, pp. 144–5).

Concluding remarks

Under these pressures welfare models in Europe evolve and change. Thus, Southern and Central Eastern European countries under the tight grip of the economic and financial crisis are proceeding to further restructuring, by cutting down on what was already very modest social protection and social assistance schemes. They are indeed espousing more of an Anglo-Saxon type of model, keeping some Continental element, rather than turning to a Social democratic high protection and high solidarity approach to face the crisis. They have lowered protection overall and scrapped benefits from status groups and professional categories, while at the same time seeking to mobilize the labour force to work for significantly decreased salaries. The reform has its positive side effects of course too, to the extent that the drying out of state resources destroys the clientelistic networks and cleanses in-built corruption from the system by default: when there is no money to go around and no privileged health coverage or pension schemes to distribute, the overall system loses its legitimacy and may thus be substantially reformed.

Liberal individualist models and social democratic ones in Northern Europe appear to face the crisis by sticking to their own recipes. Thus, Britain and Ireland adopt further welfare cuts and otherwise strive to face the crisis through increasing employment and by activating the unemployed. The Nordic countries, which actually have generally been doing rather well during the economic crisis, keep up largely with their social democratic approach (Rothstein and Steinmo, 2013).

Under these circumstances it is difficult to speak of a European social model in the sense of a set of common features that bring the different countries or the different regions of Europe together. The crisis did not have the effect of pushing countries towards the same direction as cultural and institutional specificities, and national social and political forces have managed the crisis in different ways. But we may speak of a European set of social models that persist as we have outlined in this chapter. We may also outline that these different social models have one feature in common: the formal upholding of social solidarity as a shared value, and of a national system of social protection as a state institution that may develop in different modes and configurations but that provides social protection and social assistance to the citizen. These models are brought together by the common challenge that they face: notably to reform and reorganize constantly with a view to keeping up with the fast pace of economic change and globalization.

Chapter 9

Global Europe

A very concise analysis of the role of Europe in the world can be summarized in three statements made 20 years apart. In 1982, Hedley Bull wrote, '"Europe" is not an actor in international affairs, and does not seem likely to become one...', while Ian Manners in 2002 suggested that actually Europe through the EU was redefining 'what can be "normal" in international relations. Rather than being a contradiction in terms, the ability to define what passes for "normal" in world politics is, ultimately, the greatest power of all.' Round about the same time, Philip Alston and J.H.H. Weiler (2000) were arguing that 'the Union can only achieve the leadership role to which it aspires through the example it sets to its partners and other States. Leading by example should become the leitmotif of a new EU human rights policy'.

Europe in world politics from then to now

James Gillray's classic cartoon depicting William Pitt and Napoleon Bonaparte carving Europe and the world in spheres of influence is a perfect and straightforward representation of the role held by European powers in world politics for a long period of time. Through imperial adventurism and modern colonialism, Europe's military presence and economic dominance across most of the globe was unrivalled. From the Treaty of Tordesillas in 1494, when Spain and Portugal partitioned the new world they were discovering, until the end of decolonization in the twentieth century, the European powers exerted a massive influence over the rest of the world. Of course, the colonial empires and the individual colonies also massively influenced the historical development of their European mother countries, their institutions, their economy, their politics and even their national identity. However, more than being about the interactions that Europe had with the rest of the world, the essence of Europe's colonial history is that, for centuries Europeans explored, conquered, settled and exploited the natural and human resources of large parts of the world. Although colonialism was eloquently self-legitimized as a 'civilising mission', spreading Christianity, progress and modernity to the subject peoples, in essence, during this period of imperialism, Europeans were 'the aggressors in world society' (Giddens, 2007, p. 228).

Europe's hegemony over the rest of the world ended in the twentieth century. A.J.P. Taylor (1971) has argued that what had been the centre of the world merely became 'the European question' after the First World War. The First World War marked the end of European empires and the establishment of two new poles of power located outside the European continent and with global outreach, namely Washington and Moscow. The Second World War marked the end of European colonialism and the restriction of Europe's influence over the rest of the world. However, the security shield offered by the United States during the Cold War period led to Europe largely living 'in oblivion of the rest of the world' as Zaki Laïdi has quite simply put it (2008, p. 1). The end of the Cold War brought about a new, ambitious enthusiasm about the role that Europe could carve for itself and an aspiration to 'lead by example' in international relations. Respect for democracy, human rights and the rule of law, along with tackling climate change and promoting sustainable development became the EU's flagship initiatives in its efforts to position itself as a global power at the turn of the twentieth century. The new realities of the twenty-first century, however, brought Europe into an ever less familiar and less comfortable world. Economic globalization has placed intense competition and pressures on European economies and their high labour standards, asymmetric security threats have increased perceptions of insecurity within European public opinion, and, the hallmarks of liberal internationalism and multilateralism are challenged by the non-Western powers that have emerged (Ikenberry, 2011). Pushing forward the economic and political integration of the continent was seen by some as the only way through which Europe could remain relevant in the global age.

Against this background, in this chapter we examine the role of Europe in the world. We first consider the Cold War era and the different 'Europes' existing then: Eastern Europe and the role of the Warsaw Pact as an international political actor under the hegemony of the Soviet Union; Western Europe and its development into the European Economic Community and its efforts to distinguish itself from the USA while maintaining the advantages of the Transatlantic partnership. The core of this chapter focuses on the present role of Europe in the world and particularly on the normative, economic and security dimensions. We examine the different definitions of power that have been associated with the EEC/EU in the post-1989 and post-9/11 contexts. We discuss Europe's relationship with the USA as well as how the 'others' perceive Europe's global role. Finally, we conclude by examining the sort of power the EU can be in the global twenty-first century.

The Cold War and the emergence of Europe

The end of the Second World War is portrayed as a defining period for international relations, as it ended Europe's dominance in world affairs and replaced it with the division of the world between the USA and the USSR, and the decolonization of the Third World. The pre-war multipolar system centred on Europe was replaced by a new bipolar one whose points of reference lay outside the continent.

During the first couple of decades of the post-war era, European countries were generally rather introverted, focusing mainly on their reconstruction. For the larger powers of Western Europe, this was also a period during which they had to come to terms with two new realities. The first involved digesting the loss of their remaining colonies (which was more or less easy as the very different cases of India and Algeria suggest); the second involved coming to grips with their economic and security dependency upon the USA. As for the countries on the eastern side of the Iron Curtain, their international presence and outreach was essentially channelled through the COMECON. As satellites of the USSR, however, what they did promote beyond their borders was basically the influence of Moscow and not that of Central or Eastern Europe.

Until this period, the continent's relation with the rest of the world had been a dynamic and multi-directional one. What happened in Europe affected and influenced the rest of the world, and what happened to the rest of the world was relevant for Europe. This was increasingly less the case during the first phase of the Cold War, where what was happening in Europe had very limited consequences for the rest of the world, whereas events outside the continent deeply impacted the Europeans and their integration project. For example, the Suez crisis led France to embark on a nuclear weapons production programme, it encouraged Britain to turn more towards the continent, and it contributed to the signing of the Treaty of Rome in 1957 that created the EEC (McCormick, 2007). Similarly, a few years later, the unilateral decisions of the USA to go to war in Vietnam or to suspend the convertibility of the US dollar against gold and end the Bretton-Woods system undoubtedly contributed to British membership of the EEC and encouraged further economic integration in Western Europe.

The idea of Europe as a counterweight to American and Soviet power started to take shape from very early on during the Cold War. The level of destruction that characterized the continent after the Second World War on the one hand, and the extent to which it was dependent on American economic assistance (mainly in the form of the Marshall Plan) and security guarantees on the other, meant that there was little room for this idea to materialize. Indeed the power potential of Europe was subverted by a combination of its own weaknesses and the relative American strength in the face of the Soviet threat (McCormick, 2007, p. 52). Yet what did happen during the Cold War is that the nature of power changed.

Kenneth Waltz (1979) has defined power in the international system as the capacity of a state to affect the behaviour of other states while resisting unwelcome influence from those states. Traditionally, power has been associated with military capacity; in the late twentieth century, however, we observed a relative declining value of military power and a concurrent rise of other forms of power (economic or even cultural). Threats to international peace and security increasingly came from sources that required primarily non-military solutions. Environmental degradation, international crime, terrorism, poverty, irregular migration and pandemics raised the need to address these challenges through cooperation and collaboration, through sharing knowledge and pooling resources. In this context, the EEC/EU and its model of governance became increasingly relevant.

The EEC has always had a foreign and security policy dimension, even before actually developing and institutionalizing efforts towards a *common* foreign and security policy. The Preamble of the 1951 Treaty of Paris that established the European Coal and Steel Community (ECSC, predecessor to the EEC) defined its creation as a contribution to the safeguarding of world peace. The first phase of European integration was consciously focused on the elimination of old rivalries within Western Europe rather than in world affairs. The external policies that the early EEC began to formulate were the result of its constitutive nature and the fact that it had to integrate the foreign policy patterns and priorities of the member states towards their former colonies. Gunter Burghardt has observed that the EEC's increasingly important international role was in part a by-product of its internal achievements, and in part a necessity imposed upon it by the changes in the global system (1993, p. 254). In short, the global role that the EU began to develop was the result of necessity but also of aspiration.

The 1969 Hague Summit marks a high note on the EEC/EU's path towards developing a common position and framing its engagement in world affairs as more than the actions of the individual member states. By the 1970s, the EEC had developed into a trading power with a global outreach and it had also decided to embark upon an intergovernmental effort to coordinate the foreign policy agendas of the member states through the launch of European Political Cooperation (EPC), and even to distinguish itself from the USA on certain foreign policy matters.

The core documents that set the foundation of the EPC (the 1970 Luxembourg Report, the 1973 Copenhagen Report and the 1981 London Report) did not state what the member states intended to do together through the EPC but rather laid out the modalities of cooperation, coordination and possible collective action (Smith, 2008, p. 4). The EPC was useful in terms of encouraging exchanges and links between the EEC member states and, along with the Single European Act (1987), in preparing the ground for the Common Foreign and Security Policy (CFSP) that was agreed at Maastricht (1992). Aside from this it was not able to counter the 'political insignificance' of Europe, nor to frame coordinated European responses to the security crises that erupted as the Cold War ended.

The end of the Cold War brought the end of bipolarity. With the disappearance of the Soviet threat, the Transatlantic Alliance underwent a fundamental shift. Although the USA remained the only superpower, it encountered increasing political resistance from Europe across a number of issues, including the Middle East and climate change. As the Gulf war broke out in 1990–1991, the Europeans realized that they lacked the institutional machinery and military force to act in unison. Shortly afterwards, with the disintegration of Yugoslavia leading to a full-scale war in the heart of Europe, the EEC/EU saw the dire limits of its diplomatic powers as well as its inability to formulate and implement a common foreign policy. Given that the EEC was fundamentally a peace project, the wars in the former Yugoslavia dampened its new-found enthusiasm as regards the role that 'Europe' could once again aspire to in global affairs.

The peace function of the EU has been consistently emphasized as an accomplishment of the EEC/EU, and core to its fundamental identity and to the model of regional integration and cooperation that it wishes to project in international relations. Indeed, it is often asserted that peace on the European continent was rendered possible as a result of the role of the EEC/EU. Though undoubtedly fundamental, the roles of NATO and the USA's political and military engagement have probably been much more significant, both during the Cold War period and in the years after the Soviet Union's demise. Where the EU has succeeded without a doubt is in developing and supporting institutions and frameworks within which the malign legacies of European history have been confronted and rejected.

What sort of power is the EU?

Joseph Nye's (1990) classic distinction between 'hard' and 'soft' power and the ability of a country to persuade others to do what it wants without force or coercion has been particularly influential in defining the sort of global power the EU has attempted to be in world politics. In Nye's understanding, soft power includes a range of non-military foreign policy instruments, particularly diplomacy and economic pressures that yield results in international relations. Soft diplomacy has been defined as a diplomacy that resorts to economic, financial, legal and institutional means to export values, norms and rules and achieve long-term cultural influence. Soft diplomacy is not a 'soft imperialism' as the aim is not to impose values on others, but rather to propose a deliberation as to the sort of norms and rules that are necessary to bind the international community together in the post-Cold War/ globalization era. As such it has been a useful contribution to the work of the United Nations to promote global governance (Petiteville, 2003, p. 134).

Is the concept of 'soft power' suited to Europe's global role?

Robert Kagan (2002) extrapolated and interpreted this 'soft' power as weakness, arguing that the EU has no other option than to attempt to persuade other actors through multilateralism and negotiation because it lacks the military power and strength to do otherwise. This is undoubtedly a narrow understanding of power and of the ways in which global actors project their influence, particularly in an era of globalization and interdependence. But it does reflect a rather dominant view of the limitations that the EU faced and faces in projecting its influence beyond its borders. Concerns about the limitations of the EU's global, and often too silent, role have intensely occupied the political realm. The following statement by the then President of the European Commission, Romano Prodi, in 2002 is illustrative of such concerns:

> We cannot afford to remain an economic giant and a political dwarf. We must wield more authority in international affairs. Is it not time we spoke out for our values and matched words with action? More firmness is needed on many issues: human rights, the North-South gap, sustainable development, trade, energy, especially renewable sources of energy, the Kyoto Protocol and the International Criminal Court. If we are strong, we can do much in the world. But to be strong we must be united and speak with a single voice. And that calls for a more robust common foreign and security policy. (European Commission, 2002, Speech 02/600, 3 December 2002)

However, it is necessary to elaborate on the concept of soft power a bit further because it does not in fact reflect the sort of power that the EU attempted to project in the early twenty-first century. Soft power is a normatively neutral term as economic and diplomatic pressure may be in principle used to promote 'selfish' interests, or even to oppress or dominate. Reading through the texts and declarations of EU officials who aimed to formulate the EU's global role, however, we see a very different intention. If we take for instance a speech by Benita Ferrero-Waldner, European Commissioner for External Relations and European Neighbourhood Policy in 2006, she defined the EU's soft power in these terms:

> Our soft power promotes stability, prosperity, democracy and human rights, delivering concrete results in the fight to eradicate poverty and in achieving sustainable development. The European Commission alone provides aid to more than 150 countries, territories and organisations around the world. We are a reliable partner over the long term, and as the world's biggest donor we help bring stability and prosperity to many parts of the world. And we are a champion of multilateralism, standing at the forefront of a rule-based international order. (European Commission, 2005, Speech 06/59, 2 February 2006)

These are clearly normative priorities with altruistic rather than purely selfish aims, making the description of Europe as a 'civilian power' far better suited. In 1972, François Duchene was claiming that traditional military power was giving way to progressive civilian power as the means to exert influence in international relations, and that Europe represented a 'civilian power' that was long on economic power and relatively short on armed force. Civilian power involves the centrality of economic power to achieve national goals; the primacy of diplomatic cooperation to solve international problems and the willingness to use legally binding supranational institutions to achieve international progress (Manners, 2002). This argument was refuted by Hedley Bull, one of the most eminent representatives of the English school of international relations, who argued instead that the EEC (at the time) should seek to become self-sufficient in defence and security – a military power in short. The question of the EEC assuming a military dimension was quite controversial during the Cold War and in fact it was only in 1991 with the Treaty on the European Union that the member states signalled the intent to move the Union beyond a civilian power (Whitman, 1996; Manners, 2002). For some such as Jan Zielonka (1998), militarization was unattractive as it would weaken the EU's distinct profile of having a civilian international identity. While for others, it diverted the discussion to stalemate debates on the state-like attributes that the EU ought to or ought not to have. And for others still, there was a lack of willingness to match its economic power with a military one. These challenges therefore rendered the notion of the EU as a 'normative power' more appealing. Ian Manners has worked on the ideational impact of the EU's international identity/role and has convincingly observed that the EU represents a normative power in world politics and a changer of norms in the international system (2002). The Union's historical evolution, its hybrid polity and its constitutional configuration render its normative basis rather unique.

The EU as a normative power

The EU's normative base has developed over half a century of declarations, treaties, policies, criteria and conditions, driven by a desire to establish greater legitimacy. These norms comprise peace, liberty, democracy, rule of law and respect for human rights, and may also include (though more contested) social solidarity, anti-discrimination, sustainable development and good governance. Having a normative basis is not, however, sufficient to be considered a normative power; the ability to shape norm diffusion in international relations is also a requisite. Ian Manners has used the EU's international pursuit of the abolition of the death penalty as an illustration of the EU's normative power given that this objective is not instrumental nor does it bring any material rewards to the Union and its member states. Quite the contrary; it creates tensions in the EU's relations with the USA. He concludes that:

> The EU increasingly exercis[es] normative power as it seeks to redefine international norms in its own image. These features include the willingness to impinge on state sovereignty;... interventions in support of individuals;...the absence of obvious material gain from its interventions;...and the fact that the EU often faces international opposition from the strangest partners – such as the 'unusual suspects' of the US, China, Iran, Iraq and Saudi Arabia. (Manners, 2002, pp. 252–3)

The EU has undoubtedly contributed to establishing and codifying certain global ethical standards in foreign policy-making and in international relations (Gropas, 2006; Smith, 2008).

However, in practice, on the field, its performance has tended to disappoint. Though our vision of the EU's potential role as a global actor may be trapped by Christopher Hill's famous 'capabilities-expectations' gap, the reality is that the EU's influence in world politics has been 'weak' (Gnesotto, 1999). Its foreign policy has been more uncommon than common (Gordon, 1997), and it has certainly not played the peace-building role it had intended to play in the violent conflicts that followed the tragic failures of the Yugoslav wars in the 1990s. This has largely been because the EU is not a 'strategic actor' in the way the USA is, for instance. The EU has managed to build up an institutional framework that is capable of mobilizing the resources that a civilian power needs; however, it lacks a strategic vision in spite of Javier Solana's effort to draft a European Security Strategy in 2003 when he held the post of High Representative of the EU's CFSP. In the present conjuncture of crisis, preference for intergovernmentalism and strong disintegration tendencies within the EU make it rather unlikely that a strategic vision will be formulated any time soon.

Europe as a security actor

From the outset, security was at the heart of the European integration project. It intended to protect from the Soviet Union and its ideological and military influence, and it also intended to peacefully integrate Germany into the post-war system. Throughout the Cold War, efforts to establish a common defence community in Western Europe quickly collapsed. Lack of political will to move forward on the security front, increasing opposition to military expenditure from a society that preferred to see funds channelled into social services, and Western Europe's reliance on NATO are the core reasons behind this perpetual postponement of the organization of its security dimension. The WEU, founded in 1948, obliged all members to provide the necessary military and other aid and assistance if a member was attacked (Article 51, UN Charter). But, given the modest capabilities that were assigned to the WEU by the Europeans, this was more symbolic than substantial. It is NATO, essentially through the military power of the USA, that provided security to the western and southern flanks of

Europe and that projected Europe's military might, as part of the Transatlantic Alliance, into the bipolar world. It is NATO that projected Western Europe's security in the international arena. A sort of division of labour may be considered to have taken place with security and defence assigned to NATO, and thus under the influence of the USA, and non-military aspects of foreign policy increasingly considered as an area for common positions among the countries of Western Europe. It took the end of the Cold War and the prospect of unification of the divided continent to enable European security policy, as distinct from the Transatlantic Alliance, to develop (Van Eekelen, 2013).

The eastern parts of Europe were also unable to project an autonomous security identity in international relations during the Cold War. The countries of Central and Eastern Europe joined the Warsaw Pact, which was created by the Soviet leader Nikita Khrushchev at a time of diminishing East–West tension and with the aim to eventually negotiate away both the Warsaw Pact and NATO to Moscow's advantage (Byrne, 2013). The Warsaw Pact did transform into the military counterpart of NATO, but it did not give the Soviet alliance or the Eastern European countries an important security function. Ideology often overrode realist and objective strategic planning and it was unable to achieve solid agreement among the members about the nature of the threats that they had to address together through this Pact. Under Mikhail Gorbachev's reformist leadership the Warsaw Pact managed to achieve a meaningful role in international security by providing the framework, along with NATO, through which the military confrontation apparatus between the two blocs in Europe was dismantled.

The Cold War finally provided the context for one of Europe's most influential and dynamic institutions on security matters, the Commission on Security and Cooperation in Europe (CSCE). The famous '*Helsinki effect*' which resulted from the Helsinki Process is considered to have transformed the agenda of East–West relations and provided a common platform around which opposition forces such as Solidarity (in Poland), Charter 77 (in Czechoslovakia) and other democratic movements in Eastern Europe could mobilize. It provided the political space for democratic opposition movements to emerge in the Eastern Bloc. The Final Act of the CSCE, signed in Helsinki in 1975, mainly due to the redefinition of security that the Western

European counterparts provided, essentially undermined the viability of one-party communist rule. It also developed a set of confidence-building measures and a comprehensive understanding of security beyond its military aspects that contributed to the largely peaceful transitions to democracy after 1989 (Thomas, 2001; Wenger and Mockli, 2013). The emergence of a common European identity based upon respect for human rights and fundamental freedoms has been considered a key driver to the Helsinki process that contributed to changing international relations during the bipolar era. In effect, it was the European Community that insisted on including human rights on the CSCE agenda in spite of US and Soviet objections. This insistence on the part of the EC was a continuation of their 1973 Copenhagen Declaration on European Identity that formalized the commitment of the member states to human rights as central to the European identity. For the countries of Eastern Europe, it was economic motivation to establish closer relations with Western Europe that led them to agree to accepting respect for human rights as part of the 'package'.

So, how do these distinctive security dimensions relate to the sort of power that Europe represents in international relations? Has Europe, and more specifically the EU, developed into a civilian power as argued in this section? As a proto-military power? Or as a new kind of international actor?

The moves to establishing a common security policy in the post-Cold War era through the Eurocorps, the growing string of military engagements, or the Rapid Reaction Force suggest that the EU is no longer 'just' a civilian power. There is some reticence to admitting that the EU is no longer a civilian power and analysts such as Johan Jørgen Holsten have argued that the EU has retained its civilian qualities because questions of defence remain within NATO, whereas other analysts such as Stelios Stavridis have proposed that it is thanks to its militarization that the EU can finally act as a 'real' civilian power able to promote democratic principles in global affairs.

The debate on what sort of military capabilities the EU ought to develop is a long and elaborate one. Opinions have differed as to whether the EU should develop a stronger military dimension (particularly given the high budget costs and low public opinion support for defence expenditures), and as to how this military dimension can develop as complementary to the Atlantic Alliance, or, to put it more bluntly, as complementary to US military power, rather than to overlap or rival it. The comparative advantages of the EU in development aid and humanitarian assistance, its skills in peacekeeping and monitoring and providing technical assistance have been put forward as reasons for which the EU's security character should develop to complement the USA. However, the fact that the EU may have strategic values and objectives of its own (separate from the common Transatlantic ones), and the divergence between the European and US, or between some European and some US, approaches to dealing with the current security challenges, such as international terrorism, weapons proliferation and failed-states, have been put forward as reasons for the EU to develop in part its own security identity and to continue promoting the importance of non-military aspects of security.

The wars in Iraq and Afghanistan that followed the 9/11 terrorist attacks showed the limitations of the USA's unipolar authority and unilateral use of its military might in the current global world. Given the economic interdependence that defines world affairs, up until the outbreak of the global financial crisis in 2008 it was contended that the European model, based on multilateralism and interdependence, was more suited to the changing twenty-first century. The Eurozone crisis that followed, however, saw the rise of defensive nationalism and disintegration trends within the Union that severely challenged the assumption and hope for many that the EU was offering a softer, more inclusive model for international cooperation that would inspire interstate relations in the twenty-first century.

The EU and global trade

The EU's international presence and influence goes well beyond its foreign and security policy. In the current globalization era, traditional diplomacy and foreign policy are only part of the picture. Economic policy, trade, development cooperation and humanitarian assistance are the rest.

Trade has been a Community competence for decades and the position of the EU as a major trader has ensured that the EU has been a significant actor in both the GATT and the WTO. On the EU Commission website one can find ample data and statistics confirming the global relevance of the EU and its member states. In fact, the European Commission (2014) highlights in its website that:

- The EU is the largest economy in the world... with a GDP per head of €25,000 for its 500 million consumers.
- The EU is the world's largest trading block. The EU is the world's largest trader of manufactured goods and services.
- The EU ranks first in both inbound and outbound international investments.
- The EU is the top trading partner for 80 countries. By comparison the US is the top trading partner for a little over 20 countries.
- The EU is the most open to developing countries. Fuels excluded, the EU imports more from developing countries than the USA, Canada, Japan and China put together.
- The EU benefits from being one of the most open economies in the world and remains committed to free trade. (European Commission website, 2014)

The EU is a dominant trade power, so trade policy is naturally key to how the Union engages with the rest of the world and in defining the kind of global actor it is. It has consistently favoured a stronger multilateral trading system precisely because of the fact that it is a major exporter, and also because of its nature. The challenges concerning its internal coordination across the wide range of trade areas and the complexity of the EU decision-making processes mean that the EU pursues multiple, and often contradictory, trade policies. Young and Peterson (2014) have noted that, overall, the EU favours free trade and that in recent years there has been an alignment of European policy-makers with neoliberal ideas in the economic field. Where economic interests are muted then foreign policy objectives may prevail, whereas the EU manifests a protectionist behaviour in areas where internal political dynamics demand more stringent social regulations and protective measures.

While the EU undoubtedly has significant trade power resources, the extent to which these resources translate into influence is contextually specific. As the global trade arena has undergone deep changes through the rise of the BRICS, there are increasing instances of the EU being sidelined in international negotiations. The 2008 Doha Round trade negotiations of the World Trade Organization (WTO) are one such telling instance.

Moreover, it is questionable to what extent the EU has used its global trade power as an expression of its declared desire to be a global, normative actor. Its aspiration to reinforce democratic and human rights norms and values has not been reflected in a meaningful manner in its trade relations with China or Russia, for instance, and where action was taken, as in the case of Iran (or Belarus, Myanmar and Sri Lanka, countries with less geostrategic clout), this was after intense US pressure and stands out more as the exception than the rule in EU global trade behaviour (Young and Peterson, 2014, p. 224). Similarly, its Everything But Arms (EBA) arrangement, adopted since 2001 for least developed countries (LDCs), which grants duty-free, quota-free access to all products except for arms and ammunition, has had questionable results in these countries as a result of its inadequate safeguards and checks to prevent abuses and the intensification rather than alleviation of economic injustice in the world's poorest countries. Furthermore, considering that it has been proving increasingly unable to promote its interests through multilateral negotiations in the face of opposition from the emerging countries, the EU has in practice been de-emphasizing multilateralism through launching bilateral negotiations with some of its core trading partners.

This has led many analysts to conceptualize the EU more as a 'market power' than as a 'normative power'. The size of its market and its activist trade policy undoubtedly make it a global economic power, but one whose strength is showing signs of retracting.

And how do others see Europe as a global actor?

In spite of the deep challenges that the EU currently faces, the EU has become a significant international, and rather distinctive, actor. But in order to have the entire picture of the sort of global actor it is, it is important to also understand what sort of global actor it is perceived to be. Europe's relation with the 'others' has been a constant theme running through all dimensions of Europe. The question we explore here is how do (some of these) 'others' see the EU in world politics and the role that it has been trying to shape for itself?

Why does this matter? First, because the expectations, perceptions, concerns and even prejudices that the other actors on the global scene have of 'Europe' and specifically of the EU contribute to our understanding of the sort of presence that Europe has in world affairs. Second, because the sort of power that other actors perceive it to be may also influence their behaviour towards it, and consequently may also influence the effectiveness of EU policies and initiatives, but also the scope of action that the EU may have on specific issues and policy areas. And third, because external images, the representations that others have of an actor, affect and shape their identity. As already explored in previous chapters on European identity and Europe as Culture, labelling and tracing the contours of the 'others' contributes to identity formation; so, considering the dynamic nature of Europe's global role and identity it is interesting to examine how others perceive Europe.

The EU's global role and its identity in world affairs have largely been shaped through self-representation. While it is important to be clear and understand what the EU 'says about itself', it is equally relevant to understand what the world 'thinks' of the EU. This is necessary in order to do a 'reality check' between perceptions and realities and to address any potential cognitive dissonance between the two.

Research has suggested that the EU's political and social image is fragmented in the perceptions of non-Europeans. When they do have an opinion about the purpose of the EU it is often perceived as ineffective, and even if they do feel a political and cultural affinity with Europe, the perception is that it is largely irrelevant in their regional politics. Israeli perceptions of the EU are particularly telling here, where even though they describe a cultural closeness, they consider the EU to be a non-factor in the Middle East Peace Process. The Palestinians also view the EU as a marginal actor in the Israeli–Palestinian conflict. This is quite disappointing considering that the EU is the largest donor to Palestinian state-building efforts and that along with the UN, the USA and the Russian Federation it is a member of the so-called 'Quartet', which in 2002 launched a 'road map for peace' aimed at resolving the conflict (Lucarelli and Fioramonti, 2010). Other common themes in the perceptions of non-Europeans vis-à-vis the EU are its lack of internal unity and its persistent Eurocentrism, which appears to inhibit the EU from being a full-fledged actor in world affairs, while it often endorses a subordinate position with regards to the USA. This is the case across most of the Middle East, as well as in Russia and China, and they do not consider that the EU will play a leading political role in future decades (Lucarelli and Fioramonti, 2010). This paints a pretty bleak picture for the present and certainly affects future expectations as the EU is simply not regarded as a global power that 'calls the shots'.

A similarly disconcerting perception is also shared by stakeholders in international institutions such as the UN. The core challenges are lack of unity between the EU member states and the lowest-common denominator approach, combined with a complicated bureaucracy on foreign policy matters that are widely perceived as producing ineffective and unreliable decisions in the international arena. The economic relevance and importance of the EU is much more readily acknowledged (Lucarelli and Fioramonti, 2010), although increasing criticism is raised for lack of coherence between trade and development policies, its Economic Partnership Agreement (EPA) negotiations and a rather patronizing conditionality approach.

How the normative dimension is perceived is also of particular importance. The EU's approach to democracy promotion is acknowledged and in fact its emphasis on political dialogue is contrasted with the more 'aggressive' US approach. However, talk of values can ring hollow to the countries still struggling with the structural remains of colonialism (Giddens, 2007). Political conditionality attached to development aid and trade agreements is increasingly challenged by African partners in particular. This is especially the case as the rise of China or other emerging powers has facilitated access to financing and investment with little or no strings attached, in line with China's policies of non-intervention and respect for sovereignty (regardless of the regime in the receiving country). The EU has typically conditioned loans, giving development aid and financial assistance to reforms aiming at democracy promotion, good governance and corruption reduction. Although the results of the EU's conditionality approach are hardly encouraging, China's non-interference policy in order to secure 'growth at all costs' has been labelled as a 'rogue donor', whose actions may be damaging to Africa in the long-run.

Historical and cultural variables unavoidably frame the way each actor is perceived by the rest of the international community and how its policies and actions are labelled. It comes as no surprise then that conditionality risks being interpreted within a historical context as profoundly affected by colonialism and dependency in certain cases, or that specific alliances may be framed in terms of strategic partnerships and historical bonds between countries and communities. The EU does benefit from long experience in multilateralism and mediation between different cultures and interests. These may prove to be increasingly valuable skills and experiences in today's rapidly changing and shifting globalized world.

Concluding remarks

The presence of Europe in global matters and world politics goes far beyond the European Union's common foreign and security policy and the foreign and diplomatic policies of its 28 member states. It represents more than the aggregate of the EU's policies across all sectors of activity (Hettne, 2011, p. 31). As the EU has been growing as an institutionalized polity and through enlargement, so too has its presence in the world naturally increased.

At the same time, Europe remains a (regularly expanding) community of sovereign states, making it difficult at times to extract the common themes that it represents (McCormick, 2007, p. 166). As such, wide generalizations have been made in order to identify specific traits that characterize Europe's global power. For instance, it is generally assumed that since the late twentieth century Europeans have become resistant to using military options for the pursuit of their foreign policy goals, and yet the UK, France and many other European countries from Poland to Portugal have engaged in multiple military conflicts in recent decades. One trait that undoubtedly characterizes Europe's global power is its 'transformative power', which involves attracting and inviting the 'other' to become a partner and voluntarily adopt many of its ways, values, policies and principles. The past decade, however, has shown clear signs that the EU is facing relative economic decline, a lack of strategic orientation, declining legitimacy, and a loss of attractiveness both inside and outside Europe. In this current state, it needs to revitalize the European project; if it does not then what is its added value beyond the mere preservation of past achievements? How can it defy the risks of gradual marginalization and global irrelevance? (Emmanouilidis, 2012, p. 93)

The EU has been regarded as a uniquely cosmopolitan and internationalist power. Defined as a 'liberal superpower', it has been considered particularly well equipped for navigating through a post-modern international system (Youngs, 2010, p. 3). The EU has even been referred to as the world's most committed and effective promoter of liberal political rights, collective security and multilateralism. As regards its approach to security, it is considered one of promoting global public goods with an 'international civilian agenda'. The case has also been made that the EU is essentially the 'engine' driving the global system towards a rules-based multilateralism that underpins its own integration (see McCormick, 2007; Telo, 2007; Smith, 2008; Youngs, 2010). EU foreign policy is considered to be based on a series of normative principles, generally acknowledged within the UN system as being universally applicable. In short, the EU has been associated with post-modern values of peace, multilateralism, internationalism, soft power and civilian means for dealing with conflicts. And on economic matters, the emphasis has been on sustainable development, quality of life and protection of a just welfare state. But to what extent do these actually translate into a global role for Europe?

In 2009, Giandomenico Majone described Europe, essentially referring to the EU, as the 'Would-be World Power'. This description captures rather neatly the essence of the EU's efforts to become a global power in the beginning of the twenty-first century. In other words, in spite of half a century of cooperation in the field of external relations and a background of rich legacies of diplomatic outreach of its member states, the EU has been 'punching below its weight' as regards its global presence.

The current global changes require that the European Union persuades, once again, the anxious, and even a bit distrustful, public as to what its role in the world and in their everyday life is. The democratic peace thesis was relevant and meaningful in pulling the EU through the Cold War and post-Cold War periods. But it has been challenged as insufficient for a while now, and particularly since the EU's poor management of Yugoslavia's disintegration. Sustaining a zone of peace within and around the EU remains a prime task, as does its role in minimizing the risks that stem from climate change, global terrorism, pandemics and international crime. In the present conjuncture, given the recent developments in Ukraine and the Middle East and the EU's increasingly restricted influence in climate negotiations, its powers of persuasion find themselves in rocky waters.

The relative weight of individual European countries in terms of population, income and trade has been steadily declining in what is an increasingly non-Western world. At the same time, as Europeans see their influence increasingly restricted in world affairs, they are increasingly seen as being over-represented in international institutions (Tsoukalis and Emmanouilidis, 2011). International developments have long pointed to the fact that Europe is no longer the main pivot of global concerns. Some, such as historian Niall Ferguson, are convinced that the EU is an entity on the brink of decline and destruction. Others, such as policy analyst Marc Leonard, have spoken of the twenty-first century as a New European Century 'not because Europe will run the world as an empire, but because the European way of doing things will have become the world's' (2005, p. 143). Opinions differ on whether the current crisis will mark the irrelevance and collapse of the EU or whether it will be turned into an opportunity to make the EU the vanguard for change in Europe and the world.

The EU's global role or the values that it has tried to project in global politics have also raised much scepticism. The EU has often been derided for lacking international vision and for eschewing power. And while some critics have derided the emphasis on liberal values as naive, self-defeating and harmfully utopian, risking ideological overstretch, others have increasingly criticized the EU for tilting away from liberal internationalism (see Ferguson, 2007; Gray, 2008; Youngs, 2010).

The EU has been the most innovative experiment in political institution-building. It has also been widely successful in spite of the criticism that it receives. Precisely because of this, Anthony Giddens has argued that Europe can, and should, aim to be a developed regional power, with 'some considerable clout in the world affairs' (2007, p. 211). The development of a global role for Europe has been portrayed as both a necessity and an impossibility. If it is to play a meaningful role as an influential pole in a multipolar or a-polar, rapidly changing global world it is necessary to take a more pragmatic approach. Richard Youngs has proposed that, 'A cosmopolitan European foreign policy should be built on sobriety rather than missionary zeal. A form of "realistic Wilsonianism" ... European cosmopolitanism should be pragmatic, but neither indeterminate nor inconstant' (2010, p. 138).

The EU has exhibited an impressive potential to chart innovative paths towards more liberal forms of international power. This is certainly something to be welcomed and encouraged as we go forward in the twenty-first century.

Chapter 10

Europe is...

There are two answers to the question *What is Europe?* The short answer is that Europe is a space and a place. It is a space, defined by geography. It is a continent, indeed the second smallest one on the globe. It is a place in the sense that it is a territory that is imbued with meaning – it has specific social, cultural and economic connotations. Albeit most scholars writing on Europe and politicians involved in national or European politics disagree on what these defining elements of Europe as a space actually are.

The long answer is that Europe is first and foremost a concept that takes different shapes and meanings depending on the realm of life on which it is applied and on the historical period that we are looking at. At a given point in time, depending on the perspective we adopt and the situation in which we find ourselves, Europe may represent very different things. Thus, we should better talk about *Europe*s in the plural.

An additional feature of our longer and more nuanced answer about what Europe is consists of accepting that there is no absolute truth to be found, that there is no definitive answer to be given to this question. Europe is in the eye of the beholder. Indeed it is this dynamic and constructed aspect of the definition of Europe that this book has tried to highlight. Our aim has been to provide the tools and the elements for the interested reader to dig further and make up her/his own mind as to what Europe has meant in the past, in different spheres of social, political and economic life, what it means today, and what it can possibly signify in the future.

Given the size and ambition of the project, to review the concept of Europe from different perspectives and seek to answer the question in a comprehensive, social-scientific and yet accessible manner, some compromise was necessary. Thus, in each chapter we have had to adopt and review some theoretical arguments and neglect others, to select some views and topics and disregard some thinkers or questions, to dig deeper into some challenges and discuss others more superficially. This book is the product of critical scientific inquiry but does not claim to offer an objective view of what Europe is. It rather offers a critical, though partial, perspective, our perspective, on what Europe is.

Reviewing the different definitions of Europe and its shape in different historical periods, we have organized our inquiry into eight dimensions, as if it were a scale on which to answer step by step the 'What is Europe?' question.

The historical vewpoint

We first surveyed the concept of Europe and its evolution through *history*. We argue that the concept of Europe has been rather unimportant for a good part of the last 2500 years. Even if the cradle of Europe is presumed to be classical Greece, we find that Europe as a concept hardly existed at the time. In addition, until the nineteenth century a belief in Europe as a culture, community, civilization or centre of political power has been rather weak. It was never a driving force of historical events. The concept also significantly changed in content, geographical location (shifting west and north), and points of reference, shifting from classical Greece, to ancient Rome, to Christianity, leading on to the exploratory missions of the fifteenth to seventeenth centuries. Thus, Hellenic Europe on the one hand provides the mythical foundation of today's concept of Europe, but was actually geographically located on the south-eastern part of the Mediterranean and on the area that lies largely in today's Middle East. This early reference to Europe was the centre of the opposition between Hellenes and the Barbarians or between Greeks and non-Greeks. Some classical thinkers indeed identified Greece with Europe and Persia (the Barbarians) with Asia. These proto-conceptions of Europe point to a cultural concept and are inextricably linked to the classical Greek heritage. However, they should also not be taken at face value, as what Europe meant then has been reconstructed through the lens of what Europe and the 'European civilization' is today, hence emphasizing ancient Hellas being its intellectual cradle.

While the concept of Europe survived through Hellenistic times and through the Roman Empire, it acquired some currency after the division of the Roman Empire into western and eastern. Thereby, Europe became westernized while the eastern part of the empire became orientalized, as Delanty concisely put it (1995, p. 20). Through the centuries, and although Constantinople was greeted as the new Rome, the Byzantine Empire was increasingly orientalized and Europe moved westwards. It was in the organization of Christianity into a single powerful Catholic Church in much of the European continent that Europe found a new cultural content and a reinforced unity. Christianity and the community of Christians, Christendom, became vehicles for the concept of Europe to survive and gradually also acquire some geopolitical meaning. After the birth of Islam in 700 AD, and the spread of the new religion across North Africa and in the Iberian peninsula, Europe found in the Moors and in the Muslim religion a suitable threatening 'other'. The old Persian cultural 'other' was now transformed into an actual military and political threat – that of the Arab conquerors. Christianity unified, as a cultural glue, the peoples and cultures of the former Western Roman empire and its more northern territories, including also the Barbarian tribes that had come from the north and had been converted to Christianity. Germanic Europe emerged in the tenth century, which along with the Papacy in Italy made Europe into a suitable cultural, political and geopolitical signifier that distinguished the continent from the Arabs and the Muslim world, and from the Byzantine Empire and its own eastern version of Christianity.

During the Middle Ages the concept of Europe remained, however, largely unimportant, subjugated to the much stronger cultural and political element of Christianity. It was in the centuries of the great discoveries in the fifteenth to seventeenth centuries that Europe emerged as a self-conscious concept. The kings and princes of Europe who went to discover the new lands, and later to 'civilize' the indigenous peoples that they 'discovered' there, were now considered 'Europeans'. While the motivations behind these discoveries and colonial expansion were economic and military, their justification was cultural and political, covered by the name and symbol of a Christian Europe.

Throughout this period, the racial profile of Europe as 'white' became also more visible and this racial connotation was further reinforced by opposition to the Arabs and the Turks, who were darker in complexion. However, the sixteenth and seventeenth centuries were marked also by the religious wars and divisions within Europe. Anti-Roman Catholicism culminated in the Protestant Reformation. Indeed, the notion of Europe bears in those times the seeds of its disunity: it was by incorporating but also silencing internal divisions among Christians and the Jewish traditions of Christianity that Europe managed to emerge as some sort of common cultural concept, although with limited, if any, political and geopolitical purchase.

The notion of Europe acquires importance in modern times as the nation-state emerges as the predominant form of geopolitical power. It is in the universalism of the particular, in the celebration of the nation-state and the conflicts and wars that nationalism brings, that the necessity for unity and peace and the potential of an overarching cultural and political as well as geopolitical concept of Europe emerges. The tragedies of the First World War and particularly the Second World War led to the most developed project of unifying and celebrating Europe. Perhaps one element that can be retained from the historical excursus over the meanings of the term Europe is that it is when it is most contested that Europe emerges as important – a bit like collective identity in general: it is by its absence or crisis that it becomes most visible and felt.

What we learn from this brief review of the evolution of the concept of Europe in different periods and in different realms of life is that it is fluidity, historicity and the need to adopt a critical self-reflective mode that should guide us in thinking about Europe.

A political idea of Europe

Indeed this critical and self-reflective approach is our guide for the second grid, which looks at how Europe has been transformed from a rather weak and ambivalent concept to a project, or rather *a set of different political projects* put forward in the nineteenth and twentieth century by statespersons, intellectuals and politicians with a view to uniting Europe. Our analysis shows that these projects differed greatly among themselves in terms of their political and socio-economic aspirations as well as their cultural content.

Napoleon's early conception of Europe in the early nineteenth century involved conquering the continent and attempting to unite it politically, administratively, economically and culturally but failed because it was a conquest rather than a union that he forged. Metternich, the Austrian Chancellor, took the baton after the end of the Napoleonic wars, seeking to reinstall the pre-French Revolution conservative status quo, but obviously this was no longer possible as the Spring of Nations had begun. The Holy Alliance between Prussia, the Austro-Hungarian Empire and the Russian Tsar could no longer offer a dominant narrative, and France, Britain, Spain and Portugal stood out as liberal powers seeking to have their say on pan-European matters.

The second half of the nineteenth century was characterized by the parallel disintegration of the former empires and the difficult birth of several of the largest European nation-states (Germany and Italy). Nation-states also started emerging in the south-eastern part of the continent through the dissolution of the Austro-Hungarian and Ottoman Empires, even if this process took well into the twentieth century before it was completed. While some of the positive political reforms of this period, notably democratization, parliamentarization, and expansion of franchise, can be characterized as common European traits of these socio-political processes, at the close of the nineteenth and start of the twentieth century Europe was more divided than ever, marked by aggressive nationalism, opposed state powers and spheres of influence, and a 'boiling' working class that mobilized for its rights (see Marx and Engels' reference to the spectre of communism that was haunting Europe, 1888, p. 2).

Indeed, it is no wonder that the second decade of the twentieth century brought with it the First World War and a magnitude of destruction and loss of human life that had never been imagined before. It signalled the beginning of the era of 'total war'. It is probably in the aftermath of such destruction that several unifying projects emerged in this period. One of the best known is that of Count Coudenhove-Kalergi and his Pan-Europe movement, with its dream for a United States of Europe. However, the quest for unity in Europe was to be hijacked by the fascist and Nazi projects for an ethnically cleansed totalitarian Europe. Their project, fortunately, failed and through the ashes of the Second World War the contemporary project of a united Europe emerged.

However, this project was fundamentally flawed by the internal political division between Western and Eastern Europe, between free market liberal democracies and communist regimes. Furthermore, there were also the peripheral divisions of Nordic Europe, which sought to stay outside the risky power balance of the Cold War, and the dictatorial regimes of Franco in Spain and Salazar in Portugal, which managed to stay in power well into the 1970s. The unification of Europe and its French (Jean Monnet, Robert Schuman) and Italian (Altiero Spinelli) architects was thus limp. However, the overall climate of the post-war decades was characterized by a strong pro-European movement carried forward by well-known federalists such as Henri Spaak, Fernand Dehouse, Alcide de Gasperi and Andre Philip. While the emphasis at the time was on peace and prosperity, the cultural, and later political, elements of a European unity started to be forged. It was in this perspective that the Southern European countries were incorporated into the EEC in the 1980s.

It was of course only after 1989 and the reconnection of Eastern and Western Europe and the gradual incorporation of the Nordic countries that we have reached the level of unity and, of course, also the level of internal contestation and discontent that we experience today in European politics.

Reviewing critically the different projects of uniting Europe that developed in the last two centuries, we could summarize the idea of Europe as one that has essentially taken three core approaches. The first is fundamentally one seeking the regeneration of Europe through its past grandeurs. These visions have looked into the past, often recreating or reinterpreting it, emphasizing the common roots of Europe's culture and identity, or its distinctive characteristics whose integrity had to be maintained. The second approach is one of preservation in the face of contemporary challenges from within and from the global arena. The third looks into the future and involves the generation of a new, different future; Europe frames a condition to aspire to, a political goal to be accomplished in order to break from the past or from conditions of degeneration, decline and weakness. In all the forms that the idea of Europe has taken, Europe has been the 'self' and the 'other' bound into one. Although each of its constituent parts (countries and peoples) considers itself European and rightfully claims shared ownership of Europe's history, its values and civilization, this identity is simultaneously an elusive one because the centre of power is often seen, with a certain anxiety, as being 'elsewhere'.

Is there a common culture?

Our third reading grid as to what Europe is has been that of *culture and values*. In recent decades, historians, sociologists, anthropologists, political scientists and philosophers have taken a strong interest in exploring the cultural dimensions of Europe and the signifiers of European culture, European heritage, the cultural identity of Europe and the extent to which it is different from or similar to 'Western' culture, as well as how it is perceived by Europeans in the eastern and western, northern and southern parts of the continent. For some, the idea of a European culture and set of values has been a socially constructed discourse that has transformed through time, responding to changing socio-economic and political conditions. Others have emphasized ruptures and disagreements within such historical discourses on European culture and values, pointing to the impossibility of speaking of a single European culture or set of values. Indeed, our perspective focuses on a *parcours culturel* that seeks to uncover the dominant, the alternative and the dissenting definitions of the term 'European culture'.

We thus discuss European culture as a set of cleavages along which the European cultural elements and currents can be organized. The first cleavage or the first tension in the European cultural path is that of racism versus anti-racism and equality. The enlightened modern Europe after the tragedy of the Holocaust builds its culture on the basis of a condemnation of racism in all its forms. Nonetheless, not only is there an inherent sense of 'superiority' in the construction of a European culture (seen as the 'mother' of all cultures, the archetype of modernity and progress) but racism, while in theory eradicated, still persists against specific groups, particularly in the form of a latent (or more pronounced) anti-Semitism and racism against people of Black colour, as discrimination against the Roma (who being the only European minority are constructed as non-European and non-adaptable to modernity because of their special cultural traditions), and more recently as Muslimophobia, as a fear of the Muslims and a view of Islam as incompatible to Europe's culture and values.

The second cleavage that permeates a notion of European culture is that of religion versus secularism and the appropriate degrees of the latter for liberal democratic societies in Europe. Thus, while Europe has gradually grown unchurched, the relations between church and state and the role of religion in public life remain contested matters. The tensions in this domain are manifold; they include tension between the Islamic and the Christian currents, but also among the Protestant, the Catholic and the Orthodox Christian currents, and between the atheist and religious views.

A third cleavage that marks European culture is predominantly ideological between the left and the right, between a view that privileges liberalism, individual autonomy, competition and the pursuit of freedom at all cost, and one that favours a sense of solidarity, community rights, social justice and social protection. While the distinction may take its more pronounced form in politics, it has important cultural ramifications as it defines social and personal relations, quality of life choices and views of what a good life is.

Overall, we argue that the plurality within the European culture (or European civilization) develops at two levels. First, Europe can be conceived as an 'intra-civilizational constellation' composed of a number of civilizations, which, interestingly, all appear in pairs. We thus speak of the Greco-Roman or the Judeo-Christian, the Byzantine, and the Slavic-Orthodox or Slavic and Orthodox traditions. Another version of the European culture includes the Jewish diasporic tradition, the plural realities of the Ottoman Empire and the encounters with contemporary European Islam. Second, Europe includes a transcontinental dimension of inter-civilizational encounters. This approach highlights the influence of the non-European world on the construction of a European culture through opposition or the 'mirror' effect. From trade to violent exchanges, colonization, imperialism and travel there has been a mixing, exchange and learning between European and North American, Asian, African or Latin American civilizations.

Interestingly, this plurality of cultural traditions perhaps offers the potential (but not necessarily the reality) of an open constellation that can accommodate past differences and new minorities or new populations and their own cultural traits, contributing to a new synthesis of the European culture and carrying forward the European *parcours culturel.*

So is there a European identity?

The fourth dimension addressed in this book refers to the ever-present discussion over the (non-) existence of a strong *European identity.* It is our contention that European identity is, like all collective identities, in the eye of the beholder: it is shaped by the socio-economic, national, subjective and objective circumstances of the subject that expresses it. It can be enacted or simply expressed through discourses. It is one among many collective identities that people have and is in constant evolution. There is no essence of a European identity that has always existed and that remains immutable. European identity is part of a multiple set of identity features that may form part of an individual's identity and its salience varies not only among individuals but in line with a given context and situation.

The question arises for many people whether European identity is like national identity, notably a primary political identity forged on a set of common cultural and civic features that are shared by all Europeans, or whether it is an umbrella type of higher order identity, compatible with the citizen's primary loyalty to the nation. We argue that while both cultural and civic elements are present in the constellation of a sense of European identity (and in its varied expressions), it cannot actually be considered a primary identity that would replace the national one. It rather emerges either as a higher level of identity that encompasses the national or is an intertwined level that offers a new lens through which to look at national belonging but also gives the possibility of nationally framing what Europe is. Indeed, the conflictive model in which national and European identities are understood to be in an antagonistic or zero-sum relationship risks actually misunderstanding and misrepresenting the question of what kind of a European identity exists or may further develop.

The question of whether European identity is primarily political or cultural can be answered only with reference to a specific historical moment. Thus, today, European identity is predominantly cultural in character and not political. It goes hand in hand, sometimes in tension, other times in mutual support, with different national identities, but it is nowhere near substituting them. Actually it is its cultural connotations that make European identity today compatible with strong national identities.

European identity is also stratified in terms of class and ethnicity. The possible emergence of a collective European identity appears stronger among middle class and educated people who have the opportunity to travel and be exposed to realities other than their own. At the same time, while European identity is pretty much forged on the basis of the 'unity in diversity' slogan, this *diversity* is actually ethnically and religiously circumscribed. Migrant communities or minority religions often experience European identity as an exclusionary and discriminatory concept that makes them stand out as different. The limits of what kind of diversity is included in the 'unity' has been painfully emphasized through events of the last 15 years, particularly with reference to Muslim communities whose sensitivities to freedom of expression or blasphemy have been stigmatized as illiberal and un-European. While the question of how much and what kind of diversity can fit in European unity and identity is far from settled and has no easy ready-made answer, the ways in which minorities of different kinds (ethnic, religious, linguistic) experience their 'Europeanness' remains particularly important.

Borders: both ideological and geographical

Discussing the cultural and identity dimensions of Europe, the question of *borders and boundaries* arises. Defining what Europe is involves also setting its boundaries, determining where Europe starts and ends. Borders are integral to all visions of Europe.

The first question that arises here is where does Europe end? Or also where does it start? The end or start of Europe in the West is often assumed as clear: it is defined by the Atlantic Ocean and by the Northern Sea. It is the eastern border that raises more preoccupation: what belongs to Europe in its eastern outermost corner or its southern periphery remains a little fuzzy. At the risk of developing a circular argument, we argue that the question of where do Europe's boundaries lie has significantly defined Europe's history and identity and cannot be answered in an objective way. A geographical demarcation of Europe cannot be free of cultural and geopolitical elements that are in turn historical – they are historically situated and change in time.

Perhaps what is most relevant to retain from a discussion of Europe's borders is that their importance has varied; we may speak of the rise and fall of borders and *bordering*. While at the time of Empires borders were fuzzy in general and Europe's borders were also moving and fluid, borders have hardened with the advent of nation-states. The requirement for hard and neat borders between countries has also created the necessity of defining in a hard and fast way where Europe starts and ends. However, this clearly has been a matter of power: the power of those who can decide which country belongs to Europe and which does not, and the power of those outside Europe asking to be part of it (symbolically or, today with the EU, politically). The whole twentieth century was certainly an active bordering period with the re-designing of borders as an outcome of each of the two world wars. In addition, borders were quintessential in the Cold War world order. They were also heavily militarized. At the close of the twentieth century and beginning of the twenty-first, we may, however, consider that there is a relaxation of borders as the European Union keeps expanding and embracing new territories and also engaging into what has been termed a 'neighbourhood' policy, which aims at forging close cooperative relations with those 'beyond the border'. This is of course also a period of high debate and contestation about those 'borderlands' (Turkey) who might be on the inside or the outside of the border. It is in these discourses where one realizes how much borders are a social and political, as well as economic and military, construction rather than geographical givens.

European borders today coincide with EU territorial borders. They are 'hard' and securitized with a view to controlling the mobility of people, while capital and goods are allowed to flow smoothly in either direction. This shift of Europe's edges from being frontiers and boundaries to becoming highly controlled borders is in opposition to the trends in European culture and identity outlined in this chapter, which emphasize internal diversity, plurality and different forms of engagement and exchange with the 'other(s)'.

A European political bloc?

A sixth dimension on which we can define Europe is the *political* one. Politics in Europe have been predominantly territorial, framed within the nation-state. Any political dimension of Europe has had more to do with a sum of the national political dimensions rather than with a proper European transnational political dimension. Within this national framing, political mobilization and confrontation within European societies have been characterized by cleavages as defined by Lipset and Rokkan. We have the classical core tensions between centre–periphery and between church and state, the sectoral tension between a declining agricultural sector and a developing industrial sector and their respective interests, and of course the class cleavage. In the late twentieth century, a post materialist turn in politics with the rise of the peace and environmental movements in the 1970s, and the overall post-materialist turn in politics ever since has reframed many of the issues. But economic interests and social concerns have taken a back seat in the early twenty-first century with the emergence of the cleavage between the winners and losers of globalization and European integration – what Kriesi et al. (2012) have called the integration versus demarcation cleavage. Indeed, this cleavage, while apparently socio-economic, is also motivated by cultural concerns about a loss of autonomy and authenticity. These six cleavages are European in character to the extent that they are common, even if with varying degrees of importance, across most European countries.

While politics in Europe remain remarkably tied to the national framework, there is a strong interaction and mutual influence (whether positive or negative) among European societies. It is our contention that national politics in Europe are organized along a common European political map that has shaped national political structures and political ideologies. This common European political map is organized along two main ideological axes that interact in complex ways. The first axis concerns the historic opposition between authoritarian and libertarian values, which was most distinctively expressed in the nineteenth century by attitudes to the French Revolution and the liberal and democratic movements that followed it across the continent. Second, there exists a value cleavage between individualism and collectivism, where the former is wary of big government and strong social institutions, whereas the latter stresses the need for cooperation and collective institutions that further common interests. These two axes organize politics in Europe and shape answers to the three fundamental political questions: what is the role of the state in managing the economy and the means of production? How should we manage and address social inequalities? And, how can different political identities coexist?

Against this background, we identify seven political currents that have characterized political life in contemporary Europe: liberalism, socialism and social democracy, communism, conservatism, Christian Democracy, the extreme right, and the Greens. What is perhaps common and European in these political currents is the liberal democratic tradition and its opposite, notably authoritarianism. After all, contemporary European political history is characterized by the struggle between authoritarian/totalitarian and democratic forces and currents. Indeed, the politics of the twentieth century are marked by fascism and Nazism but also by the dictatorial regimes in Southern Europe until the 1970s, and of course the totalitarian regimes in Central and Eastern Europe until 1989. From this struggle between the two forces, which is not yet completely settled if we look around at how radical right-wing parties are gaining influence in several European countries, a strong, even if not unproblematic, adherence to the principles of liberal democracy emerges as typically European. Indeed, what is special about European democracy, alongside its political features of liberalism and moderate secularism, is its social dimension.

If the opposition between democratic and authoritarian currents and legacies in Europe remains alive and kicking, we cannot of course ignore the main political feature of the end of the twentieth century, notably the dismantling of left- and right-wing ideologies as we knew them and their realignment, most forcefully during the recent, and partly still ongoing, global and specifically European financial crisis. As Gianfranco Pasquino has argued, we are not witnessing the end of ideology, however, but rather the end of ideological commitment as well as a growing disaffection of citizens with politics and a decline in electoral participation. This ideological deflation does not make the winners and losers disappear or merge with one another. It rather reinforces the integration–demarcation cleavage emphasized by Kriesi et al (2012).

Along this challenge of increasing inequality and ideological flattening, we also witness a transfer of politics from the national to the global. This shift is not one of changing allegiances of the citizens but rather of increased interdependence among states to address complex transnational challenges such as those of climate change, but also security or even diversity. This shift towards the global is partly mediated by the European, not only in institutional terms through the European Union institutions but also in symbolic terms through a sense of being an active part of a bigger whole, which shares some common political structures and values as outlined in this chapter. Indeed, what characterizes the political dimension of Europe is a strong national territorial framing, an equally strong and close interdependence and interaction, and a paradox of fading ideologies despite increasing social inequality in terms of both opportunity and outcome.

A European welfare state?

It is this political challenge for the future of Europe that brings us to our seventh dimension: the social element in the 'What is Europe?' question. The *social dimension* refers to policies that aim at taking care of the most vulnerable populations in society, on the basis of a shared notion of social solidarity. Even if the exact breadth and depth of this social solidarity may differ among European countries and so may influence the welfare systems that each supports, there is a view that European countries have put great emphasis on their systems of social protection in the post-war era in particular, thus creating a distinct European model (or indeed a set of European models) that share some common characteristics, and that are different from what happens in other parts of the Western world or in other continents.

The short answer to whether there is a social Europe or a single European social model is negative, even if in the last couple of decades an EU level of social policies has emerged. However, we may speak of a European set of social models that persist as we have outlined above. We may also outline that these different social models have one feature in common: the formal upholding of social solidarity as a shared value, and of a national system of social protection as a state institution that may develop in different modes and configurations but that provides social protection and social assistance to its citizens. These models are brought together by the common challenge that they face: notably to reform and reorganize with a view to keeping up with the fast pace of economic change and globalization. Thus, the answer here is quite ambivalent and ambiguous: there is very limited commonality among different national social models of European countries but there is a common challenge that shapes them in the same direction. However, the end product, the national welfare state, remains quite different and open-ended.

Is Europe a political player or is it on the sidelines?

Our eighth and last dimension concerns what or who Europe is in global politics. Indeed the role of Europe as a global power can be read as one of constant decline, whether our starting point is Hellenic antiquity, the Roman Empire, Byzantium, the Middle Ages, the colonialist expansion or the Cold War. Indeed, a contemporary account of Europe in global politics may start by saying that Europe's hegemony over the rest of the world ended in the twentieth century. The First World War led to the disintegration of the European empires and the emergence of two new poles of power located outside the European continent and with global influence, notably the USA and the Soviet Union. The end of colonialism was further precipitated by the Second World War, which further limited Europe's influence over the rest of the world. But it was probably the Cold War that provincialized Europe in global politics as the continent hidden behind the protective shield of the USA or under the shadow of the USSR.

However, while Europe lived in the straitjacket of the nuclear threat and in a militarized peace, important transformations have been happening in the world that contributed to the transcendence of the Cold War logic. Namely, social and political challenges, such as climate change, international crime, terrorism, irregular migration, pandemics and food security in the developing regions of the world, required a level of cooperation and pooling of resources through regional governance structures. Thus, while under the shadow of US economic assistance (through the Marshall plan) and military protection (through NATO) the idea of Europe as a new global actor timidly emerged.

It was not surprising, therefore, that in the post-Cold War era new ambition and enthusiasm emerged about the role that the reunited Europe could carve for itself as a regional actor that 'leads by example' in international relations. Respect for democracy, human rights and the rule of law, along with leadership in environmental issues and sustainable development policies became flagship initiatives of the European Union (representing Europe united) to position itself as a global power at the turn of the century.

Considering the role of Europe in the world today one has actually to replace Europe with the European Union. There are three main features of the EU as a global actor. First, the EU is a soft power in the global scene: soft in the sense that it exercises its ability to persuade other actors without force or coercion, through diplomacy and economic means. However, its softness is normatively informed. The EU has clear normative priorities that it seeks to implement such as promoting democracy, the rule of law, human rights and prosperity. As such, it therefore has better been described as a civilian rather than simply a soft power. Yet this too is in flux; even though the EU has tended to use its military forces for peace building and peace keeping purposes in a growing number of operations around the world, it has been expanding the security and defence dimensions of its external relations, making it less 'civilian' in the strict sense of the term but far from a strategic military global power. This leads to the second feature, that of the EU as a security actor, albeit a reluctant one. The internal diversity of the EU, the different past political and military experiences of its Western and Central Eastern parts, and the reluctance of member states to develop a common defence policy have so far trumped EU efforts to develop a clear security actor role in the world. Recent challenges in the Arab world and in Ukraine and the way in which the EU sees its role as a global actor testify to a growing security mind-set but it still has a limited ability to act as a single entity. A third element in the role of the EU in the world is the economic one. The rise of global trade and the emergence of bilateral trade agreements such as the TTIP point to the emergence of a new field of international economic relations where Europe probably emerges as a single and powerful actor.

On balance, Europe and the EU are best described by Giandomenico Majone's (2009) expression of 'Would-be World

Power'. There is a lot of promise and hope in it but also a lot of disunity, inability to act and scepticism.

Concluding remarks

Defining 'Europe' is an on-going story, an incessant effort to revisit core existentialist questions. Throughout the course of the continent's history, politicians, political elites, academics and thinkers have been tackling and returning to these questions in elaborate, critical, simplistic and populist ways. In this book, we have highlighted the historical and ambivalent character of the term, and have offered alternative views of Europe by putting current developments in perspective. We have adopted a critical viewpoint with regard to social and political developments in Europe today and more generally in the post-war period. We have sought to give the reader the main tools for elaborating and answering the questions her/himself. Europe is a construct of knowledge, it is a subject of inquiry, but Europe is also a *dispositif*, a device for constructing knowledge. As a construct of knowledge, Europe has taken on different forms and shapes through the centuries, and of course with different degrees of visibility and importance. As a device, it becomes a lens through which to understand the world and position ourselves in it. This book remains distinctively *European* in that it has tried tries to be self-reflexive, providing the tools for the reader to come up with their own answers rather than providing ready made 'truths', it is the beginning of an ongoing discussion.

Bibliography

Adler, E. and M. Barnett (eds.) (1998) *Security Communities,* Cambridge Studies in International Relations (Cambridge: Cambridge University Press).

Adnett, N. and S. Hardy (2005) *The European Social Model. Modernisation or Evolution?* (Cheltenham: Edward Elgar).

Adorno, T. and M. Horkheimer [1944] (1979) *Dialectic of Enlightenment* (London: Verso).

Albertazzi, D. and S. Mueller (2013) 'Populism and Liberal Democracy: Populists in Government in Austria, Italy, Poland and Switzerland', *Government and Opposition,* 48(3), 343–371.

Allen, J. and C. Hamnett (eds.) (1995) *A Shrinking World* (Oxford: Oxford University Press).

Alston, P.P. and J.H.H. Weiler (2000) *The European Union and Human Rights* (Florence: European University Institute).

Amato, G. and J. Batt (1998) 'Minority Rights and EU Enlargement to the East', Report of the First Meeting of the Reflection Group on the Long-Term Implications of EU Enlargement: The Nature of the New Border, Chairman: Giuliano Amato, Rapporteur: Judy Batt. RSC Policy Paper No 98/5, European University Institute.

Anderson, B. (1981) *Imagined Communities* (London: Verso Books).

Anderson, J. and L. O'Dowd (1999) 'Borders, Border Regions and Territoriality: Contradictory Meanings, Changing Significance', *Regional Studies,* 33(7), 593–604.

Anderson, J., L. O'Dowd and T. Wilson (eds.) (2003) *New Borders for a Changing Europe: Cross-Border Cooperation and Governance* (London: Frank Cass).

Anderson, M., D. Bigo and E. Bort (2000) 'Frontiers, Identity and Security in Europe: An Agenda for Research', in J. Brown and M. Pratt (eds.) *Borderlands Under Stress* (London: Kluwer Law International), 251–274.

Anderson, M. and E. Bort (eds.) (1998) *The Frontiers of Europe* (London: Pinter).

Andreas, P. (ed.) (2001) *Border Games, Policing the US-Mexico Divide* (Ithaca, NY: Cornell University Press).

Andreas, P. and T. Snyder (2000) *The Wall Around the West: State Borders and Immigration Controls in North America and Europe* (Lanham, MD and Oxford: Rowman & Littlefield Publishers).

Ansell, C. and G. di Palma (eds.) (2004) *Restructuring Territoriality. Europe and the United States Compared* (Cambridge: Cambridge University Press).

Appel, H. (2005) 'Anti-Communist Justice and Founding the Post-Communist Order: Lustration and Restitution in Central Europe', *East European Politics & Societies* (Summer 2005), 19(3), 37–405.

Arendt, H. (1963) *Eichmann in Jerusalem, A Report on the Banality of Evil* (London: Penguin Classics).

Armstrong, W. and J. Anderson (eds.) (2007) *Geopolitics of European Union Enlargement: The Fortress Empire* (London: Routledge).

Atkin, N. and F. Tallet (2003) *Priests, Prelates and People. A History of European Catholicism since 1750* (London: IB Tauris).

Baldwin, J.R., S.L. Faulkner, M.L. Hecht and S.L. Lindsley (2006) *Redefining Culture: Perspectives Across the Disciplines* (London: Routledge Communication Series).

Balibar, E. (2014) *Interview.* Available online at: http://www.verso books.com/blogs/1559-a-racism-without-races-an-interview-with-etienne-balibar (accessed: 24 February 2015).

Balibar, E. (2004) *We the People of Europe: Reflections on Transnational Citizenship* (Princeton, NJ: Princeton University Press).

Balibar, E. (2002) *Politics and the Other Scene* (London: Verso Books).

Balibar, E. and I. Wallerstein (2011) *Race, Nation, Class*, 2nd edn (London: Verso Books).

Ball, T. and R. Dagger (2009a) *Political Ideologies and the Democratic Ideal*, 7th edn (New York: Longman).

Ball, T. and R. Dagger (eds.) (2009b) *Ideals and Ideologies: A Reader*, 7th edn (New York: Longman).

Balme, R. and D. Chabanet (2008) *European Governance and Democracy. Power and Protest in the EU* (Lanham, MD: Rowman and Littlefield Publishers).

Bancroft, A. (2005) *Roma and Gypsy Travellers in Europe. Modernity, Race, Space and Exclusion* (Aldershot: Ashgate Publishing/ Research in Migration and Ethnic Relations Series).

Banting, K. and W. Kymlicka (2006) 'Introduction', in K. Banting and W. Kymlicka (eds.) *Multiculturalism and the Welfare State* (Oxford: Oxford University Press), 1–45.

Barbier, J.-C. (2013) *The Road to Social Europe. A Contemporary Approach to Political Cultures and Diversity in Europe* (London: Routledge).

Bartlett, R. (1993) *The Making of Europe: Conquest, Colonization, and Cultural Change, 950–1350* (Princeton, NJ: Princeton University Press).

Bartolini, S. (2005) *Restructuring Europe: Centre Formation, System Building and Political Restructuring between the Nation State and the European Union* (Oxford: Oxford University Press).

Bartolini, S. and P. Mair (1990) *Identity, Competition and Electoral Availability: The Stabilisation of European Electorates 1885–1985* (Cambridge: Cambridge University Press).

Batt, J. (2003) 'The Enlarged EU's External Borders-the Regional Dimension in: Partners and Neighbors: A CFSP for a Wider Europe.' Paris: EU Institute for Security Studies Chaillot Papers (64).

Batt, J. (2002) '"Fuzzy Statehood" versus Hard Borders: The Impact of EU Enlargement on Romania and Yugoslavia. One Europe or Several?' Working Papers No. 46, *One-Europe Programme*.

Batt, J. (2001) 'Between a Rock and a Hard Place—Multi-ethnic Regions on the EU's New Eastern Frontier', *East European Politics and Societies*, 15(3), 502–527.

Batt, J. and K. Wolczuk (2002) *Region, State and Identity in Central and Eastern Europe* (London: Routledge).

Bauman, Z. (2005) 'Freedom from, in and Through the State: T.H. Marshall's Trinity of Rights Revisited', *Theoria*, 108.

Bauman, Z. (2004) *Europe: An Unfinished Adventure* (Cambridge: Polity Press).

Bauman, Z. (2000) *Liquid Modernity* (Cambridge, MA: Polity Press).

Bauman, Z. (1989) *Modernity and the Holocaust* (Cambridge: Polity Press).

Bayly, C.A. and E.F. Biagini (2008) *Giuseppe Mazzini and the Globalization of Democratic Nationalism, 1830–1920* (Oxford: Oxford University Press/British Academy).

Bechev, D. and K. Nicolaidis (2010) *Mediterranean Frontiers: Borders, Conflict and Memory in a Transnational World* (London: I.B. Tauris).

Beck, U. (2000) *What Is Globalisation?* (Cambridge: Polity Press).

Becker, E. (1971) *The Birth and Death of Meaning*, 2nd edn (New York: Free Press).

Berger, P. and T. Luckmann (1984) *The Social Construction of Reality. A Treatise in the Sociology of Knowledge* (London: Penguin Books).

Berger, P.L. (ed.) (1999) *The Desecularization of the World: Resurgent Religion and World Politics* (Washington, DC: The Ethics and Public Policy Center).

Best, R.E. (2013) 'How Party System Fragmentation Has Altered Political Opposition in Established Democracies', *Government and Opposition*, 48(3), 314–342.

Bettiza, Go. (2014) 'Civilizational Analysis in International Relations: Mapping the Field and Advancing a "Civilizational Politics" Line of Research', *International Studies Review*, 16(1), 1–28.

Bialasiewicz, L. and J. O'Loughlin (2002) 'Galician Identities and Political Cartographies on the Polish–Ukrainian Border', in J. Halki and D. Kaplan (eds.) *Boundaries and Place: European Borderlands in Geographical Context* (Oxford: Blackwell Synergy), 217–238.

Bideleux, R. and R. Taylor (1996) *European Integration and Disintegration: East and West* (London: Routledge).

Bigo, D. (2000) 'When Two Become One: Internal and External Securitisations in Europe', in M. Kelstrup and M.C. Williams (eds.) *International Relations Theory and the Politics of European Integration* (London: Routledge), 171–204.

Blatter, J. (2001) 'Debordering the World of States: Towards a Multi-Level System in Europe and a Multi-Polity System in North America? Insights from Border Regions', *European Journal of International Relations*, 7(2), 175–209.

Blumenthal, A. (1940) 'A New Definition of Culture', *American Anthropologist*, 42(4), 571–586.

Boemeke, M.F., G.D. Feldman and E. Glaser (eds.) (1998) *The Treaty of Versailles. A Reassessment after 75 Years* (Cambridge: Cambridge University Press).

Boje, T., B. van Steenberg and S. Walby (eds.) (1999) *European Societies. Fusion or Fission?* (London and New York: Routledge).

Bonacich, E., S. Alimahomed and J.B. Wilson (2008) 'The Racialization of Global Labor', *American Behavioral Scientist*, 52(3), 342–355.

Boon, V. and G. Delanty (2007) 'Cosmopolitanism and Europe: Historical Considerations and Contemporary Applications', in C. Rumford (ed.) *Cosmopolitanism and Europe* (Liverpool: Liverpool University Press), 19–38.

Borneman, J. and N. Fowler (1997) 'Europeanization', *Annual Review of Anthropology*, 26, 487–514.

Bort, E. (ed.) (1998) *Borders and Borderlands in Europe* (Edinburgh: Edinburgh University Press).

Bourdieu, P. (1991) *Language and Symbolic Power* (Cambridge, MA: Harvard University Press).

Brown, R. (2010) *Prejudice: Its Social Psychology*, 2nd edn (Chichester: John Wiley & Sons Ltd).

Browning, C. and M. Lehti (eds.) (2010) *The Struggle for the West: A Divided and Contested Legacy* (London: Routledge).

Brunkhorst, H. (2005) *Solidarity: From Civic Friendship to a Global Legal Community* (Cambridge, MA: MIT Press).

Brusis, M. (1999) 'Re-Creating the Regional Level in Central and Eastern Europe. An Analysis of Administrative Reforms in Six Countries', in E. von Breska and M. Brusis (eds.) *Central and Eastern Europe on the Way into the European Union: Reforms of Regional Administration in Bulgaria, the Czech Republic, Estonia, Hungary, Poland and Slovakia* (München: Centrum für angewandte Politikforschung), 1–22.

Bruter, M. (2005) *Citizens of Europe? The Emergence of a Mass European Identity* (London: Palgrave Macmillan).

Bruter, M. (2004) 'On What Citizens Mean by Feeling European', *Journal of Ethnic and Migration Studies*, 30(1), 21–39.

Bull, H. (1982) 'Civilian Power Europe: A Contradiction in Terms?' *Journal of Common Market Studies*, 21(2), 149–164.

Burgess, M. (2000) *Federalism and European Union: The Building of Europe, 1950–2000* (London: Routledge).

Burgess, M. (1995) *The British Tradition of Federalism* (London: Leicester University Press).

Burgess, P. (ed.) (1997) *Cultural Politics and Political Culture in Postmodern Europe* (Amsterdam: Editions Rodopi).

Burghardt, G. (1993) 'European Union – A Global Power in the Making?' in W. Weidenfield and J. Janning (eds.) *Europe in Global Change* (Gütersloh, GE: Bertelsmann Foundation Publishers), 254–257.

Burke, P. (1980) *Sociology and History* (London: Allen and Unwin).

Byrne, M. (2013) 'The Warsaw Pact: From the Creation of a Hegemonic Alliance to its Disintegration', in V. Mastny and Z. Liqun (eds.) *The Legacy of the Cold War. Perspectives on Security, Cooperation and Conflict* (Lanham: Lexington Books), 147–170.

Cahnman, W. (1952) 'Frontiers between East and West in Europe', *Geographical Review*, 49, 605–624.

Cameron, David (2010) *Big Society speech*. Available at: https://www.gov.uk/government/speeches/big-society-speech, 19 July 2010 (accessed: 19 February 2015).

Caporaso, J.A. (2000) 'Changes in the Westphalian Order: Territory, Public Authority, and Sovereignty', *International Studies Review*, 2(2), 1–28.

Carey, S. (2002) 'Undivided Loyalties: Is National Identity an Obstacle to European Integration?' *European Union Politics*, 3, 387–413.

Casal Bertoa, F. (2013) 'Post Communist Politics: On the Divergence (and/or Convergence) of East and West', *Government and Opposition*, 48(3), 398–433.

Casanova, J. (2009) 'The Religious Situation in Europe', in H. Joas and K. Weingadt (eds.) *Secularization and the World Religions* (Liverpool: Liverpool University Press), 206–228.

Castles, F.G. (2010) 'Black Swans and Elephants on the Move: The Impact of Emergencies on the Welfare State', *Journal of European Social Policy*, 20(2), 91–101.

Castoriadis, C. (1993) 'Reflections on Racism', *Thesis Eleven*, 32, 1–13.

Castoriadis, C. (1987 [1975 in French]) *The Imaginary Institution of Society*, trans. Kathleen Blamey (Cambridge, MA: MIT Press).

Cavafy, C.P. (1975) *Collected Poems*, trans. Edmund Keeley and Philip Sherrard (Princeton, NJ: Princeton University Press).

Chadwick, O. (1993) *The Secularisation of the European Mind in the Nineteenth Century* (Cambridge: Cambridge University Press).

Checkel, J. and P. Katzenstein (eds.) (2009) *European Identity* (Cambridge: Cambridge University Press).

Christiansen, T., F. Petito and F. Tonra (2000) 'Fuzzy Politics Around Fuzzy Borders: The European Union's "Near Abroad"', *Cooperation and Conflict*, 35(4), 389–415.

Cohn, N. (1993) *Europe's Inner Demons. The Demonisation of Christians in Medieval Christendom* (London: Pimlico).

Colombo, E. (1978) 'The Decisions Facing Europe.' Second Jean Monnet Lecture by the President of the European Parliament, Emilio Colombo. Florence, 9 November 1978. [EU Speech], Available at: http://aei.pitt.edu/11188/

Comité des Sages Report (1998) *Leading by Example, a Human Rights Agenda for the European Union for the Year 2000*, Final Report (Florence: European University Institute).

Commission of the European Communities (1992) *Treaty on the European Union* (Luxembourg: EU Commission).

Conclusions of the Council and of the Representatives of the Governments of the Member States, meeting within the Council, on a Work Plan for Culture (2015–2018) (2014), *OJ C 463*, 23.12.2014, 4–14.

Coudenhove-Kalergi, R. (1926) *Pan Europe* (New York: Alfred Knopf).

Coudenys, W. (2007) *Frontiers and Limits of European Culture*. Available online at: www.uneecc.org/userfiles/File/sibiu_wim_coude nys_full%20text.doc (accessed: 24 February 2015).

Council of Europe (2008) *White Paper on Intercultural Dialogue. Living Together as Equals in Dignity*. Available online at: http:// www.coe.int/t/dg4/intercultural/source/white%20paper_final_revised_ en.pdf (accessed: 24 February 2015).

Council of Europe (1954) *European Cultural Convention*. Available online at: http://conventions.coe.int/Treaty/en/Treaties/Html/018.htm (accessed: 20 March 2015).

Cox, R.H. (1999) *The Consequences of Welfare Reform: How Conceptions of Social Rights Are Changing* (Norman, OK: University of Oklahoma).

Crampton, R.J. (1997) *Eastern Europe in the Twentieth Century – And After*, 2nd edn (London: Routledge).

Cuban, S. (2013) *Deskilling Migrant Women in the Global Care Industry* (London: Palgrave Macmillan).

D'Appollonia, A.C. (2002) 'European Nationalism and European Union', in A. Pagden (ed.) *The Idea of Europe* (Cambridge: Cambridge University Press), 171–190.

Dahrendorf, R. (2005) *Reflections on the Revolution in Europe* (New Brunswick, NJ: Transaction Publishers).

Dahrendorf, R. (1979) *A Third Europe?* Jean Monnet Lecture. Florence, 26 November 1979. Available online at: http://cadmus.eui. eu/handle/1814/22157

Dalby, S. (1993) 'Post-Cold War Security in the New Europe', in J. O'Loughin and H. van der Wusten (eds.) *The New Political Geography of Eastern Europe* (London: Belhaven Press), 71–85.

Davies, N. (1996) *Europe: A History* (Oxford: Oxford University Press).

Davison, A. and H. Muppidi (eds.) (2009) *Europe and Its Boundaries: Words and Worlds, Within and Beyond* (Plymouth, MA: Lexington Press).

Dawson, C. (1952) *Understanding Europe* (London: Sheed and Ward).

DeBardeleben, J. (ed.) (2005) *Soft or Hard Borders? Managing the Divide in An Enlarged Europe* (Aldershot: Ashgate Publishers).

Delanty, G. (2013) *Formations of European Modernity. A Historical and Political Sociology of Europe* (London: Palgrave Macmillan).

Delanty, G. (ed.) (2012) *Routledge International Handbook of Cosmopolitan Studies* (London: Routledge).

Delanty, G. (2006a) 'Borders in a Changing Europe: Dynamics of Openness and Closure', *Comparative European Politics*, 4, 183–202.

Delanty, G. (ed.) (2006b) *Europe and Asia Beyond East and West* (London: Routledge).

Delanty, G. (2004) 'Conceptions of Europe. A Review of Recent Trends', *European Journal of Social Theory*, 6(4), 471–488.

Delanty, G. (1995) *Inventing Europe: Idea, Identity, Reality* (New York: St Martin's Press).

Delanty, G. and C. Rumford (2005) *Rethinking Europe. Social Theory and the Implications of Europeanization* (London: Routledge).

Dell'Olio, F. (2005) *The Europeanization of Citizenship: Between Ideology of Nationality, Immigration and European Identity* (Aldershot: Ashgate).

Derrida, J. (1992) *The Other Heading. Reflections on Today's Europe* (Bloomington, IN: University of Indiana Press).

Diamandouros, N. (1993) 'Politics and Culture in Greece, 1974–1991: An Interpretation', in R. Clogg (ed.) *Greece 1981–1989. The Populist Decade* (New York: St Martin's Press), 1–25.

Donnan, H. and T.M. Wilson (1999) *Borders: Frontiers of Identity, Nation & State* (Oxford: Berg Publishers).

Dostoyevsky F. (1973) *The Diary of a Writer* (New York: Octagon Books).

Dowe, D. et al. (eds.) (2001) *Europe in 1848: Revolutions and Reform* (New York: Berghahn Books).

Drake, H. (2000) *Jacques Delors: A Political Biography* (London: Routledge).

Duchene, F. (1972) 'Europe's Role in World Peace', in R. Mayne (ed.) *Europe Tomorrow: Sixteen Europeans Look Ahead* (London: Fontana), 32–47.

Duchesne, S. (2008) 'Waiting for a European Identity. Reflections on the Process of European Identification', *Perspectives on European Politics and Society*, 9(4), 397–410.

Duchesne, S., E. Frazer, F. Haegel and V. van Ingelgom (eds.) (2013) *Overlooking Europe: Citizens' Reactions to European Integration Compared* (London: Palgrave Macmillan).

Eder, K. and W. Spohn (eds.) (2005) *Collective Memory and European Identity: The Effects of Integration and Enlargement* (London: Ashgate Publishing).

Emmanouilidis, J.A. (2012) 'Europe's Role in the Twenty-First Century', in T. Renard and S. Biscop (eds.) *The European Union and Emerging Powers in the 21st Century. How Europe Can Shape a New Global Order* (Aldershot: Ashgate Publishing).

Emmanouilidis, J.A. and L. Tsoukalis (eds.) (2011) *The Delphic Oracle on Europe: Is There a Future for the European Union?* (Oxford: Oxford University Press).

Erdenir, B. (2012) 'Islamophobia qua racial discrimination: Muslimophobia', in A. Triandafyllidou (ed.) *Muslims in 21st Century Europe: Structural and Cultural Perspectives* (London: Routledge), 45–59.

Esping-Andersen, G. (ed.) (1996) *Welfare States in Transition: National Adaptations in Global Economies* (London: Sage).

Esping-Andersen, G. (1990) *The Three Worlds of Welfare Capitalism* (Cambridge: Polity Press).

EU-MIDIS (2011) *European Union Minorities and Discrimination Survey Run by the Fundamental Rights Agency*. Available online at: http://fra.europa.eu/en/project/2011/eu-midis-european-union-minorities-and-discrimination-survey (accessed: 24 February 2015).

European Commission (2014) *EU Position in World Trade*. Available online at: http://ec.europa.eu/trade/policy/eu-position-in-world-trade/ (accessed: 26 February 2015).

European Commission (2005) *EU in the World*. Available online at: http://europa.eu/rapid/press-release_SPEECH-06-59_en.htm?locale=en (accessed: 26 February 2015).

European Commission (2002) *Europe in Transition, Hopes and Fears*. Available online at: http://europa.eu/rapid/press-release_SPEECH-02-600_en.htm?locale=EN (accessed: 26 February 2015).

European Commission (2001) *A Community of Cultures. The European Union and the Arts*. Available online at: http://ecoc-doc-athens.eu/attachments/1423_A_community_of_cultures_eu&arts.pdf (accessed: 24 February 2015).

European Monitoring Centre on Racism and Xenophobia (2006) *Muslims in the European Union. Discrimination and Islamophobia*, Report. Available at: http://fra.europa.eu/sites/default/files/fra_uploads/156-Manifestations_EN.pdf (accessed: 26 February 2015).

Evans, E.J. (2004) *Thatcher and Thatcherism*, 2nd edn (London: Routledge).

Fanon, F. (1952) *Black Skin, White Masks* (New York: Grove Press).

Featherstone, K. and G. Kazamias (eds.) (2001) *Europeanization and the Southern Periphery* (London: Frank Cass).

Fekete, L. (2003) 'Death at the Border – Who Is to Blame?' *European Race Bulletin* (London: Institute for Race Relations), 44, 1–12.

Ferguson, N. (2007) *The War of the World. History's Age of Hatred* (London: Penguin Books).

Fligstein, N. (2008) *Euro-Clash* (Oxford: Oxford University Press).

Foucher, M. (1998) 'The Geopolitics of European Frontiers', in E. Bort and M. Anderson (eds.) *The Frontiers of Europe* (London: Pinter Press), 235–250.

Franceschi, M. and B. Weider (2007) *The Wars Against Napoleon, Debunking the Myth of the Napoleonic Wars* (New York: Savas Beatie LLC).

Freudenstein, R. (2000) 'Río Odra, Río Buh: Poland, Germany, and the Borders of Twenty-First-Century Europe', in P. Andreas and T. Snyder (eds.) *The Wall Around the West: State Borders and Immigration Controls in North America and Europe* (Lanham, MD: Rowman & Littlefield), 173–183.

Fukuyama, F. (1992) *The End of History and the Last Man* (London: Penguin Books).

Fulbrook, M. (1993) *National Histories and European History* (London: UCL Press).

Geddes, A. (2000) *Immigration and European Integration, Towards Fortress Europe?* (Manchester: Manchester University Press).

Geertz, C. (1973) *The Interpretation of Cultures: Selected Essays* (New York: Basic Books).

Genet, J. (1958) *Les negres* (Paris: L'Arbalète).

Giddens, A. (2007) *Europe in the Global Age* (Cambridge: Polity Press).

Gilroy, P. (1987) *'There Ain't No Black in the Union Jack': The Cultural Politics of Race and Nation* (London: Hutchinson).

Giuliani, G. and C. Lombardi-Diop (2013) *Bianco E Nero. Storia Dell'identità Razziale Degli Italiani* (Milano: Mondadori Education).

Gnesotto, N. (1999) 'L'OTAN et l'Europe', *Politique Etrangère*, été.

Goetz, K., P. Mair and G. Smith (eds.) (2008) 'European Politics: Pasts, Presents, Futures', *West European Politics*, Special Issue, 31(12), available online at: http://www.tandfonline.com/toc/fwep20/31/1-2# (accessed: 14 May 2015).

Goffman, H. (1963) *Stigma: Notes on the Management of Spoiled Identity* (Englewood Cliffs, NJ: Prentice-Hall).

Goffman, H. (1961) *Asylums: Essays on the Social Situations of Mental Patients and Other Inmates* (New York: Doubleday Anchor).

Goldstein, L.J. (1957) 'On Defining Culture', *American Anthropological Association*, 59(6), 1075–1081.

Gorbachev, M.S. (1988) *Perestroika: New Thinking for Our Country and the World* (London: Harper & Row).

Gordon, P.H. (1997) 'Europe's Uncommon Foreign Policy', *International Security*, 22(3), 74–100.

Gray, J. (2008) *Black Mass: Apocalyptic Religion and the Death of Utopia* (London: Penguin Books).

Green, D.M. (2007) *The Europeans: Political Identity in an Emerging Polity* (Boulder, CO: Lynne Rienner).

Gropas, R. (2006) *Human Rights and Foreign Policy: The Case of the EU* (Brussels and Athens: Bruyant and Sakkoulas).

Gunther, R., N. Diamandouros and H.J. Puhle (eds.) (1995) *The Politics of Democratic Consolidation: Southern Europe in Comparative Perspective* (Baltimore, MD: Johns Hopkins University Press).

Habermas, J. (2006) *The Divided West* (Cambridge, MA: Polity Press).

Habermas, J. (1987 [1981 in German]) *The Theory of Communicative Action: Vol. 2: Lifeworld and System: A Critique of Functionalist Reason*, trans. T. McCarthy (Boston, MA: Beacon Press).

Habermas, J. (1984 [1981 in German]) *The Theory of Communicative Action: Vol. 1: Reason and the Rationalization of Society*, trans. T. McCarthy (Boston, MA: Beacon Press).

Hall, S. (1981) 'Notes on Deconstructing the Popular', in R. Samuel (ed.) *People's History and Social Theory* (London: Routledge & Kegal Paul), 227–240.

Handler, R. (1988) *Nationalism and the Politics of Culture in Quebec* (Madison, WI: University of Wisconsin Press).

Hann, C. (2011) 'Back to Civilization', *Anthropology Today*, 27(6), 1–2.

Hay, D. (1957/1968) *Europe. The Emergence of an Idea* (Edinburgh: Edinburgh University Press).

Hay, C. and D. Wincott (2012) *The Political Economy of European Welfare Capitalism* (London: Palgrave Macmillan).

Hemerijck, A. (2001) 'Prospects for Effective Social Citizenship in an Age of Structural Inactivity', in C. Crouch, K. Eder and D. Tambini (eds.) *Citizenship, Markets and the State* (Oxford: Oxford University Press), 134–170.

Herb, H. and D. Kaplan (1999) *Nested Identities: Nationalism, Territory, and Scale* (Lanham, MD: Rowman & Littlefield Publishers).

Herrmann, R., T. Risse and M. Brewer (eds.) (2004) *Transnational Identities. Becoming European in the EU* (Lanham, MD: Rowman & Littlefield Publishers).

Herrschel, T. (2011) *Borders in Post-Socialist Europe: Territory, Scale, Society* (Aldershot: Ashgate Publishers).

Hettne, B. (2011) 'The EU as an Emerging Global Actor', in J.-U. Wunderlich and D.J. Bailey (eds.) *The European Union and Global Governance. A Handbook* (London: Routledge).

Hewitson, M. and M. D'Auria (eds.) (2012) *Europe in Crisis. Intellectuals and the European idea, 1917–1957* (New York and Oxford: Berghahn Books).

Hobsbawm, E. (1996) *The Age of Capital* (London: Vintage).

Hobsbawm, E. (1994) *The Age of Extremes. The Short Twentieth Century, 1914–1991* (New York: Vintage Books).

Hobsbawm, E. (1990) *Nations and Nationalism since 1780* (Cambridge: Cambridge University Press).

Hobsbawm, E. (1989) *The Age of Empire, 1875–1914* (New York: Vintage Books).

Hobsbawm, E. (1975) *The Age of Capital 1848–1875* (New York: Vintage Books).

Höfele, A. and W. von Koppenfels (eds.) (2005) *Renaissance Go-Betweens. Cultural Exchange in Early Modern Europe* (Berlin: Waler de Gruyter GmbH & Co).

Hofstede, G. (2001) *Culture's Consequences: Comparing Values, Behaviors, Institutions and Organizations Across Nations*, 2nd edn (Thousand Oaks, CA: Sage Publications).

Hooghe, L. and G. Marks (2008) 'European Union?', *West European Politics*, 31(1), 108–129.

Ichijo, A. and W. Spohn (eds.) (2005) *Entangled Identities. Nations and Europe* (London: Routledge).

Ikenberry, J.G. (2011) 'The Future of the Liberal World Order', *Foreign Affairs*. May/June 2011. Available online at: http://www.foreignaffairs.com/articles/67730/g-john-ikenberry/the-future-of-the-liberal-world-order (accessed: 26 February 2015).

Inglehart, R. (1977) *The Silent Revolution: Changing Values and Political Styles among Western Publics* (Princeton, NJ: Princeton University Press).

Inglehart, R.F. and C. Welzel (2005) *Modernization, Cultural Change, and Democracy: The Human Development Sequence* (New York: Cambridge University Press).

Institute of Race Relations (2008) 'Cultural Cleansing', *European Race Bulletin*, 62. Available at: http://www.irr.org.uk/pdf/ERB_62.pdf (accessed: 26 February 2015).

Jacobs, D. and R. Maier (1998) 'European Identity: Construct, Fact and Fiction', in M. Gastelaars and A. de Ruijter (eds.) *A United Europe: The Quest for a Multifaceted Identity* (Maastricht, NL: Shaker), 13–34.

Jansen, R.S. (2011) 'Populist Mobilization: A New Theoretical Approach to Populism', *Sociological Theory*, 29(2), 75–96.

Jenkins, R. (1996) *Social Identity*, 3rd edn (London: Routledge).

Jepsen, M. and A. Serrano Pascual (2006) *Unwrapping the European Social Model* (Bristol: The Policy Press).

Jones, R.B. (1980) *The Making of Contemporary Europe* (London: Hodder and Stoughton).

Jordan, B. (1998) *The New Politics of Welfare: Social Justice in a Global Context* (London: Sage Publications).

Jordan, B., B. Stråth and A. Triandafyllidou (2003) 'Contextualising Immigration Policy Implementation in Europe', *Journal of Ethnic and Migration Studies*, 29(2), 195–224.

Jordan, W.C. (2002) '"Europe" in the Middle Ages', in A. Pagden (ed.) *The Idea of Europe. From Antiquity to the European Union* (Washington, DC: Woodrow Wilson Centre Press and Cambridge University Press), 72–90.

Judt, T. (2005) *Postwar: A History of Europe since 1945* (London: William Heinemann).

Kagan, R. (2002) 'Power and Weakness', *Policy Review*, 113 (June and July 2002), 3–28.

Kaya, A. (2013) *Europeanization and Tolerance in Turkey: The Myth of Toleration* (London: Palgrave).

Keating, M. (1993) *The Politics of Modern Europe: The State and Political Authority in the Major Democracies* (Aldershot: Edward Elgar Press).

Keating, M. and J. Hughes (eds.) (2003) *The Regional Challenge in Central and Eastern Europe: Territorial Restructuring and European Integration, Regionalism & federalism*, Vol. 1 (Brussels: Peter Lang).

Kennedy, M. (2012) 'For Illegal Immigrants, Greek Border Offers a Back Door to Europe', *International Herald Tribune*, 14 June 2012. Available online at: http://www.nytimes.com/2012/07/15/world/europe/illegal-immigrants-slip-into-europe-by-way-of-greek-border.html?_r=1 (accessed: 25 February 2015).

Kershaw, I. (2000) *The Nazi Dictatorship. Perspectives of Interpretation*, 4th edn (London: Bloomsbury Academic).

King, R., G. Lazaridis and C. Tsardanidis (eds.) (2000) *Eldorado or Fortress. Migration in Southern Europe* (London: Macmillan).

Kitschelt, H. (1995) 'Formation of Party Cleavages in Post-Communist Democracies: Theoretical Propositions', *Party Politics*, 1, 447.

Kitschelt, H. (1992) 'The Formation of Party Systems in East Central Europe', *Politics and Society*, 20, 7–50.

Kluckhohn, C. (1949) *Mirror for Man. The Relation of Anthropology with Modern Life* (New York: McGraw-Hill Education and Whittlesey House).

Kohli, M. and M. Novak (eds.) (2002) *Will Europe Work? Integration, Employment and the Social Order* (London: Routledge).

Körner, A. (2000) *1848: A European Revolution? International Ideas and National Memories of 1848* (Basingstoke: Palgrave Macmillan).

Kraus, P. (2011) 'The Politics of Complex Diversity. A European Perspective', *Ethnicities*, 12(1), 3–25.

Kriesi, H. (2014) 'The Populist Challenge', *West European Politics*, 37(3), 361–378.

Kriesi, H., E. Grande, M. Dolezal, M. Helbling, D. Höglinger, S. Hutter and B. Wüest (eds.) (2012) *Political Conflict in Western Europe* (Cambridge: Cambridge University Press).

Kriesi, H., E. Grande, R. Lachat, M. Dolezal, S. Bornschier and T. Frey (2008) *West European Politics in the Age of Globalization* (Cambridge and New York: Cambridge University Press).

Kriesi, H., E. Grande, R. Lachat, M. Dolezal, S. Bornschier and T. Frey (2006) 'Globalization and the Transformation of the National Political Space: Six European Countries Compared', *European Journal of Political Research*, 45(6), 921–957.

Kroeber, A. and C. Kluckhohn (1952) *Culture* (New York: Meridian Books).

Krzyzanowski, M. (2010) *The Discursive Construction of European Identities, A Multi Level Approach to Discourse and Identity in the Transforming European Union* (Brussels: Peter Lang).

Kundera, M. (1984) 'The Tragedy of Central Europe', *The New York Review of Books*, 31(7). Available at: http://www.nybooks.com/articles/archives/1984/apr/26/the-tragedy-of-central-europe/

Kuus, M. (2004) 'Europe's Eastern Expansion and the Re-Inscription of Otherness in East Central Europe', *Progress in Human Geography*, 28(4), 472–489.

Laclau, E. (1977) *Politics and Ideology in Marxist Theory; Capitalism, Fascism, Populism* (London: Verso).

Lahav, G. (2004) *Immigration and Politics in the New Europe. Reinventing Borders* (Cambridge: Cambridge University Press).

Laïdi, Z. (ed.) (2008) *EU Foreign Policy in the Globalized World. Normative Power and Social Preferences* (London: Routledge/ GARNET Series: Europe in the World).

Laïdi, Z. (1998) *A World without Meaning: The Crisis of Meaning in International Politics* (London: Routledge).

Lavenex, S. (2005) 'Politics of Exclusion and Inclusion in the Wider Europe', in J. de Bardeleben (ed.) *Soft or Hard Borders? Managing the Divide in an Enlarged Europe* (Aldershot: Ashgate), 123–144.

Lawler, P. (1997) 'Scandinavian Exceptionalism and European Union', *Journal of Common Market Studies*, 35(4), 565–594.

Lawson, D., C. Armbruster and M. Cox (eds.) (2010) *The Global 1989: Continuity and Change in World Politics* (Cambridge: Cambridge University Press).

Leconte, C. (2010) *Understanding Euroscepticism, The European Union Series* (Basingstoke: Palgrave MacMillan).

Lee, R. (2011) 'Modernity, Solidity and Agency: Liquidity Reconsidered', *Sociology*, 45(4), 650–664.

Le Goff, J. (2005) *The Birth of Europe: 400–1500* (Malden, MA: Blackwell Publishing).

Lehti, M. and D.J. Smith (eds.) (2005) *Post-Cold War Identity Politics, Northern and Baltic Experiences* (London: Taylor & Francis e-Library).

Leonard, M. (2005) *Why Europe Will Run the 21st Century* (London: Fourth Estate).

Levine, L. (1990) *Highbrow/Lowbrow: The Emergence of Cultural Hierarchy in America* (Boston, MA: Harvard University Press).

Levitt, P. (2007) *God Needs No Passport: Immigrants and the Changing American Religious Landscape* (New York: The New Press).

Lijphart, A. (ed.) (1969) *Politics in Europe. Comparisons and Interpretations* (New Jersey: Prentice-Hall Inc).

Lipgens, W. (1982) *A History of European Integration: 1945–1947*, Vol. 1 (Oxford: Clarendon Press).

Lipset, S. and S. Rokkan (eds.) (1967) *Party Systems and Voter Alignments: Cross-National Perspectives* (London and New York: Free Press).

Lowenhardt, J., R. Hill and M. Light (2001) 'A Wider Europe, the View from Minsk and Chisinau', *International Affairs*, 77(3), 605–620.

Lucarelli, S. and L. Fioramonti (eds.) (2010) *External Perceptions of the European Union as a Global Actor* (London: Routledge/ GARNET Series: Europe in the World).

MacLaughlin, J. (1999) 'Nation-Building, Social Closure and Anti-Traveller Racism in Ireland', *Sociology*, 33(1), 129–151.

Macmaster, N. (2001) *Racism in Europe* (Basingstoke: Palgrave Macmillan).

Magone, J.M. (2011) *Contemporary European Politics. A Comparative Introduction* (London: Routledge).

Magone, J.M. (2005) *The New World Architecture. The Role of the European Union in the Making of Global Governance* (New Brunswick, NJ: Transaction Publishers).

Mair, P. (2009) 'Representative versus Responsible Government', MPIfG Working Paper 09/8. Cologne, available at: http://www.mpifg.de/pu/workpap/wp09-8.pdf (accessed: 12 May 2015).

Mair, P. (1997) *Party System Change* (Oxford: Oxford University Press).

Majone, G. (2009) *Europe as the Would-Be World Power* (Cambridge: Cambridge University Press).

Mali, J. and R. Wokler (eds.) (2003) *Isaiah Berlin's Counter-Enlightenment* (Philadelphia, PA: American Philosophical Society).

Af Malmborg, M. and B. Stråth (eds.) (2002) *The Meaning of Europe: Variety and Contention Within and Among Nations* (Oxford: Berg Publishers).

Manners, I. (2002) 'Normative Power Europe: A Contradiction in Terms?' *Journal of Common Market Studies*, 40(2), 235–258.

Marshall, T.H. (1950) *Citizenship and Social Class* (London: Pluto Press).

Martens, W. (2006) *Europe: I Struggle, I Overcome* (Berlin: Springer).

Martin, L.G. and D. Keridis (2004) (eds.) *The Future of Turkish Foreign Policy*, Belfer Center for Science and International Affairs (Cambridge, MA: The MIT Press).

Marx, K. and F. Engels (1998) *The Communist Manifesto* (1888 translation by Samuel Moore) (London: Verso).

Maslow, A. (1962) *Towards a psychology of being* (New York: Van Nostrand).

Matsaganis, M. (2013) 'The Crisis and the Welfare State in Greece. A Complex Relationship', in A. Triandafyllidou, R. Gropas and H. Kouki (eds.) *The Greek Crisis and European Modernity* (London: Palgrave Macmillan), 152–178.

Mazower, M. (2000) *Dark Continent. Europe's Twentieth Century* (New York: Vintage Books).

McCormick, J. (2007) *The European Superpower* (London: Palgrave Macmillan).

McKay, S. (2013) 'Disturbing Equilibrium and Transferring Risk: Confronting Precarious Work', in N. Countouris and M. Freedland (eds.) *Resocialising Europe in a Time of Crisis* (Cambridge: Cambridge University Press), 191–212.

McLaren, L. (2006) *Identity, Interests and Attitudes to European Integration* (Basingstoke: Palgrave Macmillan).

McMahon, D.M. (2001) *Enemies of the Enlightenment. The French Counter-Enlightenment and the Making of Modernity* (Oxford: Oxford University Press).

Medrano, Diez J. (2003) *Framing Europe. Attitudes to European Integration in Germany, Spain and the UK* (Princeton, NJ and Oxford: Princeton University Press).

Medrano, Diez J. and P. Gutierrez (2001) 'Nested Identities and European Identity in Spain', *Ethnic and Racial Studies*, 24(5), 753–778.

Meret, S. and B. Siim (2013) 'Multiculturalism, Right-Wing Populism and the Crisis of Social Democracy', in M. Keating and D. McCrone (eds.) *The Crisis of Social Democracy in Europe* (Edinburgh: Edinburgh University Press), 125–140.

Meyer, H. and J. Rutherford (eds.) (2012) *The Future of European Social Democracy. Building the Good Society* (London: Palgrave Macmillan).

Miera, F. (2012) 'Ethnic Statistics in Europe: The Paradox of Colourblindness', in A. Triandafyllidou, T. Modood and N. Meer (eds.) *European Multiculturalisms* (Edinburgh: Edinburgh University Press), 213–238.

Mikkeli, H. (1998) *Europe as an Idea and as an Identity* (London: Palgrave Macmillan).

Miliband, Ed (2014) *One Nation Economy*. Available online at: http:// labourlist.org/2014/01/ed-miliband-one-nation-economy-speech-full-text/, 17 January 2014 (accessed: 19 February 2015).

Milward, A.S. (1992) *The European Rescue of the Nation-State* (London: Routledge).

Minghi, J.V. (1963) 'Boundary Studies in Political Geography', *Annals of the Association of American Geographers*, 53, 407–428.

Moch, L.P. (2003) *Moving Europeans: Migration in Western Europe since 1650* (Bloomington, IN: Indiana University Press).

Modood, T. (2013) *Multiculturalism*, 2nd edn (London: Polity Press).

Modood, T. (2010) *Still Not Easy Being British. Struggles for a Multicultural Citizenship* (Oxford: Trentham Books).

Modood, T. (2007) *Multiculturalism: A Public Policy Idea* (London: Polity Press).

Modood, T. (1992) *Not Easy Being British. Colour, Culture and Citizenship* (Oxford: Trentham Books).

Modood, T., A. Triandafyllidou and R. Zapata-Barrero (eds.) (2006) *Multiculturalism, Muslims and Citizenship. European Approaches* (London: Routledge).

Monnet, J. Memorandum to Robert Schuman and George Bidault, 4 May 1950, in D. Welch (1995) *Modern European History 1871–2000. A Documentary Reader*, 2nd edn (London and New York: Routledge), 135.

Moravcsik, A. (1998) *The Choice for Europe. Social Purpose and State Power from Messina to Maastricht* (Ithaca, NY: Cornell University Press).

Moravcsik, A. (1991) 'Negotiating the Single European Act: National Interests and Conventional Statecraft in the European Community', *International Organization*, 45(1), 19–56.

Morgan, P. (2003) *Fascism in Europe: 1919–1945* (London: Routledge).

Morin, E. (1987) *Penser l'Europe* (Paris: Gallimard).

Morley, D. and K. Robins (2002) *Spaces of Identity: Global Media, Electronic Landscapes and Cultural Boundaries* (London: Routledge).

Moscovici, S. (1981) 'On Social Representations', in J. Forgas (ed.) *Social Cognition: Perspectives on Everyday Understanding* (London and New York: Academic Press), 181–200.

Mosse, G. (1999) *The Fascist Revolution. Towards a General Theory of Fascism* (New York: Howard Ferting).

Mudde, C. (2004) 'The Populist Zeitgeist', *Government and Opposition*, 39(4), 541–563.

Mudimbe, V.Y. (1988) *The Invention of Africa: Gnosis, Philosophy and the Order of Knowledge* (Bloomington, IN: Indiana University Press).

Murray, G. (2007) 'Who Is Afraid of T.H. Marshall? Or What Are the Limits of the Liberal Vision of Rights?' *Societies without Borders*, 2, 222–242. Available online at: http://www98.griffith.edu.au/dspace/bitstream/handle/10072/17742/47191_1.pdf?sequence=1 (accessed: 24 February 2015).

Nauert, C.G. (2006) *Humanism and the Culture of Renaissance Europe*, 2nd edn (Cambridge: Cambridge University Press).

Nelson, K. (2010) 'Social Assistance and Minimum Income Benefits in Old and New Democracies', *International Journal of Social Welfare*, 19(4), 367–378.

Neumann, I.B. (1999) *Uses of the Other: 'The East' in European Identity Formation* (Minneapolis, MN: University of Minnesota Press).

Neuwahl, N. (2005) 'What Borders for Which Europe?', in J. de Bardeleben (ed.) *Soft or Hard Borders? Managing the Divide in an Enlarged Europe* (Aldershot: Ashgate), 23–45.

Newman, D. (2006) 'Borders and Bordering. Towards an Interdisciplinary Dialogue', *European Journal of Social Theory*, 9(2), 171–186.

Nicolet, C. (1988) *L'inventaire du monde. Géographie et politique aux origines de l'empire romain* (Paris: Fayard).

Nodia, G. (2000) 'Chasing the Meaning of "Post-Communism": A Transitional Phenomenon or Something to Stay?' *Contemporary European History*, 9(2), 269–283.

Nye, J.S. Jr (1990) 'Soft Power' in *Foreign Policy*, No. 80, Twentieth Anniversary (Autumn, 1990), 153-171.

Nye, J.S. (2004) *Soft Power: The Means to Success in World Politics* (New York: Public Affairs).

Nye, J.S. (2002) *The Paradox of American Power* (Oxford: Oxford University Press).

Nye, J.S. (2000) 'Soft Power', in *Foreign Policy*, No. 80, Twentieth Anniversary (Autumn 1990), 153–171.

O'Dowd, L. (2003) *Culture, Cooperation and Conflict at International Borders in Europe* (Amsterdam: Rodopi).

O'Dowd, L. (2002) 'State Borders, Border Regions and the Construction of a European Identity', in M. Kohli and M. Novak (eds.) *Will Europe Work? Integration, Employment and the Social Order* (London: Routledge), 95–110.

O'Dowd, L. and T. Wilson (eds.) (1996) *Borders, Nations and States, Frontiers of Sovereignty in the New Europe* (Aldershot: Avebury).

O'Loughlin, J. and H. Van der Wusten (1993) *The New Political Geography of Eastern Europe* (London: Belhaven Press).

Ohmae, K. (1995) *The End of the Nation-State: The Rise of Regional Economies* (New York: Simon and Schuster Inc.).

Ohmae, K. (1990) *The Borderless World* (New York: Harper Business).

Orluc, K. (2007) 'Caught Between Past, Present and Future. The Idea of Pan-Europe in the Interwar Years', in H.-Å. Persson and B. Stråth (eds.) *Reflections on Europe: Defining a Political Order in Time and Space* (Brussels: Peter Lang), 95–120.

Pagden, A. (ed.) (2002) *The Idea of Europe. From Antiquity to the European Union* (Washington, DC: Woodrow Wilson Centre Press and Cambridge University Press).

Pappas, T. (2014) *Populism and Crisis Politics in Greece* (London: Palgrave Macmillan).

Pasquino, G. (2002) 'The Italian National Election of 13 May 2001', *Journal of Modern Italian Studies*, 6(3), 371–387.

Passerini, L. (2002) 'From the Ironies of Identity to the Identities of Irony', in A. Pagden (ed.) *The Idea of Europe* (Cambridge: Cambridge University Press), 191–208.

Passerini, L. (ed.) (1998) *The Question of European Identity: A Cultural Historical Approach* (Florence: European University Institute).

Patterson, T. (2002) 'The Vanishing Voter: Why Are the Voting Booths So Empty?' *National Civic Review* (Winter 2002), 91(4), 367–378.

Peckham, R.S. (2003) *Rethinking Heritage: Cultures and Politics in Europe* (London: I.B. Taurus).

Perkins, M.A. (2004) *Christendom and European Identity. The Legacy of a Grand Narrative since 1789* (Berlin: Walter de Gruyter).

Perkins, M.A. and M. Liebscher (eds.) (2006) *Nationalism versus Cosmopolitanism in German Thought and Culture 1789–1914. Essays on the Emergence of Europe* (Lewiston and Queenston: The Edgar Mellen Press).

Perkmann, M. (2003) 'Cross-Border Regions in Europe. Significance and Drivers of Regional Cross-Border Co-Operation', *European Urban and Regional Studies*, 10(2), 153–171.

Perrin, M. (1994) *L'idée de l'Europe au fil de deux millénaires* (Paris: Editions Beauchesne).

Persson, H.-Å. and B. Stråth (eds.) (2007) *Reflections on Europe: Defining a Political Order in Time and Space* (Brussels: Peter Lang).

Petiteville, F. (2003) 'Exporting "Values"? EU External Co-Operation as a "soft diplomacy"', in M. Knodt and S. Princen (eds.) *Understanding the European Union's External Relations* (London: Routledge/ ECPR Studies in European Political Science), 127–141.

Petmesidou, M. (2013) 'Is the Crisis a Watershed Moment for the Greek Welfare State? The Changes for Modernization Amidst an Ambivalent EU Record on "Social Europe"', in A. Triandafyllidou, R. Gropas and H. Kouki (eds.) *The Greek Crisis and European Modernity* (London: Palgrave Macmillan), 178–208.

Picht, R. (1993) 'Disturbed Identities. Social and Cultural Mutations in Contemporary Europe', in S. Garcia (ed.) *European Identity and the Search for Legitimacy* (London: Pinter), 81–94.

Pocock, J.G.A. (2002) 'Some Europes in Their History', in A. Pagden (ed.) *The Idea of Europe: From Antiquity to the European Union* (Cambridge: Cambridge University Press), 55–72.

Polanyi, K. (1957) *The Great Transformation*, 1st edn 1944 (London: Beacon Press, this edition 2001).

Radeljic, B. (ed.) (2014) *Debating European Identity* (Brussels: Peter Lang).

Rand, A. (1982) *Philosophy. Who Needs It?* (New York: Penguin).

Regulation (EU) No 1295/2013 of the European Parliament and of the Council (11.12.2013) establishing the Creative Europe Programme (2014 to 2020) and repealing Decisions No 1718/2006/EC, No 1855/2006/EC and No 1041/2009/EC, available at: http://eur-lex. europa.eu/legal-content/EN/TXT/HTML/?uri=CELEX:32013R1295 &from=EN (accessed 19 June 2015)

Reitbergen, P. (2014) *Europe. A Cultural History*, 3rd edn (London: Routledge).

Rhodes, M. (2013) 'Labour Markets, Welfare States and the Dilemmas of European Social Democracy', in M. Keating and D. McCrone (eds.) *The Crisis of Social Democracy in Europe* (Edinburgh: Edinburgh University Press), 140–156.

Risse, T. (2010) *A Community of Europeans? Transnational Identities and Public Spheres* (Ithaca, NY: Cornell University Press).

Risse, T. (2004) 'European Institutions and Identity Change', in R.K. Herrmann, T. Risse and M.B. Brewer (eds.) *Transnational Identities: Becoming European in the EU* (New York: Rowman and Littlefield), 247–271.

Risse, T. (2003) 'Towards a European Public Sphere? Theoretical Considerations'. Paper presented at the European Union Studies Association, Nashville TN, 20 March 2003.

Roberts, J.M. (1967) *Europe: 1880–1945*, 3rd edn (London: Longman).

Robins, K. (2006) 'Towards a Transcultural Policy for European Cosmopolitanism', in U.H. Meinhof and A. Triandafyllidou (eds.) *Transcultural Europe. Cultural Policy in a Changing Europe* (Basingstoke: Palgrave Macmillan), 254–283.

Rogowski, R. and C. Turner (eds.) (2006) *The Shape of the New Europe* (Cambridge: Cambridge University Press).

Rothstein, B. and S. Steinmo (2013) 'Social Democracy in Crisis? What Crisis?' in M. Keating and D. McCrone (eds.) *The Crisis of Social Democracy in Europe* (Edinburgh: Edinburgh University Press), 87–106.

Ruggie, J.G. (1993) 'Territoriality and Beyond: Problematizing Modernity in International Relations', *International Organization* (Winter 1993), 47(1), 139–174.

Ruiz-Jiménez, A. et al. (2004) *European and National Identities in EU's Old and New Member States: Ethnic, Civic, Instrumental and Symbolic Components, European Integration Online Papers*, (EIoP)

8(11). Available online at: http://eipo.or.at/eiop/texte/2004-011a.htm (accessed: 24 February 2015).

Rumford, C. (ed.) (2009) *The SAGE Handbook of European Studies* (London: Sage Publishers).

Saint-Blancat, C. and O. Schmidt di Friedberg (eds.) (2005) 'Mosque Conflicts in Europe, Special Issue', *Journal of Ethnic and Migration Studies*, 31(6).

Sapir, A. (2006) 'Globalisation and the Reform of the European Social Models', *Journal of Common Market Studies*, 44(2), 369–390.

Sassatelli, M. (2002) 'Imagined Europe: The Shaping of a European Cultural Identity Through the EU Cultural Policy', *European Journal of Social Theory*, 5(4), 435–451.

Schieder, T. (1962) 'Bismarck und Europa', in T. Schieder (ed.) *Begegnungen mit der Geschicte* (Gottingen: Vandenhoeck & Ruprecht), S. 254.

Schopflin, G. and N. Wood (eds.) (1989) *The Search for Central Europe* (London: Polity Press).

Schulz-Forberg, H. and B. Stråth (eds.) (2010) *The political history of European integration* (London: Routledge).

Sennett, R. (1996) *Flesh and Stone. The Body and the City in Western Civilization* (New York: W.W. Norton Company reprint).

Shohat, E. and R. Stam (2014) *Unthinking Eurocentrism: Multiculturalism and the Media* (London: Routledge).

Shore, C. (2000) *Building Europe. The Cultural Politics of European Integration* (London: Routledge).

Smith, A. (1995) *Nations and Nationalism in a Global Era* (Cambridge: Polity Press).

Smith, A. (1992) 'National Identity and the Idea of Europe', *International Affairs*, 68(1), 129–135.

Smith, A.D. (1991) *National Identity* (London: Penguin).

Smith, A.D. (1986) *The Ethnic Origins of Nations* (Oxford: Blackwell Publishers).

Smith, K.E. (2008) *European Union Foreign Policy in a Changing World*, 2nd edn (Cambridge: Polity Press).

Snow, D. and L. Anderson (1987) 'Identity Work among the Homeless. The Verbal Construction and Avowal of Personal Identities', *American Journal of Sociology*, 92(6), 1336–1371.

Soage, A.B. (2006) 'The Danish Caricatures Seen from the Arab World', *Totalitarian Movements and Political Religions*, 7(3), 363–369.

Sotiropoulos, D.A. and T. Veremis (eds.) (2002) *Is Southeastern Europe Doomed to Instability?* (London: Frank Cass).

Spohn, W. and A. Triandafyllidou (eds.) (2003) *Europeanisation, National Identities and Migration: Changes in Boundary Constructions between Western and Eastern Europe* (London: Routledge).

Stolcke, V. (1995) 'Talking Culture. New Boundaries, New Rhetorics of Exclusion in Europe', *Current Anthropology*, 36(1), 1–24.

Stråth, B. (ed.) (2000) *Europe and the Other and Europe as the Other* (Brussels: Peter Lang).

Taylor, A.J.P. (1971) *The Struggle for Mastery in Europe* (Oxford: Oxford University Press).

Taylor-Gooby, P. (2013) *The Double Crisis of the Welfare State and What to Do About It* (Basingstoke: Palgrave Macmillan).

Telo, M. (2007) *Europe: A Civilian Power? European Union, Global Governance, World Order* (Basingstoke: Palgrave Macmillan).

Thernborn, G. (1995) *European Modernity and Beyond* (London: Sage Publications).

Thomas, D.C. (2001) *The Helsinki Effect: International Norms, Human Rights and the Demise of Communism* (Princeton, NJ: Princeton University Press).

Tilly, C. (1993) *European Revolutions 1492–1992* (Oxford: Blackwell).

Tilly, C. (1992) *Coercion, Capital, and European States: A.D. 990–1992* (Cambridge, MA: Blackwell).

Touraine, A. (1977) *The Self-Production of Society* (Chicago: University of Chicago Press).

Triandafyllidou, A. (2011) Addressing Cultural, Ethnic and Religious Challenges in Europe. A Comparative Overview of 15 European Countries, ACCEPT-PLURALISM project report, available at http://ec.europa.eu/research/social-sciences/pdf/accept-pluralism-addressing-cultural-ethnic-religious-diversity-challenges-in-eu_en.pdf (accessed: 12 May 2015).

Triandafyllidou, A. (2001) *Immigrants and National Identity in Europe* (London: Routledge).

Triandafyllidou, A. and S. Marchetti (2014) *Paying for Care. The Employers' Perspective on Migrant Domestic Work* (Aldershot: Ashgate).

Triandafyllidou, A. and W. Spohn (2003) 'Introduction', in W. Spohn and A. Triandafyllidou (eds.) *Europeanisation, National Identities and Migration* (London: Routledge), 1–19.

Triandafyllidou, A. and I. Ulasiuk (2014) *Diversity Partnerships. Towards a Common Framework for Migrants and Minorities in Europe*, European University Institute, Global Governance Programme, February 2014.

Triandafyllidou, A. and R. Wodak (2003) 'Focus: Studying Identity: Theoretical and Methodological Challenges', *Language & Politics*, 2(2), 205–223.

Triandafyllidou, A., R. Gropas and H. Kouki (eds.) (2013) *The Greek Crisis and European Modernity* (London: Palgrave).

Triandafyllidou, A., T. Modood and N. Meer (eds.) (2012) *European Multiculturalisms. Cultural, Religious and Ethnic Challenges* (Edinburgh: Edinburgh University Press).

Tsoubarian, A. (1994) *The European Idea in History in the Nineteenth and Twentieth Centuries: A View from Moscow* (London: Frank Cass).

Tsoukalas, C. (2002) 'The Irony of Symbolic Reciprocities: The Greek Meaning of "Europe" as an Historical Inversion of the European Meaning of "Greece"', in M. Af Malmborg and B. Stråth (eds.) *The Meaning of Europe* (Oxford: Berg Publishers), 27–51.

Tsoukalis, L. and J. Emmanouilidis (eds.) (2011) *The Delphic Oracle on Europe: Is There a Future for the European Union?* (Oxford: Oxford University Press).

UNESCO World Cultural Heritage Web site (n.d.) Available online at: http://whc.unesco.org/en/list/669 (accessed: 23 February 2015).

Vachudova, M.A. (2000) 'Eastern Europe as Gatekeeper: The Immigration and Asylum Policies of an Enlarging European Union', in P. Andreas and T. Snyder (eds.) *The Wall Around the West: State Borders and Immigration Control in North America and Europe* (Boulder, CO: Rowman and Littlefield).

van Biezen, I. and H. Wallace (2013) 'Old and New Oppositions in Contemporary Europe', *Government and Opposition*, 48(3), 289–313.

Van Eekelen, W.F. (2013) 'The Construction of Europe's Security Policy: Slow but Steady', in V. Mastny and Z. Liqun (eds.) (2013) *The Legacy of the Cold War. Perspectives on Security, Cooperation and Conflict* (Langham, MD: Lexington Books), 171–198.

Van Houtum, H. (2000) 'An Overview of European Geographical Research on Borders and Border Regions', *Journal of Borderlands Studies*, 15(1), 57–83.

Van Houtum, H. and F. Boedeltje (2009), 'Europe's shame, Death at the borders of the EU', *Antipode*, 41: 2, 226–230.

Van Houtum, H. and R. Pijpers (2007) 'The European Union as a Gated Community: The Two-faced Border and Immigration Regime of the EU', *Antipode*, 39, 291–309.

Van Houtum, H. and A. Strüver (2002) 'Where Is the Border?' *Journal of Creative Geography*, 4(1), 20–23.

Van Houtum, H. and T. van Naerssen (2002) 'Bordering, Ordering and Othering', *Tijdschrift voor Economische en Sociale Geografie* (TESG), 93(2), 125–136.

Van Houtum, H., O. Kramsch and W. Zierhofer (eds.) (2005) *B/ordering Space* (Aldershot: Ashgate).

Vaughan, R. (1979) *Twentieth Century Europe: Paths to Unity* (London: Croom Helm).

Wæver, O. (1992) 'Nordic Nostalgia: Northern Europe After the Cold War', *International Affairs*, 68(1), 77–102.

Waites, B. (1993) *What Is Europe? Europe and the Wider World* (London: Routledge).

Walters, W. (2009) 'Europe's Borders', in C. Rumford (ed.) *Sage Handbook of European Studies* (London: Sage), 485–505.

Waltz, K. (1979) *Theory of International Politics* (Boston, MA: Addison-Wesley Publishing).

Weiler, J.H.H. (1999) *The Constitution of Europe. 'Do the New Clothes Have an Emperor?' and Other Essays on European Integration* (Cambridge: Cambridge University Press).

Weiss, G. (1973) 'A Scientific Concept of Culture', *American Anthropologist*, 75(5), 1376–1413.

Wenger, A. and D. Mockli (2013) 'The Conference on Security and Cooperation in Europe as a Regional Model', in V. Mastny and Z. Liqun (eds.) *The Legacy of the Cold War. Perspectives on Security, Cooperation and Conflict* (Langham, MD: Lexington Books), 199–230.

Weyland, K. (2001) 'Clarifying a Contested Concept: Populism in the Study of Latin American Politics', *Comparative Politics*, 34(1), 1–22.

Whitefield, S. (2002) 'Political Cleavages and Post-Communist Politics', *Annual Review of Political Science*, 2002(5), 181–200.

Whitman, R. (ed.) (2011) *Normative Power Europe: Empirical and Theoretical Perspectives* (Basingstoke: Palgrave Macmillan).

Whitman, R. (1996) *The International Dimension of Democratisation: Europe and the Americas* (Oxford: Oxford University Press).

Wolff, L. (1994) *Inventing Eastern Europe: The Map of Civilization on the Mind of the Enlightenment* (Stanford, CA: Stanford University Press).

Woodley, D. (2010) *Fascism and Political Theory. Critical Perspectives on Fascist Ideology*, Routledge Issues in Contemporary Political Theory (London: Routledge).

Yapp, M.E. (1992) 'Europe in the Turkish Mirror', *Past and Present*, 137(1), 134–155.

Young, A.R. and J. Peterson (2014) *Parochial Global Europe. 21st Century Trade Politics* (Oxford: Oxford University Press).

Youngs, R. (2010) *The EU's Role in World Politics. A Retreat from Liberal Internationalism* (London: Routledge).

Zapata-Barrero, R. (ed.) (2010) *Shaping the Normative Contours of the European Union: a Migration-Border Framework* (Barcelona: CIDOB-GRITIM UPF).

Zapata-Barrero, R. (2006) 'The Muslim Community and Spanish Tradition: Maurophobia as a Fact, and Impartiality as a Desideratum', in T. Modood, A. Triandafyllidou and R. Zapata-Barrero (eds.) *Multiculturalism, Muslims and Citizenship: A European Approach* (London: Routledge), 143–162.

Zaslove, A. (2008) 'Here to Stay? Populism as a New Party Type', *European Review*, 16(3), 319–336.

Zielonka, J. (2006) *Europe as Empire. The Nature of the Enlarged European Union* (Oxford: Oxford University Press).

Zielonka, J. (1998) *Explaining Euro-Paralysis: Why Europe Is Unable to Act in International Politics* (Basingstoke: Palgrave Macmillan).

Index

Made in the USA
Middletown, DE
28 March 2020

87409926R00179